Companion
To The
San Francisco
Bay Area

7TH
EDITION

Maria Goodavage

AVALON
TRAVEL

THE DOG LOVER'S COMPANION
TO THE SAN FRANCISCO BAY AREA
THE INSIDE SCOOP ON WHERE TO TAKE YOUR DOG

Published by
Avalon Travel
a member of the Perseus Books Group
1700 Fourth Street
Berkeley, CA 94710, USA

Printing History
1st edition—1993
7th edition—June 2011
5 4 3 2 1

ISBN-13: 978-1-59880-744-8
ISSN: 1078-8921

Editor: Shaharazade Husain
Designer: Jacob Goolkasian
Graphics Coordinator: Elizabeth Jang
Production Coordinator: Elizabeth Jang
Map Editor: Albert Angulo
Cartographers: Kat Bennett, Kaitlin Jaffe
Proofreader: Naomi Adler Dancis

Cover and Interior Illustrations by Phil Frank

Printed in Canada by Friesens

ABOUT THE AUTHOR

Jake the Yellow-Lab-sort-of-dog and Maria Goodavage have traveled throughout the state to check out some of the most dog-friendly parks, beaches, lodgings, and restaurants in the world. As part of their research, they've ridden on ferries, horse-drawn carriages, cable cars, gondolas, and steam trains. They've visited chichi art galleries, dumpy drive-in movies, kitschy tourist attractions, dog-friendly wineries, high-end  stores, ski resorts, major-league ballgames, and even had high tea together. They've eaten at restaurants where dogs are treated almost like people (except they never get the bill). They've stayed at the best hotels, the worst flea-bitten motels, and everything in between. Jake's favorite saying: "You're not really gonna leave the house without me, are ya?" (This is usually accompanied by all his extra folds of neck skin drooping forward into his face, his floppy ears hanging especially low, his tail sagging dejectedly, and his big seal-like eyes looking wet and wide and oh-so-woeful.)

Since Jake still doesn't have a driver's license after all these years, he relies on Maria, former longtime *USA Today* correspondent, to be his chauffeur. Maria is well qualified—she started chauffeuring dogs many years back, when her intrepid Airedale, Joe, joined her during some of her travels for the newspaper. With all of their experiences on the road, it was only a matter of time before a book was born, followed by a series of books. Both *The Dog Lover's Companion to California* and *The Dog Lover's Companion to the San Francisco Bay Area* are now in their seventh editions.

Maria is a freelance writer, and an editor and blogger for Dogster.com, one of the most widely read dog websites in the world. Check out her blog at www.dogblog.dogster.com.

Jake lives near the beach in San Francisco with Maria, her husband, and their daughter. He encourages his fans to write to him, care of Maria (who won't let him online anymore—long story), and tell him about new dog-friendly places he should sniff out for this book's next edition. You can find contact info at www.caldogtravel.com. And you can follow Jake's tweets at @dog_trips_calif.

In Memoriam
PHIL FRANK
1943–2007

Just before my deadline for the sixth edition of this book, Phil Frank, who illustrated this book and the entire *Dog Lover's Companion* series, died of a brain tumor. He was only 64. Phil was best known for his perennially popular *San Francisco Chronicle* comic strip, Farley, and a nationally syndicated strip, The Elderberries.

In 1991 he took on the illustration job for the first edition of *The Dog Lover's Companion to the Bay Area* pretty much as a favor to my then-co-author, Lyle York, a colleague at the *Chronicle*. If not for his delightful, humorous, sweet, fun illustrations of dogs and their people, I'm not sure the series would have taken off as it did. His illustrations are an integral part of these books—sometimes the main selling point for browsers too busy to read the text.

But beyond his talent as an illustrator, Phil was one of the kindest, most humble, most decent human beings I've come across. I'll never forget when my daughter was an aspiring cartoonist at the age of 6, and Phil invited us to come to his Sausalito studio to give her a little cartooning tutelage. She was transfixed by his gentle humor, his grandfatherly demeanor, and his drawing style. They worked together for nearly two hours, and he invited us to come back any time she needed a refresher. Sadly, life got busy, and although we emailed a few times, that was the last time I saw him.

I am comforted that Phil's illustrations—and thus a part of him—will live on in these books. But I wish he were still here to make the world a better place for all who knew him.

CONTENTS

Contra Costa County 93

Alameda County. 111

Marin County 139

San Francisco County 179

San Mateo County 225

Santa Clara County. 253

Index. 278

Introduction

Now, Charley is a mind-reading dog. There have been many trips in his lifetime, and often he has to be left at home. He knows we are going long before the suitcases come out, and he paces and worries and whines and goes into a state of mild hysteria, old as he is.

John Steinbeck, *Travels with Charley*

There was a time when dogs could go just about anywhere they pleased. Well-dressed dogs with embarrassing names attended afternoon teas, while their less-kempt counterparts sauntered into saloons without anyone's blinking a bloodshot eye.

No one thought it strange to see a pug-nosed little snookum-wookums of a dog snuggled on his mistress's lap on a long train journey. Equally accepted were dogs prancing through fine hotels, dogs at dining establishments, and dogs in almost any park they cared to visit.

But then there came a time (a period perhaps best referred to as the Doggy Dark Ages) when dogs came to be seen as beasts not fit for hotels, restaurants, or even many parks. The world was getting more crowded, patience growing thinner; there was only so much room, and, dangit, four-legged varmints weren't going to be sharing it. They were just *dogs* after all—animals who eat from bowls on the floor and lick their heinies at unfortunate moments. Dogs were for the house, the backyard, sidewalks (with canines being "curbed"), and some tolerant parks. So we got used to leaving our dogs behind when we took off for an afternoon, or for a road trip. It hurt—oh, how it hurt—but what could you do?

Many of us know that guilt too well. The guilt that stabs at you as you push your dog's struggling body back inside the house and tug the door shut can be so painful that sometimes you just can't look back. Even a trip to the grocery store can become a heart-wrenching tale of woe. A survey by the American Animal Hospital Association shows that the vast majority of us feel guilty when leaving pets at home. Thirty-nine percent of pet people call to talk to their pets when they're away. I've tried that, but it always made me feel even worse.

Joe, the Airedale terrier who inspired not only this book but the entire *Dog Lover's Companion* series, was born with an unparalleled gift for making people feel guilty—and not your ordinary, run-of-the-mill guilt where you smart for a couple of hours after seeing your dog's moping eyes follow your car as you speed away. It's that deep-in-the-gut-for-days guilt, where the sight of that pouting snout, those drooping ears, and that tail lowered to half-mast hangs with you until you return home.

John Steinbeck's blue poodle, Charley, was a master of powerful pleas that were carefully designed to allow him to accompany his people on trips. Eventually, his hard work paid off and he won himself a seat in Steinbeck's brand-new truck/house on their epic journey across America. They sought and found the heart of this country in their adventures across 34 states.

Joe's guilt-inducing expertise won him a spot in my rusty, beat-up, hiccupping pickup truck in our sporadic little journeys around the Bay Area, and later, California. We sought and found thousands of dog-friendly places in our adventures and misadventures.

Joe and I were frequently joined by two other experts in the field of rating parks and sniffing out good dog attractions. Nisha, our old-lady springer spaniel, insisted on standing in the back of the truck, under the camper top, madly wagging her tail for hours on end as we drove and drove and drove. She was a real asset to have around when it came to checking out beaches, lakes, rivers, and ponds—any area with water. (Joe hated to get his paws wet, so he couldn't be impartial in his rating of watery attractions.)

Bill, a big, lovable galoot of a dog, was my other original canine researcher. I found him partway through my travels. He was trembling in the middle of a Northern California road, with a big chain tight around his neck. He'd evidently broken loose, because the last link of the thick chain was mauled.

I came to find out that his owner beat him regularly. Bill went back to San Francisco with me that afternoon. During the months when I was looking for the perfect home for him (oh, and did he ever get the perfect home!), he became one of the friendliest, most outgoing dogs I've ever had the pleasure to meet. His presence during my journeys was invaluable. He lifted my spirits when I was tired, and his 85 pounds of muscle kept away bad spirits when we visited questionable areas.

Time marches on. All journeys have to end someday. Joe, Nisha, and Bill have gone to that giant off-leash beach in the sky. They're dearly missed, but their legacy—that of helping other dogs lead better lives by sniffing out places they're allowed to go with their humans—lives on. I'm pretty sure that now Joe is chasing—and finally catching—cats (in Dog Heaven, in case you didn't know, all cats are slow), and eating all the horse manure he wants.

Before I choke up, I'd like to introduce you to a dog you'll be seeing plenty of throughout this book. His name is Jake, and we figure he's about 97 percent yellow Lab, leaving 3 percent hound or Great Dane or some other big thing with short fur. When he was about six months old, we were asked to foster him for a week. That was back in 2002.

Jake now weighs 90 pounds or so, and is one of the sweetest, most noodley dogs I've ever met. When we're home, he can usually be found reposing on his chair (despite our best attempts to keep him off it, the big comfy Ikea chair is now referred to as "Jake's chair"), jowls sprawled over the windowsill (which is half chewed away from his younger days—a very attractive sight), big brown eyes staring off into the distance as if longing for another road trip.

We've had some terrific trips together. Since traveling with a giant furry termite is a bad idea, I waited until his penchant for chewing furniture, windowsills, and floorboards had disappeared. Then we hit the road, enjoying dog-friendly lodgings, restaurants, and parks around the Bay Area.

As a water dog, he excels at checking out liquidy attractions, from wading pools at dog parks to ponds, lakes, and beaches. Fortunately, I never have to worry about him going after ducks, per his breed's instinct. For some reason, when swimming ducks see him dogpaddling, they make a beeline right for him. This gives Jake the creeps, and he swims away, with the ducks fast on his tail. It's a sight that would make a duck hunter cry.

On a similar note, he's always glad when we visit a dog park that has a separate section for small dogs. Tiny dogs become giants with Jake, yapping a couple of times while giving him the chase. He tucks his tail between his legs and runs away, glancing nervously behind him to make sure he's escaped before relaxing enough to be his big doggy self again.

Jake and I (the "we" you will be reading about throughout the book) are happy to announce that the seventh edition of the book finds the Doggy Dark Ages further behind us than ever. Dog travel is scorching hot. Everyone's getting in on it. For many reasons, dogs have become a real part of our families ("fur kids" is a common name for their status), and businesses have seen the golden opportunities. Witness the dog travel agents, dog road-trip accessories, and even an upstart doggy airline.

Many lodgings, from the humblest cabins to the most regal luxury suites and chichi vacation rentals, are now allowing dog guests. "If we have a house that doesn't permit dogs, they're just not going to do very well," a Sonoma County vacation rental agent told me. A Bay Area innkeeper's policy sums up this dog-loving travel trend: "Come here with a young child, I'll probably turn you away. Come here with a dog, I go all gaga."

Many upscale chains have taken the dog-friendly policy all the way. Loews has its "Loews Loves Pets" program. Kimpton hotels all welcome dogs, and most provide them some sort of VIP package. And Starwood Hotels, one of the leading hotel companies in the world, started its Starwood LTD (Love That Dog) program in its Sheraton, Westin, and W hotels in the United States and Canada.

"Dog owners are a market niche that's been underserved by the travel industry," a Starwood press release announced. And Barry Sternlicht, Starwood's founder, chairman, and CEO, has lofty goals for Starwood. "We intend to become the most dog-friendly hotel company in the land, and not just allow dogs to stay, but actually pamper and spoil them," says Barry, who has two dogs of his own.

The vacation industry is truly going to the dogs. And the San Francisco Bay Area is rife with dog-friendly destinations.

We've tried to find the very best of everything you can do with your dog in the Bay Area, so you'll never again have to face the prospect of shutting the door on your dog's nose. This book is crammed to the breaking point with descriptions of thousands of dog-friendly parks, restaurants with outdoor tables, and lodgings. The book also describes dozens of unusual adventures you and your dog can share. You can ride on steam trains, cable cars, and surreys. You can sip chardonnay at a winery where dogs are adored, attend a San Francisco Giants game, go to church, cruise the San Francisco Bay in luxury, enjoy concerts by world-renowned performers, and shop at high-fashion stores.

The seventh edition of this book is the most fun-packed yet. We've added countless new places to go with your dog, many of them discovered through readers whose dogs insist on writing to tell us about their favorite new park, cool eatery, or pooch-loving hotel. We're so grateful to these dogs that, whenever possible, we acknowledge them under the new listing. (See the imprint page for easy ways to get in touch with us with your hot dog tips. Better yet, go to my website, www.caldogtravel.com, and click on the "contact" button.)

Bay Area dogs are lucky dogs indeed: Since the last edition, oodles more dog parks have sprung up. Dog parks are a huge trend, one that shows no signs of slowing. We personally prefer being out of the confines of a fenced area, and on a leash-free beach or trail, but these parks do put a wag in many a dog's tail. Dog parks run the gamut from very basic (often just bones city governments throw to appease their dog-bearing constituents) to gorgeous, perfectly manicured, custom-designed doggy playgrounds. I can't describe them all, because of space limitations, so if I'm missing one you'd love to see in the pages of the book, let me know. There's always a way to make room.

A traveling dog's life has changed significantly from the days when John Steinbeck and Charley traversed the country together. Dogs have less freedom, but, ironically, more choices.

And you can pretty much rest assured that no one will look askance when he or she realizes that your traveling companion is none other than the furry beast at your side. "Used to be odd when someone wanted a room to stay in with their dog," says a rural innkeeper. "Now it doesn't even make us blink."

The Paws Scale

At some point, we've got to face the facts: Humans and dogs have different tastes. We like eating oranges and smelling lilacs and covering our bodies with soft clothes. They like eating roadkill and smelling each other's unmentionables and covering their bodies with horse manure.

The parks, beaches, and recreation areas in this book are rated with a dog in mind. Maybe your favorite park has lush gardens, a duck pond, a few acres of perfectly manicured lawns, and sweeping views of a nearby skyline. But unless your dog can run leash-free, swim in the pond, and roll in the grass, that park doesn't deserve a very high rating.

The very lowest rating you'll come across in this book is the fire hydrant symbol 🐾. This means the park is merely "worth a squat." Visit one of these parks only if your dog just can't hold it any longer. These parks have virtually no other redeeming qualities for canines.

Beyond that, the paws scale starts at one paw 🐾 and goes up to four paws 🐾🐾🐾🐾. A one-paw park isn't a dog's idea of a great time. Maybe it's a tiny park with few trees and too many kids running around. Or perhaps it's a magnificent-for-people park that bans dogs from every inch of land except paved roads and a few campsites. Four-paw parks, on the other hand, are places your dog will drag you to visit. Some of these areas come as close to dog heaven as you can imagine. Many have lakes for swimming or zillions of acres for hiking. Some are small, fenced-in areas where leash-free dogs can tear around without danger of running into the road.

This book is *not* a comprehensive guide to all of the parks in the Bay Area. If I included every single park, it would be ridiculously unportable. Instead, I tried to find the best, largest, and most convenient parks—and especially parks that allow dogs off leash. Some counties have so many wonderful parks that I had to make some tough choices in deciding which to include and which to leave out. Other counties have such a limited supply of parks that, for the sake of dogs living and visiting there, I ended up listing parks that wouldn't otherwise be worth mentioning.

I've provided specific directions to the major parks and parks near highways. Other parks are listed by their cross streets. If you don't have GPS, I highly recommend checking an Internet map site such as Mapquest.com or picking up detailed street maps from the AAA—California State Automobile Association (maps are free for members)—before you and your dog set out on your adventures.

He, She, It

In this book, whether neutered, spayed, or au naturel, dogs are never referred to as "it." They are either "he" or "she." I alternate pronouns so no dog reading this book will feel left out.

To Leash or Not to Leash...

This is not a question that plagues dogs' minds. Ask just about any normal, red-blooded American dog whether she'd prefer to visit a park and be on leash or off, and she'll say, "Arf!" No question about it, most dogs would give their canine teeth to frolic about without a cumbersome leash.

Whenever you see the running dog symbol 🐕 in this book, you'll know that under certain circumstances, your dog can run around in leash-free bliss. Fortunately, the Bay Area is home to hundreds of such parks. The rest of the parks demand leashes. I wish I could write about the parks where dogs get away with being scofflaws. Unfortunately, those would be the first parks the

animal control patrols would hit. I don't advocate breaking the law, but if you're going to, please follow your conscience and use common sense.

Also, just because dogs are permitted off leash in certain areas doesn't necessarily mean you should let your dog run free. In large tracts of wild land, unless you're sure your dog will come back when you call or will never stray more than a few yards from your side, you should probably keep her leashed. An otherwise docile homebody can turn into a savage hunter if the right prey is near. Or your curious dog could perturb a rattlesnake or dig up a rodent whose fleas carry bubonic plague. In pursuit of a strange scent, your dog could easily get lost in an unfamiliar area. (Some forest rangers recommend having your dog wear a bright orange collar, vest, or backpack when out in the wilderness.)

There's No Business Like Dog Business

There's nothing appealing about bending down with a plastic bag or a piece of newspaper on a chilly morning and grabbing the steaming remnants of what your dog ate for dinner the night before. It's disgusting. Worse yet, you have to hang onto it until you can find a trash can. And how about when the newspaper doesn't endure before you can dispose of it? Yuck! It's enough to make you wish your dog could wear diapers. But as gross as it can be to scoop the poop, it's worse to step in it. It's really bad if a child falls in it, or—*gasp!*—starts eating it. And have you ever walked into a park where few people clean up after their dogs? It's so whiffy even the dogs look vaguely discomfited.

Unscooped poop is one of a dog's worst enemies. Public policies banning dogs from parks are enacted because of it. And not all poop woes are outside. A dog-loving concierge at an upscale hotel told us that a guest came up to her and said there was some dirt beside the elevator. The concierge sent someone to clean it up. The dirt turned out to be dog poop. The hotel, which used to be one of the most elegant dog-friendly hotels around (it even had a Pampered Pet Program), now bans dogs. (There were other reasons, including a new boss, but the poop was the last straw.)

Just be responsible and clean up after your dog everywhere you go. (And obviously, if there's even a remote chance he'll relieve himself inside, don't even bring him into hotels or stores that permit dogs!) Anytime you take your dog out, stuff plastic bags in your jacket, purse, car, pants pockets—anywhere you might be able to pull one out when needed. Or, if plastic isn't your bag, newspapers will do the trick. If it makes it more palatable, bring along a paper bag, too, and put the used newspaper or plastic bag in it. That way you don't have to walk around with dripping paper or a plastic bag whose contents are visible to the world. If you don't enjoy the squishy sensation, try one of those cardboard or plastic bag pooper-scoopers sold at pet stores. If you don't feel like bending down, buy a long-handled scooper. There's a scooper for every taste.

This is the only lecture you'll get on scooping in this entire book. To help keep parks alive, I should harp on it in every park description, but that would take another 100 pages—and you'd start to ignore it anyway. And, if I mentioned it in some park listings but not others, it might imply that you don't have to clean up after your dog in the parks where it's not mentioned.

A final note: Don't pretend not to see your dog while he's doing his bit. Don't pretend to look for it without success. And don't fake scooping it up when you're really just covering it with sand. I know these tricks because I've been guilty of them myself—but no more. I've seen the light. I've been saved. I've been delivered from the depths of dog-doo depravity.

Etiquette Rex: The Well-Mannered Mutt

While cleaning up after your dog is your responsibility, a dog in a public place has his own responsibilities. Of course, it really boils down to your responsibility again, but the burden of action is on your dog. Etiquette for restaurants and hotels is covered in other sections of this chapter. What follows are some fundamental rules of dog etiquette. I'll go through it quickly, but if your dog's a slow reader, he can read it again: no vicious dogs; no jumping on people; no incessant barking; no leg lifts on surfboards, backpacks, human legs, or any other personal objects you'll find hanging around beaches and parks; dogs should come when they're called; dogs should stay on command.

Joe Dog managed to violate all but the first of these rules at one point or another. (Jake followed in his pawsteps to an amazing extent, considering he never even met Joe.) Do your best to remedy any problems. It takes patience, and it's not always easy. For instance, there was a time during Joe's youth when he seemed to think that human legs were tree trunks. Rather than pretending I didn't know the beast, I strongly reprimanded him, apologized to the victim from the depths of my heart, and offered money for dry cleaning. Joe learned his lesson—many dry-cleaning bills later.

Safety First

A few essentials will keep your traveling dog happy and healthy.

Heat: If you must leave your dog alone in the car for a few minutes, do so only if it's cool out and if you can park in the shade. *Never, ever, ever* leave a dog in a car with the windows rolled up all the way. Even if it seems cool, the sun's heat passing through the window can kill a dog in a matter of minutes. Roll

down the window enough so your dog gets air, but not so much that there's danger of your dog getting out or someone breaking in. Make sure your dog has plenty of water.

You also have to watch out for heat exposure when your car is in motion. Certain cars, such as hatchbacks, can make a dog in the backseat extra hot, even while you feel OK in the driver's seat.

Try to time your vacation so you don't visit a place when it's extremely warm. Dogs and heat don't get along, especially if the dog isn't used to heat. The opposite is also true. If your dog lives in a hot climate and you take him to a freezing place, it may not be a healthy shift. Check with your vet if you have any doubts. Spring and fall are usually the best times to travel.

Water: Water your dog frequently. Dogs on the road may drink even more than they do at home. Take regular water breaks, or bring a heavy bowl (the thick clay ones do nicely) and set it on the floor so your dog always has access to water. I use a nonspill bowl, which comes in really handy on curvy roads. When hiking, be sure to carry enough water for you *and* a thirsty dog.

Rest Stops: Stop and unwater your dog. There's nothing more miserable than being stuck in a car when you can't find a rest stop. No matter how tightly you cross your legs and try to think of the desert, you're certain you'll burst within the next minute… so imagine how a dog feels when the urge strikes, and he can't tell you the problem. There are plenty of rest stops along the major California freeways. I've also included many parks close to freeways for dogs who need a good stretch with their bathroom break.

How frequently you stop depends on your dog's bladder. If your dog is constantly running out the doggy door at home to relieve himself, you may want to stop every hour. Others can go significantly longer without being uncomfortable. Watch for any signs of restlessness and gauge it for yourself.

Car Safety: Even the experts differ on how a dog should travel in a car. Some suggest doggy safety belts, available at pet-supply stores. Others firmly believe in keeping a dog kenneled. They say it's safer for the dog if there's an accident, and it's safer for the driver because there's no dog underfoot. Still others say you should just let your dog hang out without straps and boxes. They believe that if there's an accident, at least the dog isn't trapped in a cage. They say that dogs enjoy this more, anyway.

I'm a follower of the last school of thought. Jake loves sticking his snout out of the windows to smell the world go by. The danger is that if the car kicks up a pebble or angers a bee, his nose and eyes could be injured. So far, he's been OK, as has every other dog who has explored the Golden State with us, but I've seen dogs who needed to be treated for bee stings to the nose because of this practice. If in doubt, try opening the window just enough so your dog can't stick out much snout.

Whatever travel style you choose, your pet will be more comfortable if he has his own blanket with him. A veterinarian acquaintance brings a faux-sheepskin blanket for his dogs. At night in the hotel, the sheepskin doubles as the dog's bed.

The Ultimate Doggy Bag

Your dog can't pack his own bags, and even if he could, he'd probably fill them with dog biscuits and chew toys. It's important to stash some of those in your dog's vacation kit, but here are other handy items to bring along: bowls, bedding, a brush, towels (for those muddy days), a first-aid kit, pooper-scoopers, water, food, prescription drugs, tags, treats, toys, and—of course—this book.

Make sure your dog is wearing his license, identification tag, and rabies tag. Bringing along your dog's up-to-date vaccination records is a good idea, too. If you should find yourself at a park or campground that requires the actual rabies certificate, you'll be set. In addition, you may unexpectedly end up needing to leave your dog in a doggy day care for a few hours so you can go somewhere you just can't bring your dog. A record of his shots is imperative. (You'll also have to get him a kennel-cough shot if boarding is a possibility.)

It's a good idea to snap a disposable ID on your dog's collar, too, showing a cell phone number or the name, address, and phone number either of where you'll be vacationing or of a friend who'll be home to field calls. That way, if your dog should get lost, at least the finder won't be calling your empty house. Paper key-chain tags available at hardware stores offer a cheap way to change your dog's contact info as often as needed when on vacation. Dog-book author and pet columnist Gina Spadafori advises always listing a local number on the tag. "You'd be surprised how many people don't want to make a long-distance phone call," she writes in her book *Dogs for Dummies.*

Some people think dogs should drink only water brought from home, so their bodies don't have to get used to too many new things. I've never had a problem giving my dogs tap water from other parts of the state, nor has anyone else I know. Most vets think your dog will be fine drinking tap water in most U.S. cities.

"Think of it this way," says Pete Beeman, a longtime San Francisco veterinarian. "Your dog's probably going to eat poop if he can get hold of some, and even that's probably not going to harm him. I really don't think that drinking water that's OK for people is going to be bad for dogs." (Jake can attest to the poop part. But let's not talk about that.)

Bone Appétit

In some European countries, dogs enter restaurants and dine alongside their folks as if they were people, too. (Or at least they sit and watch and drool while their people dine.) Not so in the United States. Rightly or wrongly, dogs are considered a health threat here. But many health inspectors I've spoken with say they see no reason why clean, well-behaved dogs shouldn't be permitted inside a restaurant. "Aesthetically, it may not appeal to Americans," an environmental specialist with the state Department of Health told me. "But the truth is, there's no harm in this practice."

Ernest Hemingway made an expatriate of his dog, Black Dog (a.k.a. Blackie), partly because of America's restrictive views on dogs in dining establishments. In "The Christmas Gift," a story published in *Look* magazine in 1954, he describes how he made the decision to take Black Dog to Cuba, rather than leave him behind in Ketchum, Idaho.

This was a town where a man was once not regarded as respectable unless he was accompanied by his dog. But a reform movement had set in, led by several local religionists, and gambling had been abolished and there was even a movement on foot to forbid a dog from entering a public eating place with his master. Blackie had always tugged me by the trouser leg as we passed a combination gambling and eating place called the Alpine where they served the finest sizzling steak in the West. Blackie wanted me to order the giant sizzling steak and it was difficult to pass the Alpine.… We decided to make a command decision and take Blackie to Cuba.

Fortunately, you don't have to take your dog to a foreign country to eat together at a restaurant. The state is full of restaurants with outdoor tables, and hundreds of them welcome dogs to join their people for an alfresco experience. The law on outdoor dining is somewhat vague, and each county has

different versions of it. In general, as long as your dog doesn't go inside a restaurant (even to get to outdoor tables in the back) and isn't near the food preparation areas, it's probably legal. The decision is then up to the restaurant proprietor.

The restaurants listed in this book have given us permission to tout them as dog-friendly eateries. But keep in mind that rules can change and restaurants can close, so I highly recommend phoning before you set your stomach on a particular kind of cuisine. Since some restaurants close during colder months, phoning ahead is a doubly wise thing to do. (Of course, you can assume that where there's snow or ultracold temperatures, the outdoor tables will move indoors for a while each year.) If you can't call first, be sure to ask a server or the manager for permission before you sit down with your sidekick. Remember, it's the restaurant proprietor, not you, who will be in trouble if someone complains to the health department.

Some basic rules of restaurant etiquette: Dogs shouldn't beg from other diners, no matter how delicious their steaks look. They should not attempt to get their snouts (or their entire bodies) up on the table. They should be clean, quiet, and as unobtrusive as possible. If your dog leaves a good impression with the management and other customers, it will help pave the way for all the other dogs who want to dine alongside their best friends in the future.

One day, well-behaved California dogs may find themselves treated much like their European counterparts. A couple of restaurants in upscale hotels here have already figured out a way around the no-dogs-inside law. They simply set up tables in the hotel lobby, just outside the official restaurant. People with dogs get table service as if they were in the restaurant itself, and everyone is happy. It's a toe in the door, at least.

In our neighbor to the north, Oregon state lawmaker Brian Clem (D-Salem) has sponsored a bill that would allow well-behaved dogs inside restaurants that want to let them in. The bill hasn't exactly been well received by state health officials, whom the Associated Press quoted as arguing that dogs are "quite naturally a vector for a variety of pathogens, including salmonella and campylobacter." (Er, raw meat is a major vector for these organisms, and I don't see health officials running to ban this in restaurants. Health officials I've talked with said it would be "extremely difficult" to get these germs from a dog.) If Clem's bill makes it one day, it could lead the way to the Europeanization of restaurants. Until then (and don't hold your breath) enjoy all the dog-friendly alfresco eateries the Golden State offers.

A Room at the Inn

Good dogs make great hotel guests. They don't steal towels, and they don't get drunk and keep the neighbors up all night. The Bay Area is full of lodgings whose owners welcome dogs. This book lists dog-friendly accommodations of all types, from motels to bed-and-breakfast inns to elegant hotels—but the basic dog etiquette rules are the same everywhere.

Dogs should never be left alone in your room. Leaving a dog alone in a strange place invites serious trouble. Scared, nervous dogs may tear apart drapes, carpeting, and furniture. They may even injure themselves. They might also bark nonstop and scare the daylights out of the housekeeper. Just don't do it.

Only bring a house-trained dog to a lodging. How would you like a houseguest to go to the bathroom in the middle of your bedroom?

Make sure your pooch is flea-free. Otherwise, future guests will be itching to leave.

It helps to bring your dog's bed or blanket along for the night. Your dog will feel more at home and won't be tempted to jump on the hotel bed. If your dog sleeps on the bed with you at home (as 47 percent do, according to the American Animal Hospital Association survey), bring a sheet and put it on top of the bed so the hotel's bedspread won't get furry or dirty.

Don't wash your dog in the hotel tub. "It's very yucky," I was told by one motel manager who has seen so many furry tubs that she's thinking about banning dogs.

Likewise, refrain from using the ice bucket as a water or food bowl. Bring your own bowls, or stay in a hotel that provides them, as many of the nicer ones do these days.

After a few days in a hotel, some dogs come to think of it as home. They get territorial. When another hotel guest walks by, it's "Bark! Bark!" When the housekeeper knocks, it's "Bark! Snarl! Bark! Gnash!" Keep your dog quiet, or you'll both find yourselves looking for a new home away from home.

For some strange reason, many lodgings prefer small dogs as guests. All I can say is, "Yip! Yap!" It's really ridiculous. Large dogs are often much calmer and quieter than their tiny, high-energy cousins.

If you're in a location where you can't find a hotel that will accept you and your big brute (a growing rarity these days), it's time to try a sell job. Let the manager know how good and quiet your dog is (if he is). Promise he won't eat the bathtub or run around and shake all over the hotel. Offer a deposit or sign a waiver, even if they're not required for small dogs. It helps if your sweet, soppy-eyed dog is at your side to convince the decision-maker.

In the early days of my exploring the Bay Area with dogs, I sometimes had to sneak dogs into hotels because so few allowed them. I don't recommend it. A lodging might have a good reason for its rules. Besides, you always feel as if you're going to be caught and thrown out on your hindquarters. You race in and out of your room with your dog as if ducking sniper fire. It's better to avoid feeling like a criminal and move on to a more dog-friendly location. With the numbers of lodgings that welcome dogs these days, you won't have to go far.

The lodgings described in this book are for dogs who obey all the rules. I list a range of rates for each lodging, from the least expensive room during low season to the priciest room during high season. Most of the rooms are doubles, so there's not usually a huge variation. But when a room price gets into the thousands of dollars, you know we're looking at royal suites.

Many lodgings charge extra for your dog. If you see "Dogs are $10 (or whatever amount) extra," that means $10 extra per night. Some charge a fee for the length of a dog's stay, and others ask for a deposit. These details are also noted in the lodging description. A few places still ask for nothing more than your dog's promise that she'll be on her best behavior. So, if no extra charge is mentioned in a listing, it means your dog can stay with you free.

A final note. You may be tempted to make your reservations with one of the popular discount reservation websites like Expedia or Travelocity. But if you're traveling with a dog, you need to make your reservations directly with hotels so they will know ahead of time that you're bringing a pooch. Too many people have made the mistake of reserving without mention of a dog, arrived at the hotel, and found out there was no room at the inn for a dog. It would be great if in the future, dogs were taken into account on these sites so you could get their deep discounts. In fact, since most hotel sites don't have an online reservation option to indicate dog guests, your best bet is to phone the hotel directly to make your rezzies. You don't want to be expecting a night at the top of the Ritz and end up spending the night in the back of a Toyota.

Ruffing It Together

Whenever we go camping, big Jake insists on sleeping in the tent. He gets in before we do, sprawls out and doesn't budge until morning. The dog of our camping buddies keeps guard over their tent nearby while Jake dreams sweet doggy dreams about his cozy chair at home.

It may not be the most macho place to be, but Jake has the right idea. Your tent or vehicle is the safest place for a dog at night. Some experts say it's dangerous to leave even a tethered dog outside your tent at night. The dog can escape or become a late dinner for some hungry creature.

All state parks require dogs to be kept in a tent or vehicle at night. Some county parks follow suit. Other policies are more lenient. Use good judgment.

If you're camping with your dog, chances are you're also hiking with him. Even if you're not hiking for long, watch out for your dog's paws, especially those who are fair of foot. Rough terrain can cause a dog's pads to become raw and painful, making it almost impossible for him to walk. Several types of dog boots are available for such feet. It's easier to carry the booties than to carry your dog home.

Be sure to bring plenty of water for you and your pooch. Stop frequently to wet your whistles. Some veterinarians warn against letting your dog drink out of a stream because of the chance of ingesting giardia and other internal parasites, but it's not always easy to stop a thirsty dog.

A Dog in Need

If you don't have a dog but could provide a good home for one, or if you have a dog but you're thinking of getting another, I'd like to make a plea on behalf of all the unwanted dogs who will be euthanized today—and tomorrow, and the day after that, and the day after that. Animal shelters are overflowing with dogs who would devote their lives to being your best buddy, your faithful traveling companion, and a dedicated listener to all your tales of bliss and woe.

If you can't adopt a dog, consider fostering one. Most shelters and rescue groups are in great need of people who can foster dogs until the dog is adopted, or ready for adoption. (Beware, fostering is how we originally got hold of Jake. You may not be able to say good-bye once you say hello.)

Fostering is free, fun, and fulfilling. Go ahead. Make a dog's day—or life.

Keep in Touch

Our readers mean everything to us. We explore the San Francisco Bay Area so you and your dogs can spend true quality time together. Your input to this book is very important. In the last several years, we've heard from many wonderful dogs and their people about new dog-friendly places or old dog-friendly places we didn't know about. If you have any suggestions or insights to offer, please contact us using the information listed in the front of this book, or via my website, www.caldogtravel.com. If your tip pans out and becomes a listing, we'll try to give you and/or your dog credit in the next edition.

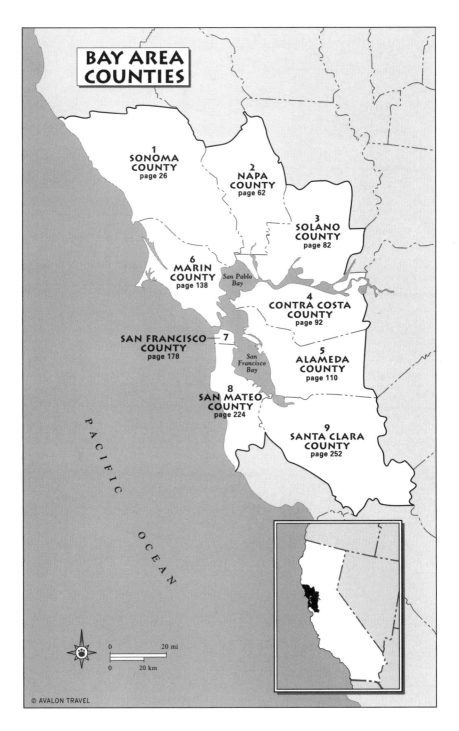

BAY AREA COUNTIES

1 SONOMA COUNTY page 26

2 NAPA COUNTY page 62

3 SOLANO COUNTY page 82

6 MARIN COUNTY page 138

San Pablo Bay

4 CONTRA COSTA COUNTY page 92

7 SAN FRANCISCO COUNTY page 178

San Francisco Bay

5 ALAMEDA COUNTY page 110

8 SAN MATEO COUNTY page 224

9 SANTA CLARA COUNTY page 252

PACIFIC OCEAN

0   20 mi

0   20 km

© AVALON TRAVEL

26

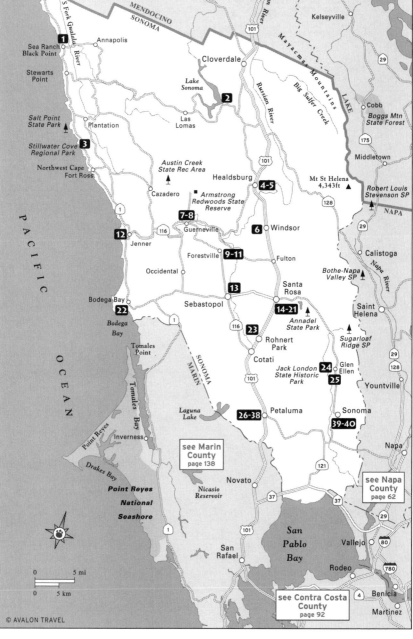

SONOMA COUNTY

CHAPTER 1

Sonoma County

Dog-friendly wineries. Off-leash parks galore. Sumptuous resorts and cute cottages that welcome dogs. French bistros and casual wine-country dining where dogs no one bats an eye at a dog, except to say, "Would you like some more water, pooch?"

Sonoma County is getting to be so dog friendly that dogs have become almost de rigueur here. "I visited Sonoma and felt naked without a dog," a reader, Kim, wrote me after she and her husband spent a romantic weekend exploring the region. (They'd been wanting a dog for years, and upon returning home they adopted a mellow malamute mix, Edna, who now travels with them regularly.)

Sonoma County has everything a dog's heart could desire, including the occasional ripe whiff of agriculture at its finest. Practically anything will grow here. It's the Bay Area capital for trees, flowers, and vegetables, as well as

PICK OF THE LITTER—SONOMA COUNTY

BIGGEST DOG PARK
Rocky Memorial Dog Park, Petaluma (page 56)

BEST BEACH
Sonoma Coast State Beaches, Jenner (page 43)

MOST DOG-FRIENDLY PLACES TO EAT
Willi's Seafood Restaurant, Healdsburg (page 34)
Bistro des Copains, Occidental (page 44)
Garden Court Cafe, Glen Ellen (page 52)

BEST PEOPLE WATCHING
Harmony Lounge, Sonoma (page 60)

BEST ANTIQUE-Y PLACE TO STAY
Camellia Inn, Healdsburg (page 36)

BEST LODGING SWIMMING POOL THAT ALLOWS DOGS
(ONLY ONE IN THE STATE!)
Casita Carneros' 20x40-foot pool, Sonoma (page 61)

MOST BEAUTIFUL OCEANFRONT HOUSE
Robinsong, rented through **Sea Ranch Vacation Homes,**
Sea Ranch (page 30)

LODGING WITH BIGGEST ACREAGE
Relais du Soleil, Glen Ellen (page 53)

MOST DOG-FRIENDLY PLACES TO STAY

Fern Grove Cottages, Guerneville (page 39)

Larissa House, Guerneville (page 39)

Wagging Woods, rented through **Russian River Getaways,** Guerneville (page 40)

Dock Calm, rented through **Russian River Vacation Homes,** Guerneville (page 41)

Sonoma Orchid Inn, Guerneville (page 41)

Sheraton Sonoma County, Petaluma (page 59)

COOLEST WINERY DOG EVENTS

Lambert Bridge Winery's Yappy Hour, Healdsburg (page 34)

Kunde Family Estate's Eco-Tour Dog Hikes, Kenwood (page 35)

MOST FUN ON A RIVER

Renting a Dog-Friendly Canoe at Russian River Adventures, Healdsburg (page 33)

goats, sheep, cattle, chickens, pigs, and probably a few farm animals that are being invented right now. Horticulturist Luther Burbank called the county "the chosen spot of all the Earth as far as nature is concerned." Dogs love this proximity to Mother Earth and Mother Cow Patty and Mother Chicken Manure. (See the Diversion *Sniff Out the Farm Trail* for ways to get close to this delightful aspect of Sonoma County.)

Sea Ranch

PARKS, BEACHES, AND RECREATION AREAS

◼ Sea Ranch Beach Trails

🐾 🐾 🐾 (See Sonoma County map on page 26)

Sea Ranch is a private development, but seven public foot trails cross the property leading to the beach, which is also public property. The smooth, wide dirt trails are managed by Sonoma County Regional Parks, and they offer incomparable solitary walks through unspoiled grassy hills.

All the trails are clearly marked on Highway 1. Each trailhead has restrooms and a box where you are asked to deposit $7 for parking. No motorcycles, bicycles, or horses are allowed. Keep your dog on leash.

Here are the distances to the beach, listing trails from north to south: Salal Trail, 0.6 mile; Bluff-Top Trail, 3.5 miles; Walk-On Beach Trail, 0.4 mile; Shell Beach Trail, 0.6 mile; Stengel Beach Trail, 0.2 mile; Pebble Beach Trail, 0.3 mile; Black Point Trail, 0.3 mile. 707/785-2377.

PLACES TO STAY

Sea Ranch Vacation Homes beach rentals: The Sea Ranch Vacation Homes rental agency offers 16 beautiful, dog-friendly homes for rent in the glorious oceanfront community of Sea Ranch. Some homes are almost on the water, some are set in wooded areas, and some next to meadows. All are attractive, but our favorite is Robinsong, a stellar example of how a seaside home can live up to its landscape. The fireplace flanked by smartly cushioned "window

seats" is worth the price of admission. You will love reading there, and your dog will adore snoozing on a blanket beside you. The look of the interior is clean and crisp, yet amazingly cozy. The spacious kitchen, which boasts an island, is set up for the chef in you.

Rates for the Robinsong are $315 nightly (there's a two-night minimum) and $1,890 for the week. It's one of the more expensive dog-friendly homes, but if you have it in your budget, it's worth it. Rates for the variety of dog-friendly homes are $160–350. Weekly rates are $960–2,100. Dogs are $40 extra nightly. For reservations and information, call 707/884-4235; www.sea ranchrentals.com.

Cloverdale

PARKS, BEACHES, AND RECREATION AREAS

◪ Lake Sonoma Recreation Area

🐾🐾🐾 (See Sonoma County map on page 26)

This is the only recreation site in the nine counties of the Bay Area run by the U.S. Army Corps of Engineers, and it's too bad. The Corps has a liberal attitude toward dogs, and this park is beautifully developed and managed, not to mention clean. It's also free. You must keep your dog on a six-foot leash, and he's not allowed on the swimming beach at the north end, but rangers told us there's no rule against dogs swimming anywhere else.

If you're the type who doesn't clean up after your dog, here's a warning: Change your act, or stay far from here. Rangers have been known to charge a cleanup fee for owners who ignore the deposits of their dogs.

A large lawn with picnic tables, some shaded, is at the visitors center. You can rent a boat from the private concession on the lake, which allows leashed dogs on all boats. Follow signs from the visitors center. To reserve a boat, call 707/433-2200. Waterskiing and camping are also popular here.

For a good dog hike, pick up a map at the visitors center and drive west on Dry Creek Road to the trailheads, which have their own parking lots. There are 40 miles of trails. Here are two of our favorites: There's a bit of shade at the Gray Pine Flat Trailhead. This smooth foot trail goes down to the lake through an unusual forest of foothill pines, madrone, manzanita, and blooming desert brush. The buzz of motorboats on the lake blends with the hammering of woodpeckers. You get a good view of the lake fairly quickly. If you'd prefer less of a climb back to the trailhead, take the Little Flat Trail, which starts lower down.

Horses are allowed on these trails, but bikes aren't—a plus for your dog's safety. Unfortunately, it gets bone-dry here in summer, and poison oak is common.

Camping is available at 113 sites at Liberty Glen Campground and several primitive boat-in sites on the lake. None of these sites has water. (Campers at Liberty Glen can stock up nearby.) Rates are $10–14. For reservations (advised in summer), phone 877/444-6777.

Take U.S. 101 to the Canyon Road exit. Go west to Dry Creek Road and turn right into the entrance. Take a right at the only fork. 707/433-9483 or 707/431-4533.

Timber Cove
PARKS, BEACHES, AND RECREATION AREAS

❸ Stillwater Cove Regional Park
😸😸😸 (See Sonoma County map on page 26)

This is a tiny but delightful beach at the foot of spectacular pine-covered cliffs. Park in the small lot beside Highway 1, leash your dog, and walk down. There is a larger picnic area above the highway, where a $6 day-use fee is charged. From here, you have to cross the highway to get to the cove. Look both ways!

There are 23 campsites. Two are available on a first-come, first-served basis. For the others, phone 707/565-2267 for reservations. Sites are $25. Dogs are $2 extra. The turnout is about one mile north of Fort Ross State Park (where dogs are banned). 707/847-3245.

Healdsburg
PARKS, BEACHES, AND RECREATION AREAS

❹ Villa Chanticleer Dog Park
😸😸😸😸🐕 (See Sonoma County map on page 26)

This 1.5-acre fenced dog park is a great place to take your dog whether you live here or you're just visiting. It's within a beautiful oak grove setting, so it's easy on the eyes, plus there's plenty of shade. Lucky dogs who come here have it all: trees, enough room to romp, and the smells of nature. It has all the good dog-park amenities, including benches and water. The ground cover is wood chips, which adds to the woodsy feeling here, but Jake thinks each wood chip is a delicacy and is content to plop himself down and gnaw away until an interesting dog or errant tennis ball catches his eye. Note that if you have an older or smaller dog, you might be better off at Badger Park.

The park is set within the larger Villa Chanticleer Park, which has buildings and backdrops that are popular for weddings. Be sure your dog is on leash if you explore beyond the dog area: You don't want your dog interfering with any nuptials. The address is 1248 Chanticleer Way.

DIVERSION

Canoe with Canine: Plenty of companies rent canoes to people who want to explore lakes and rivers. But very few advertise that they love dogs and that dogs love canoes. Meet **Russian River Adventures.** The company that expounds on the great variety of wildlife you'll see while paddling down the Russian River is the same one that says "Bring Fido!" This section of the river is terrific for viewing birds, including egrets, osprey, and owls. It's also one of the best for going swimming and playing in the water. Most dogs do indeed love it. When we take Jake on a canoe, though, he won't sit down. It seems he feels it's his duty to keep the canoe balanced just so. He looks like a misplaced figurehead of a dog-loving ship. He never wants to leave, though, so I assume he is having fun. Either that, or he's too petrified that he'll tip the canoe and land in the water (heaven forbid for a water dog with webbed feet).

A big thanks to Denise and Kelly for letting us know about this place. Their dog Fergus apparently loves swimming, but screams the whole time he's in the water. "A bit alarming, to say the least," says Denise. Rates for a few hours with the canoe are $49 per person. Children 2–12 are $24. Dogs are $10. 20 Healdsburg Avenue, Healdsburg; 707/433-5599; www.soar1.com/rradventures/welcome.htm.

5 Badger Dog Park

🐾🐾🐾🦮 (See Sonoma County map on page 26)

If your dog is small, old, or on the inactive side for whatever reason, this is the Healdsburg dog park to visit. Your elderly dog won't need an AARP card to enter, but if you have a dog like Jake (big, youngish, and very active), you should take your business to Villa Chanticleer Dog Park. Badger Dog Park is a lovely little fenced park, with one gorgeous large oak that people tend to congregate under. The ground is grassy, which dog paws appreciate. If only this park were bigger than a quarter acre we could give it an extra paw. It's set within Badger Park, which is at 750 Heron Drive. 707/431-3384.

PLACES TO EAT

Costeaux French Bakery: Stroll around Healdsburg's good-looking town square, with its old buildings and benches for shady rest stops, and then drop in here for dinner or a wonderful pastry snack at an outdoor table. 417 Healdsburg Avenue; 707/433-1913.

Oakville Grocery: This gourmet grocer is the home of a terrific alfresco café where dogs are welcome. The outdoor café features a wood-burning fireplace, which makes for cozy evenings. Jake loves sniffing the rotisserie chicken, and the pizzas are to drool for. Wine is big here, too, but dogs should stick with water: There's always a doggy bowl here for thirsty pooches. (Don't let the "No Dogs Allowed" sign scare you off. "That's only for yappy or dangerous dogs," says a friendly manager.) 124 Matheson Street; 707/433-3200.

Willi's Seafood Restaurant: Like starters? This seafood restaurant is all about starters/tapas with a seafood bent. Blissfully, the seafood is oh-so-fresh.

DIVERSIONS

Merlot Over and Play Dead: I didn't make up this pun. (Mine are usually worse.) It's the name of a wine made by a Healdsburg vintner who owns the Mutt Lynch Winery. Other "doggone good wines," as Brenda Lynch calls them, are Canis Major and Portrait of a Mutt.

Sonoma County wineries are going to the dogs. Some have their own lines of dog-labeled wines. Several allow well-behaved dogs in their tasting rooms and at their picnic areas. I don't list which ones allow pooches in the tasting rooms because the health department doesn't necessarily approve, and I don't want to get anyone in trouble. Below is a taste of some of Sonoma's more dog-friendly wineries, listed by area. Phone the individual wineries for hours, prices, and dog-friendly specifics. (Some are by appointment only.) For a more complete list go to www.sonomacounty.com/what-to-do/wineries, and look for the symbol for dog-friendly wineries.

GEYSERVILLE

Raymond Burr Vineyards, 8339 West Dry Creek Road; 888/900-0024; www.raymondburrvineyards.com.

Stryker Sonoma, 5110 Highway 128; 707/433-1944; www.strykersonoma.com.

HEALDSBURG

Acorn Winery, 2040 Old Redwood Highway; 707/433-6440; www.acornwinery.com.

Lambert Bridge Winery, 4085 West Dry Creek Road; 707/431-9600; www.lambertbridge.com. (Note: Friday late afternoons/early evenings there's a Yappy Hour, with pizza for humans and treats for dogs! Call for hours.)

Matrix Winery, 3291 Westside Road; 888/884-1288; www.matrixwinery.com.

Montemaggiore, 2355 West Dry Creek Road; 707/433-9499; www.montemaggiore.com.

Mutt Lynch Winery, 602 Limerick Lane; 707/942-6180; www.muttlynchwinery.com.

People who like ceviche say this is one of the best places to get it. The scallops wrapped in bacon are droolworthy. Chicken and other meaty dishes are also available, if you're not lured by fish. Nadia Stafford, who recommended this place to us, says the lobster rolls are to die for. What really puts a smile on a dog's snout is that the waitstaff will bring your dog a little treat and a bowl of water. Dine together on the mostly shaded patio. 403 Healdsburg Avenue; 707/433-9191.

Quivira Vineyards, 4900 West Dry Creek Road; 707/431-8333; www.quivirawine.com.

KENWOOD
Kunde Family Estate, 9825 Sonoma Highway; 707/833-5501; www.kunde.com. (See Diversion, *Hike and Drink With Your Dog,* for a fantastic outing offered by this marvelously dog-friendly winery.

VJB Vineyards & Cellars, 9077 Sonoma Highway; 707/833-2300; www.vjbcellars.com.

SANTA ROSA
De Loach Vineyards, 1791 Olivet Road; 707/526-9111; www.deloachvineyards.com.

Hanna Winery & Vineyards, 5353 Occidental Road; 707/575-3371; www.hannawinery.com.

Martin Ray Winery, 2191 Laguna Road; 707/823-2404; www.martinray-winery.com.

SEBASTOPOL
Graton Ridge Cellars, 3561 Gravenstein Highway North; 707/823-3040; www.gratonridge.com.

Taft Street Winery, 2030 Barlow Lane; 707/823-2049; www.taftstreetwinery.com.

SONOMA
Homewood Winery, 23120 Burndale Road; 707/996-6353; www.homewoodwinery.com.

Imagery Estate Winery, 14335 Highway 12; 707/935-4500; www.imagerywine.com.

Ledson Winery & Vineyards, 7335 Highway 12; 707/537-3810; www.ledsonwinery.com.

Nicholson Ranch Vineyards & Winery, 4200 Napa Road; 707/938-8822; www.nicholsonranch.com.

Sebastiani Vineyards and Winery, 389 4th Street East; 707/933-3230; www.sebastiani.com.

PLACES TO STAY

Best Western Dry Creek Inn: This is one of the more upscale Best Westerns we've visited. It has a Tuscan ambiance, and the rooms are lovely and comfy. The heated pool beckons, but keep water dogs out. Ditto for the occasional wine tastings they have here. (Dogs are sloppy drunks.) Rates are $115–199. Dogs are $30 extra. 198 Dry Creek Road 95448; 707/433-0300; www.drycreekinn.com.

Camellia Inn: Jake's and my jaws dropped at the same time (not a pretty sight) when we learned that dogs are welcome to stay in two rooms at this exquisite 1871 Italianate Victorian. The rooms look like they're straight out of the 1800s, only with modern, super comfy bedding and amenities. A walk around the grounds is a must. There are more than 50 varieties of camellias around the inn. The inn's website has a garden directory, so you'll be able to identify all the foliage and trees. Canines have no problem sniffing out the dogwoods.

The inn may be an antique wonder, but it splashes into the present with a lovely pool, which is a blessing on summer days. In warmer months, an evening wine and cheese social is held poolside. In cooler months, they bring the goodies inside the inn's cozy parlor. A delightful breakfast comes with your stay. "But we don't make dog breakfasts," an innkeeper explained apologetically. That's OK. Dogs are thrilled to be able to set paw here. Rates for the dog-friendly rooms are $199–289. 211 North Street 95448; 707/433-8182 or 800/727-8282; www.camelliainn.com.

The Irish Rose Inn: This small, quaint inn in the heart of Dry Creek Valley is pink, and it's surrounded by 95 rose bushes. But even the manliest of dogs enjoys a stay here, thanks to owner Chris Matson's hospitality and a relaxed, friendly atmosphere. (Oh, and because dogs are fairly color-blind.) Dogs also get treats if their parents—you—are OK with that.) The two guest rooms in the main house are pleasant and airy. We like Michael's room for its mosquito-netting-draped king bed. There's also the Chateau Margi, a one-bedroom cottage with a small kitchen.

My favorite part of the Irish Rose is the pretty porch, where you can sit and relax in one of the wicker chairs after coming back from a day of wine-tasting. There's an afternoon wine and cheese social and a full, tasty breakfast. Rates are $160–200, but management says they frequently have specials, so be sure to inquire. 3232 Dry Creek Road 95448; 707/431-2801 or 707/696-0751; www .theirishroseinn.com.

Windsor

Until 1992, Windsor wasn't anything but an unincorporated county area. Then it became a town, thanks to the "d" word (development). In 1997, it spawned its very first park, and with that park came a fenced-in dog park. Dogs think Windsor's movers and shakers are very smart people, indeed.

DIVERSION

Hike and Drink With Your Dog: If you enjoy a vigorous hike and good food and company, you must put a **Kunde Family Estate Eco-Tour Dog Hike** on your list of things you really need to do this summer. Fourth-generation winegrower Jeff Kunde leads a pack of happy dogs and people on a three-mile hike through this 1,850-acre wine-growing estate and up to breathtaking panoramic views about 800 feet higher than where you started. This hike isn't for the fair of paw, but it's worth the effort. It's great fun, you'll meet wonderful dogs and people, and after the hike you'll be treated to a wine-tasting and yummy box lunch while overlooking the beautiful Sonoma Valley from your scenic perch. Dogs get a "water bar" and treats.

The fee is $45 per person. A portion of the fee is donated to Canine Companions for Independence and the Sonoma County Humane Society. Great causes, to be sure. Hikes meet in the winery's tasting room, at 9 A.M. Dates are on the winery's website: www.kunde.com. Reserve at Kunde's hospitality department at 707/833-5501, ext. 334. The winery is at 9825 Sonoma Highway.

PARKS, BEACHES, AND RECREATION AREAS

6 Pleasant Oak Park

🐾🐾🐕 (See Sonoma County map on page 26)

This is a fine example of how a fenced-in dog park can become a decent place, despite a rather austere start. In the park's early days, it was little more than a dirt lot surrounded by a very high fence with double gates. But now it's really something to wag about. It has water, grass, and enough trees to cast a cooling shade in the summer. Dogs from miles around come to socialize. Their humans have been known to follow suit. The park is at Old Redwood Highway and Pleasant Avenue. 707/838-1260.

Guerneville

Guerneville is the largest town on the Russian River. The river area is both a longstanding family vacation destination and a gay/lesbian-friendly resort area. What really counts, though, is that it's so dog-friendly. Behold!

PARKS, BEACHES, AND RECREATION AREAS

🐾 Armstrong Redwoods State Reserve

🐾🐾 (See Sonoma County map on page 26)

As is usual in state parks, you can take a dog only on paved roads and into picnic areas. But here you can give your dog and yourself an exceptional treat. The picnic grounds are a cool, hushed redwood cathedral. You can walk on Armstrong Woods Road, which winds along Fife Creek (usually lush, but dry in the heart of summer) all the way to the top of McCray Mountain, about three miles.

The drive is fairly terrifying, so you may prefer to walk anyway. Hikers, bicycles, and autos all share the road, so be very careful. Your dog must be leashed everywhere in the park. From Guerneville, go about 2.5 miles north on Armstrong Woods Road. The day-use fee is $8, but if you park out front you can walk in for free. 707/869-2015 or 707/865-2391.

🐾 Vacation Beach

🐾🐾🐾 (See Sonoma County map on page 26)

Vacation Beach is not really a beach, but an access point where the Russian River is dammed by two roads across it. It's one of several public spots where you and your dog used to be able to legally jump into the drink, but leashes seem to be the law here now. It's still fun. People and pooches picnic, swim, put in canoes, and cool their feet and paws in the cool river.

From Highway 116 between Guerneville and Monte Rio, turn south at the unmarked road where you see Old Cazadero Road veering north. You can park at the approaches to the dams but not on the crossing itself. 707/869-9000.

PLACES TO EAT

Triple R Bar & Grill: You'll cluck for the chicken cobbler. You'll melt for the house-made mac and cheese (made with crispy onions). The home-style food here is great, and you can also get some lighter cuisine. The three R's in the Triple R stand for the dog-friendly Russian River Resort, of which the restaurant is part. Dogs can dine with you at the outdoor tables here. 16390 Fourth Street; 707/869-0691.

PLACES TO STAY

Creekside Inn and Resort: Dogs get to stay at three of several cottages and rooms at this fun inn near the Russian River. Bird dogs enjoy lounging in the Quail Cottage, a small, bright cottage with a fireplace. The Deck House, another poochy haven, is a little larger, with a sunny deck. The sweet one-bedroom Apple House is separated from the inn by a very old apple tree.

The inn's land is dotted with several large redwoods. The property spans three acres, and dogs are welcome to cruise around on leash. Human guests may hang out in the inn's main dining room and lounge, both of which have fireplaces. Humans can also swim in the pool here. Dogs have to be content to do the dog paddle in the Russian River, not too far away.

Rates are $125–210. Weekly rates are available. 16180 Neeley Road, P.O. Box 2185 95446; 707/869-3623 or 800/776-6586; www.creeksideinn.com.

Fern Grove Cottages: Sleep in one of 20 charming cabins under 200-foot redwoods here! The friendly owners, Mike and Margaret Kennett, welcome good pooches in five of the 20 rooms here. "We've had some great dogs stay here," says Margaret, who doles out biscuits at check-in and provides old blankets for your dog's sleeping pleasure.

The cottages are simple but cozy, with tasteful decor. Most have fireplaces, and some have kitchens. A delicious continental breakfast comes with your stay. The homemade granola and scones are divine. Rates are $89–259. Dogs are $25 extra. 16650 Highway 116 95446; 707/869-8105; www.ferngrove.com.

Dawn Ranch Lodge: The cottages on this 15-acre redwood-festooned property (formerly Fifes Guest Ranch) will melt your heart if you like older abodes. These were built in 1905, and they still have the charm of their day, updated with a simple, light, airy decor. They're super comfy, too. Dogs think they're the cat's meow, but truth be told, they really like walking around the ranch better. The meadows, the trees, the river, all speak to a dog's soul.

Cottages are $99–325. Dogs are $25 for the length of their stay. 16467 Highway 116, P.O. Box 45 95446; 707/869-0656 or 800/734-3371; www.dawn ranch.com.

Highlands Resort: If your dog has never been to a bar, ask to stay in the Highland's studio: The large room not only has a cozy fireplace, but it has its own wet bar. Teetotaling dogs might prefer the three larger cabins that allow dogs. The cabins have fireplaces, and some have kitchenettes, but no bar.

The Highlands, known as "a straight-friendly gay resort," is set on three wooded acres (which dogs can explore on leash) and has the feel of a country retreat. It has a swimming pool and outdoor hot tub—both clothing-optional. In the resort's brochure there's a bird's-eye–view picture of a fellow standing in the hot tub, with just a bit of bun showing. Joe Dog blushed and came back for another look.

Rates are $66–195. Dogs are $25 extra for the length of their stay. 14000 Woodland Drive 95446; 707/869-0333; www.highlandsresort.com.

Larissa House: This sweet one-bedroom home has a fenced garden/yard and private dock on the river. Nadia, the owner, lives next door and adores dogs. In fact, you pretty much have to have a dog to stay here. It's so dog-gone dog-friendly that the shower is designed so that you and your dog can shower at the same time (if your dog isn't too shy about these things). Nadia makes sure all dogs receive a welcoming bag of treats when they arrive. Dogs fall instantly in love when they meet Nadia, and the love-fest often continues year-round, when she sends them (note: *them,* not *you*) a Christmas card. Rates are $1,000 per week. 17798 Orchard Avenue 95446; 707/869-3651.

Russian River Getaways: If you and your dog want a home away from home while you vacation in the Russian River area, you've hit the jackpot. Russian River Getaways has dozens of beautiful dog-friendly homes for rent on a nightly or weekly basis. The homes are generally quite upscale, but the prices are fairly down to earth. (An aside that will put a smile on your dog's snout: The majority of the homes rented through Russian River Getaways permit dogs. "We tell them that if they don't allow dogs, they're not going to do such good business," says an employee. "They really can't compete.")

Most of the homes are very attractive, and some go the extra mile for dogs. Wagging Woods, for instance, is set on three acres, and one full acre is securely fenced so dogs can trot about leashless. Boy dogs are smitten with the "faerie ring" of redwood trees on the property. Some homes provide kayaks, others have their own spas or pools, and a few are historic beauties.

Rates for the homes range $160–3,300 nightly, and there's a two-night minimum. There's also a cleaning fee, which varies with each house. Weekly rates are available. 707/869-4560 or 800/433-6673; www.rrgetaways.com.

Russian River Resort: This is a great place to meet a man, especially if you are a man. When we swung by for a peek at the resort, the saline pool was chock full of guys. Unlike at another clothing-optional dog-friendly resort down the road, everyone was wearing a swimsuit. Jake, who has been known to make friends with sunbathers who opt for no clothes (see *Baker Beach* in the *San Francisco County* chapter), may have been disappointed, but he didn't show it: Cheering him up was the dog-loving attitude of the guests and staffers. (Dogs aren't allowed in the pool area, but Jake had a peek.) "What a GORGEOUS dog!" was a refrain Jake frequently reveled in during his visit.

This is an adults-only resort, and a manager says that while most of the guests are gay or lesbian, everyone is welcome here. (Just not children of the human variety.) Jake wasn't the only visitor wearing a collar and a leash when we visited. "Looks like we have something in common," said a man whose outfit matched Jake's, except for the leather vest and chaps he was wearing. His big bear of a friend, who was holding the other end of the leash, gave Jake a friendly head rub and chest scratch, but I refrained from giving *his* leashed friend the same treatment.

The rooms have been attractively redone since a flood did a number on them, and they have comfy beds, microwaves, and little fridges, and some even feature pellet stoves. And here's a real boon for the canine set: There's a small lawn area at the rear of the property where dogs can exercise and play. An attractive restaurant with a dog-friendly patio is also part of the setup here.

Dogs aren't allowed at the resort on weekends or holidays. The good news is that it's less expensive here midweek. Rates are $65–180. Dogs are $25 per stay. 16390 Fourth Street 95446; 707/869-0691 or 800/417-3767; www.russian riverresort.com.

Russian River Vacation Homes: Spend your Russian River–area vacation in your own charming private house. This is an ideal way to vacation with your pooch. Russian River Vacation Homes offers 35 beautiful, quaint houses for pets and their people. From a one-bedroom rustic log cabin on the river to a three-bedroom riverside home complete with hot tub, you and your holiday hound will find the home of your dreams.

Scooter the Dog contacted us to tell us about a lovely two-bedroom rental home she co-owns with her people, Ed and Nancy. It's called Dock Calm, and sure enough, it has a river dock, and you'll feel very calm here. All rooms have river views. It's a very dog-friendly place, with nice furniture that's mostly fine for pooches. There's even a doggy door. Dogs also get to use a big doggy bed. Jake, a hearth dog if ever there was one, recommends putting it by the fire on a chilly evening. You could spend the day with your dog just lazing on the deck, with its outdoor couch and lounge chairs. A wonderful hot tub graces a second deck, and the river views from here are droolworthy. And speaking of drool, visiting dogs get complimentary dog treats with their stay.

Rates for the range of Russian River Vacation Homes are $145–535. Weekly rates are $750–2,450. Dock Calm falls somewhere in the middle. 707/869-9030; www.riverhomes.com.

Sonoma Orchid Inn: The rooms here are beg for glowing adjectives. They're homey, elegant, well appointed, cozy, and very dog-friendly. Six of the inn's nine rooms welcome pooches, who get treats and a list of dog-friendly wineries and beaches upon arrival. Some rooms have little fridges, some have gas fireplaces, and all the dog rooms have private entrances. (It's great for dogs being pursued by paparazzi.) The inn can arrange for an on-site or off-site dog sitter, should you be going to a spa or other destination where dogs aren't allowed. Not that you'll even want to think about it while you're here, but there's free Wi-Fi for those who need to stay plugged in.

Other fun treats: The inn has a swimming pool, which is a godsend in the summer. A sumptuous gourmet breakfast–centered around eggs from the inn's organically raised chickens, and other fresh local ingredients—is served in the Farmhouse Greatroom. In the afternoon you can nibble fresh-baked goodies (like cookies, not Milk-Bones). Rates are $149–229. Dogs are $30 extra nightly, but the owners really like to try to waive or reduce the fee, so if you keep your room nice and unhairy and ungrimey, you may have a shot of them waving their magic "no dog fee" wand over your wallet. But if they don't, don't take it personally. It takes quite a bit to make dog rooms perfectly spotless. 12850 River Road 95446; 707/869-4466 or 888/877-4466; www.ridenhour inn.com. (Yes, that's the website.)

Forestville

This beautiful town's motto is: "Where wine country meets the redwoods." This is Russian River country, and dogs love sniffing around some terrific beaches here. Be sure to visit the historic community's little "downtown." It's an eclectic charmer.

PARKS, BEACHES, AND RECREATION AREAS

If you have a dog who likes splashing in water, prepare for a very happy pooch: Forestville is home to three county beaches that permit leashed dogs. They're all Russian River havens, with good river access, old black walnut forests, German ivy, and lots of birds. Dogs need to be leashed, but there's plenty to enjoy, even tethered together. Since this pretty much describes all three river access locales, below we'll just list the pertinent info for each.

9 Steelhead Beach
😺 😺 😺 (See Sonoma County map on page 26)

At 50 acres, with lots of picnic areas and flat grassy territory, this is the largest and most developed of the three county beach access areas in Forestville. If you drive in, you pay $6. Walk in and it's free. The park is at 9000 River Road. 707/565-2041.

10 Forestville River Access/Mom's Beach
😺 😺 😺 (See Sonoma County map on page 26)

It's 10 acres of on-leash fun here. This is an undeveloped area, at 10584 River Drive, off River Road, but it'll cost you $5 to enter, developed or not. 707/565-2041.

11 Sunset Beach
😺 😺 😺 (See Sonoma County map on page 26)

This is a wild and lovely river access location, with about 10 acres to explore with your leashed dog. Entry costs $5. 11057 Sunset Drive. 707/565-2041.

PLACES TO EAT

Russian River Pub: This log-cabin pub is known for its chicken wings ("Ain't no Thing but a Chicken Wing," read the t-shirts that adorn the servers), but much of the food here isn't typical pub grub; it's quality cuisine. You can order items like a seared ahi tuna salad, house-made pesto on a chicken sandwich, and meats that have been lovingly brined and coddled for hours. There are even some vegetarian options. Many regulars lovingly call the pub a dive, but you can't dive too deep with food like this. Dine with your dog on the patio. 11829 River Road; 707/887-7932.

Jenner

PARKS, BEACHES, AND RECREATION AREAS

1 2 Sonoma Coast State Beaches

🐾🐾🐾🐾 (See Sonoma County map on page 26)

A string of beautiful, clean beaches runs south from Jenner to Bodega Bay, and you can't go wrong from Goat Rock Beach south to Salmon Creek Beach: Gorgeous bluff views, stretches of brown sand, gnarled rocks, and grassy dunes welcome you. Always keep an eye on the surf and a leash on your dog.

Dogs are not allowed on any of the trails that run on the bluffs above the beaches, on Bodega Head, in the Willow Creek area east of Bridgehaven, or in the seal rookery upriver from Goat Rock Beach. (Watch for the warning sign.) No camping is permitted on any of the beaches, except Bodega Dunes and Wright's Beach, which have campgrounds. These two also charge a $6 day-use fee. Day use of all other beaches is free. 707/875-3483.

The Bodega Dunes Campground has 99 developed sites, and Wright's Beach Campground has 27 developed sites. Sites are $35 at Bodega, and $35–45 at Wright's. Reservations are highly recommended. Call 800/444-7275. For general beach info, call 707/875-3483.

PLACES TO STAY

Jenner Inn: This area is a black hole for cell phone reception, and only a few of the rooms and cottages have phones or TVs, so this is a great place to visit if you really want to get away from it all. (That said, they do have Internet access in the parlor these days.)

There's so much relaxing to be done here that you'll scarcely notice that you're not doing anything. The early-20th-century rooms and cottages are comfy and furnished with antiques. Some have fireplaces, some have kitchens, and some have river views. The Russian River is just a bone's throw away, and it's a fairly quick walk to the ocean, should you want to see big water. The best part of staying here with a dog is the big three-acre meadow in the back: Pooches are welcome to trot around off leash! You won't need to worry about finding a local dog park if you stay here. Rates are $118–298. Dogs are $25 extra. Highway 1, Box 69 95450; 707/865-2377; www.jennerinn.com.

Duncan's Mills

This cute little town on the Russian River is home to a general store, a candy store, a couple of restaurants, a wine-tasting store, several antiques shops, and a smattering of other sweet little places. It's a good, old-fashioned town that's had some new life breathed into it in recent years. Seventy percent of the 20 or so businesses here are run by women. Many of them are dog friendly.

PLACES TO EAT

Cape Fear Cafe: I hope this fun eatery is named for the beautiful Cape Fear coast of North Carolina, and not the disturbing movie where a dog gets poisoned (among other gruesome incidents). The people here are friendly, and the food—mostly of the American genre, mixed with some fun international renditions—is quite tasty. Dogs are welcome to dine with you at the umbrella-topped tables on the patio, but only on uncrowded weekdays. (It's a pretty small eating area.) 25191 Highway 116; 707/865-9246.

Occidental

If you become an accidental Occidental tourist, you and your leashed pooch can enjoy a stroll through this historic landmark town, with its interesting assortment of shops and galleries. If you want to eat great food and/or spend the night, there's a dog-friendly restaurant and lodging.

PLACES TO EAT

Bistro des Copains: Ooh la la, dogs love this French bistro. Is it the *Bauf en Daube à la Provençale* (for you non-French-speaking dogs, that's beef braised in red wine with lots of good stuff)? Is it the *Magret de Canard* (dog French lesson No. 2: duck breasts with more good stuff)? Who knows? It could even be the creamy risottos served with delectable ingredients. Maybe they just love it because they're welcome here, and they get biscuits and water when they join you on the pretty patio. The wine selection is lovely, too, but dogs don't generally care about this. 3782 Bohemian Highway; 707/874-2436.

PLACES TO STAY

Negri's Occidental Hotel: This is a very basic, although decent, motel. It's close to the village, and there's a pool, should you feel like doing the dog paddle. (Your dog needs to stay dry here.) Rates are $85–190. Dogs are $15 extra. 3610 Bohemian Highway 95465; 707/874-3623 or 877/867-6084; www.occidentalhotel.com.

DIVERSION

Sniff Out the Farm Trail: This area is replete with fun little farms, selling everything from apples to wine to Christmas trees to meat and cheese. Well-behaved leashed dogs are often invited to join you at the many different farms that are part of the **Sonoma County Farm Trails.** Phone ahead to make sure it's OK. You can get a Farm Trails map and info at www.farmtrails.org.

Sebastopol

Dogs enjoy sniffing out this sweet semirural community. It's got oodles of little Farm Trails farms (see the Diversion *Sniff Out the Farm Trail*), should you be drooling for some fresh produce. (Some sell meat, too, should that interest your dog.)

PARKS, BEACHES, AND RECREATION AREAS

13 Ragle Ranch Regional Park Dog Park/ Animal Care Center Dog Park

🐾 🐾 🐕 (See Sonoma County map on page 26)

It's only a half-acre, but this simple little fenced park provides a welcome relief for dogs longing to run around without a leash. A doggy/human water fountain with a bone-shaped pad is a refreshing sight. Ground cover is hay—fitting for the area's rural feel. Trees, shrubs, benches, and other park accommodations will follow with more donations of time and money.

The park is within Ragle Ranch Regional Park, which has a lovely nature trail that will take you and your leashed dog to Atascadero Creek. Hang onto that leash, because this is a primo bird-watching area. Boy dogs love the oak grove that shades this area. From Highway 12, drive north on Ragle Road. The dog park is at 500 Ragle Ranch Road. 707/565-2041.

PLACES TO EAT

West Side Cafe: This eatery used to be called the Animal House Café, which struck us as odd for an Asian restaurant, but apparently that was left over from its days as a crazy deli. You can get an assortment of Asian foods, from Chinese to Japanese to Thai. The curries are particularly tasty. Dogs are welcome to join you on the patio. 171 Pleasant Hill Avenue; 707/823-1800.

Santa Rosa

PARKS, BEACHES, AND RECREATION AREAS

This sprawling city welcomes dogs off leash at several of its parks.

14 DeTurk Round Barn Park

🐾🐾🐾🐕 (See Sonoma County map on page 26)

This is one of the more interesting parks to peruse with your pooch. It's a smallish park in the historic west-side district of town, and it's home to a wonderful rare round barn that was built in the 1870s. Dogs have to be leashed to explore around the barn area.

What dogs like best about this park is a relatively small (9,000 square feet) dog park where they can throw their leashes to the wind. It's fenced with attractive white wood and has some young trees working to become shade trees. The dog park is actually called Maverick Park, in honor of a valuable member of the K-9 Corps of the Sonoma County Sheriff's Department who was killed in the line of duty in Santa Rosa. We won't forget you, Maverick.

The park is at Donahue and 8th Streets. 707/543-3292 or 707/539-5979.

15 Doyle Park

🐾🐾🐾🐾🐕 (See Sonoma County map on page 26)

Doyle Park is a very stately place to take a pooch. A little stone bridge takes you over a stream and into the park's main entry area. The trees here have an elegant, deep-rooted look. The grass is like a cool, plush green carpet. At Doyle, even the squirrels don't look squirrelly.

Dogs think it's all grand. But what they think is even better is the fact that they can run around all this splendor without a leash 6–8 A.M., thanks to a great program run by the city. Dogs who can't make these hours don't have to mope around on leash, though: Doyle Park is graced not only with the off-leash program, but with its very own fenced doggy park. It's not as riveting as the rest of the park, but it's got water and some trees, and it's a very safe place to take even an escape artist. Like Rincon Park's dog run, Doyle's dog run closes during winter rains to keep the grass happy.

In addition to the rules mentioned in the beginning of this section, there's one that's a little tough if you're a parent of a dog and a young child: No children under 10 years old are allowed in the dog run, whether accompanied by a parent or not. The park users devised this rule, apparently meant to protect kids from getting mowed over by herds of dogs, and also to protect herds of dogs from lawsuits.

For the main entrance, take Sonoma Avenue to Doyle Park Drive and turn south, driving a few hundred feet over insufferable speed bumps to the parking area. The dog run will be way over to the left. To park closer to the dog run, take Sonoma Avenue to Hoen Avenue and turn south. The parking lot is on the right, and the dog run is on the other side of the ball field. 707/543-3292 or 707/539-5979.

16 Franklin Park

👣👣🐕 (See Sonoma County map on page 26)

Dogs can run off leash here during very limited hours: 6–8 A.M. It's green and slopey, with enough trees to make any boy dog happy. Be careful, because it's not as safe from traffic as some of the other parks (though it's not exactly Indy 500 territory around here).

The park is at Franklin Avenue and Gay Street. 707/543-3292 or 707/539-5979.

17 Galvin Community Park

👣👣👣🐕 (See Sonoma County map on page 26)

Yahoo! This is yet another addition to Santa Rosa's growing legion of dog parks. The fenced dog park is where your pooch can run free here. It's about 0.75 acre. Amenities include benches for your tired tush and water for your thirsty pooch. The ground cover is mostly wood chips, and it smells so good when it's first brought in. Sometimes it can be a little hard to tell the poop from the wood chips, but you get used to it. Jake always poops in the grass, which is easy to see, but so hard to clean up. (This is more than you needed to know about Jake.)

The park is at Yulupa Avenue and Bennett Valley Road. 707/543-3292 or 707/539-5979.

18 Northwest Community Park

👣👣👣🐕 (See Sonoma County map on page 26)

The fenced dog park within Northwest Park has doubled in size since its inception and is once again up and running—and so are the neighborhood dogs. (No, smarty, the dogs haven't actually doubled in size.)

The dog area is now an acre and has two sections, grass, some shade, and benches. The dog park is just northwest of Northwest Park's soccer fields. The park is on Marlow Road, behind Comstock Junior High School, north of Guerneville Road. 707/543-3292 or 707/539-5979.

19 Rincon Valley Community Park

👣👣👣👣🐕 (See Sonoma County map on page 26)

The fenced dog park here is one of the more attractive dog parks in these parts. That's mostly because it has grass. Real grass. Not just a few green sprigs fighting their way through the tough dirt, but good ol' carpety grass. That's not because the dogs here pussyfoot around. In fact, dogs are so happy to be here that they tear around with great gusto. We're not exactly sure why there's so much grass, but we do know that the dog run closes during the rainy winter months, so that could have something to do with it.

A few trees grace the dog-run area, and the views of the surrounding hills make it seem as if it's in the middle of the countryside. As of this writing, it's actually on the edge of the countryside.

The dogs who come to Rincon's dog run are a friendly lot, running to the fence and sniffing all newcomers, tails wagging exuberantly. The people who come here are much the same, except they chat rather than sniff. A parks department spokesman says park users made up the rule. So apparently if you've got a kid and a dog, you'll have to hire a sitter to bring your dog here. Boo!

But now here's something to cheer about: The dog park includes a little wading pond! This puts some big wag in a water dog's tail. There's also a separate section for large and small dogs. The park is on Montecito Boulevard, west of Calistoga Road. Don't forget that it's closed during rainy winter weather. 707/543-3292 or 707/539-5979.

20 Spring Lake Regional Park
🐾🐾🐾 (See Sonoma County map on page 26)

In winter, this county park doesn't offer dogs much more than a leashed trot around the lake. But in summer, it's leafy and full of the sounds of kids yelling and thumping oars. It's more fun here for people than dogs, who must be leashed. This is a good spot for a picnic, in-line skating, working out on a parcourse fitness trail, a boat ride, or human swimming (no dogs allowed in the swim area). The path around the lake is paved for skaters, strollers, and bicyclists, and there are short dirt paths off into the open oak and brush woods. You can fish from the banks, where they're cleared of tules and willows.

The parking fee is $6 in winter, $7 in summer; the large lot has some shady spots. Campsites are $25, plus $2 extra for a dog. Most of the 30 sites are reservable, and a few are first-come, first-served. For reservations phone 707/565-2267. Dogs must have proof of a rabies vaccination. The campground is open daily May 1–September 30, weekends and holidays the rest of the year.

From Highway 12, on the Farmer's Lane section in Santa Rosa, turn east on Hoen Avenue. Take Hoen four stoplights to Newanga Avenue. Turn left on Newanga, which goes straight to the entrance. 707/539-8092.

21 Youth Community Park
🐾🐾🐾 (See Sonoma County map on page 26)

If you like oak trees, come here. Big oaks hang out all over the park. Some really big, really old oaks even have their own fences, so no one can do leg lifts or initial carving on their trunks.

Dogs used to be allowed to run leash-free in the lawn area here during limited hours, but leashes are now the law 24/7. A word of warning: Skateboarders abound here. A little skateboard area is in front of the park, and kids love skateboarding around the parking lot, too. Some dogs don't even notice them; others get nervous about the sound of board crashing on pavement.

The park is in the far west reaches of the city, on the west side of Fulton Road, about 0.25 mile south of Piner Road. 707/543-3292.

PLACES TO EAT

Flying Goat Coffee: Dine with your dog at the four umbrella-topped tables outside. There's usually a bowl of water out here, too. (For your dog, not your feet.) 10 4th Street; 707/575-1202.

Juice Shack: In the summer, come here with your hot pooch and cool off with a creamy smoothie or a fresh organic juice. In cooler months, you can enjoy hot juices here. Hmm… I'd rather go for the hot soup served here, or the wrap sandwiches. Dine with your dog at the outdoor area under the big pine tree. Thirsty dogs will get water on request. 1810 Mendocino Avenue; 707/528-6131.

PLACES TO STAY

Best Western Garden Inn: If you want to keep things cool and then nuke them, you'll be happy to know all rooms come with a mini-fridge and a micro-wave. Rates are $89–194. Dogs are $15 extra. 1500 Santa Rosa Avenue 95404; 707/546-4031.

Days Inn: Rates are $60–129. Dogs are $10 extra. 3345 Santa Rosa Avenue 95401; 707/568-1011.

TraveLodge Santa Rosa: Rates at this TraveLodge are $55–139. Dogs are $15 extra; a second pet will run you $10 more. 1815 Santa Rosa Avenue 95407; 707/542-3472.

Bodega Bay

PARKS, BEACHES, AND RECREATION AREAS

22 Doran Beach Regional Park

🐾 🐾 🐾 (See Sonoma County map on page 26)

This Sonoma County regional park offers leashed dogs access to marshland full of egrets, herons, and deer, as well as to the Pinnacle Gulch Trail. The plain but serviceable beach has almost no surf (which is great for dog swims), and there are picnic tables near the beach.

The fee for day use is $6. Campsites are $18 plus $2 for each dog. The camp-ground has 134 sites. Reservations are recommended. The park is on High-way 1, one mile south of Bodega Bay. Phone 707/565-2041 for more info, or 707/565-2267 for camping reservations.

PLACES TO EAT

The Boat House: This restaurant in downtown Bodega Bay will allow you to sit with your dog as you eat fish-and-chips, oysters, and calamari at one of the six unshaded tables on its patio. If fish isn't your dog's wish, he can order a burger. 1445 Highway 1; 707/875-3495.

The Dog House: The name of the restaurant says it all. But if you need more, here are the words of one of the servers: "Dogs are treated better than people here." The Dog House is indeed a very dog-friendly place to dine. The food is unpretentious (hot dogs, burgers, etc.), and the servers love seeing a dog come to one of the eight outdoor tables. They often offer a bowl of water before the pooch even gets a chance to peruse the menu. 537 Highway 1; 707/875-2441.

Lucas Wharf: Your dog's nose will flare and drip with excitement as you dine at the outdoor tables here. That's partly because of the tasty deli specials, but it's mostly because your dog will be getting high on sea smells at this place right on the water. Speaking of water, the folks here love dogs and will provide your pooch with water, should she need to wet her whistle. 595 Highway 1; 707/875-3522.

Kenwood

PLACES TO STAY

Kenwood Oaks Guest House: This charming, comfortably appointed A-frame guesthouse is set on a two-acre horse ranch in the Sonoma Valley. Two friendly horses call the fields around the cottage home, and your dog will be so welcome she'll feel right at home, too. "I love dogs," says owner Joan Finkle, who is the proud mom of dogs Honey and Ella and who lives in a larger house across the property. "They're welcome off leash here, as long as they don't go in with the horses." (While the horses are friendly, some dogs don't know how to react when near these "giant dogs.")

The one-bedroom guesthouse is set back from the road about 300 yards, so there's ample buffer zone for fairly well voice-controlled dogs. It's fun to peruse the grounds, especially for boy dogs, who are agog at the giant valley oak by the house, and the other oaks nearby. A narrow, fenced doggy area sidles up to part of the length of the house and is accessible via a sliding glass door. It's about 20 feet long by six feet wide and has a gravelly ground cover. When the weather's right, guests sometimes use it if they want to hit the wineries or head to a restaurant and give their furry friends a break from touring.

You get free Wi-Fi here, should you need to get in touch with the non-rural world. Rates for the house are $195–275. There may be a cleaning deposit. The house is on Warm Springs Road. You'll get the address when you make your reservation. 707/833-1221; www.kenwoodoaksguesthouse.com.

Rohnert Park

PARKS, BEACHES, AND RECREATION AREAS

23 Robert's Lake Dog Park/Rohnert BARK

😾😾😾🐕 (See Sonoma County map on page 26)

The fenced dog park here is kind of long and narrow, but it's perfect for dogs who like to play fetch. It's pretty, and grassy, and has water, and a separate area for small dogs. It's adjacent to the lake in the larger Robert's Lake. Dogs may be leashed in the park area outside the dog park. The park is at 5010 Roberts Lake Drive; 707/565-2041.

PLACES TO STAY

Best Western Rohnert Park: This hotel is right next door to a huge veterinary center that is nationally renowned for its neurology department. If you find yourself taking your dog there, stay here. The manager, Johnny, loves dogs and brings his own pooch to work with him. According to Baron, a quesadilla-loving German shorthaired pointer who wrote to me, Johnny and the staff bent over backward making his stay as comfortable as possible when Baron was getting MRIs next door. Rates are $88–105. Dogs are $25 extra. 6500 Redwood Drive 94928; 707/584-7435.

Glen Ellen

PARKS, BEACHES, AND RECREATION AREAS

24 Jack London State Historic Park

😾😾😾 (See Sonoma County map on page 26)

The extensive backcountry trails here are off-limits to dogs, but the parts of historic interest are not. You're free to take your leashed dog the half mile to Wolf House, visiting Jack London's grave en route, and around the stone house containing the museum of Londoniana (open 10 A.M.–5 P.M., no pets inside). The trail is paved and smooth up to the museum, but then it becomes dirt and narrow.

Oaks, pines, laurels, and madrones cast dappled light, and the ups and downs are gentle. Signs warn of poison oak and rattlesnakes. The ruins of the huge stone lodge that was London's dream Wolf House are impressive and sad. A fire of unknown origin destroyed it in 1913. London planned to rebuild it, but he died three years later.

Dogs are also allowed in the picnic areas by the parking lot and the museum. From Highway 12, follow signs to the park. Turn west on Arnold Drive, then west again on London Ranch Road. The fee is $8 for day use. 707/938-5216.

25 Sonoma Valley Regional Park/ Elizabeth Anne Perrone Dog Park

🐾🐾🐾🐾🐕 (See Sonoma County map on page 26)

This large, welcoming park has a paved, level trail that winds alongside a branch of Sonoma Creek. Better yet for dogs who like to roll, it sports many dirt trails that head off into the oak woodlands above. Varied grasses, wildflowers, madrones, and moss-hung oaks make this a scenic walk. Dogs like to chew some of the grasses, roll on the wildflowers (don't let them do this!), and do leg lifts on the madrones and oaks. They may enjoy the park even more than you. If you start at the park entrance off Highway 12 and walk westward across the park to Glen Ellen for about a mile, you'll end up at Sonoma Creek and the old mill, with its huge working waterwheel.

Dogs need to be on leash for all that fun. But the big fenced dog park within the park is an exception. The Elizabeth Anne Perrone Dog Park is only about an acre, but it feels like more. It's totally landscaped, with grass and trees. "A dog lover's paradise," as reader Robin Domer and her furry children, Max and Oliver, wrote us. Pooper-scoopers, poop bags, and water are supplied.

The park is just south of Glen Ellen between Arnold Drive and Highway 12. The entrance is off Highway 12. The parking fee is $6. 707/539-8092.

PLACES TO EAT

Garden Court Cafe: This sweet café used to be right across the street from the leash-free Elizabeth Anne Perrone Dog Park, but it up and moved to downtown Glen Ellen. Fortunately it's every bit as dog-friendly as it used to be. Well-behaved dogs can join you on the patio, where they can drink from dog water bowls and even choose from a few items on a dog menu. Jake likes the Bleu Plate Special, a kind of egg scramble with burger, zucchini, and garlic. (His dog breath is rather interesting after such a meal.) If your dog hankers for something Italian, try the Babaloo pizza, which is a biscuit crust topped with ketchup, jack cheese, and fresh herbs. It's good-looking enough that you might be tempted to share it with your dog, but the human food here is tasty, too, and your dog will like you better if you order your own. If your dog doesn't feel like paying for one of these dishes, he can get a free house-made pooch biscuit. (Far from a consolation prize, judging by the blissful expression on Jake's face.) 13647 Arnold Drive; 707/935-1565.

PLACES TO STAY

The Chauvet: Is your wallet feeling very fat right now? How would you like a luxurious three-bedroom condo to call your own for a night or a week? The units at this gorgeous historic landmark in downtown Glen Ellen are huge–about 2,000 square feet each–with fabulous furnishings and gourmet kitchens. I won't spend too much time drooling over the details, because it's beyond reach for most dogs reading this book. You can look at the website and drool on your own keyboard. Rates are $545–595. Weekly rates are available. Dogs are allowed in certain units with prior approval. A big thanks to Barbara Steinberg for letting us know about this well-heeled option. 13756 Arnold Drive 95442; 707/996-6720; www.chauvetcondominium.com.

Relais du Soleil: This lodging's name translates to "a place in the sun." And what a place it is! It's a turn-of-the-previous-century spread that features two accommodations. Dogs get to stay in the more modern bunkhouse suite, a three-room cottage with everything you'll need for a comfy stay. Your room comes with a great breakfast (the specialty is Grand Marnier French toast), and it comes with something dogs like even better: 160 acres! That's a lot of place in the sun! Enjoy, because acreage like this is hard to find around here these days.

You'll be treated royally upon arrival, with a glass of champagne, and fresh flowers in your cottage. If you're lucky, you'll get to meet Mammie, the resident dog. She's a sweet mix of black lab and Rhodesian ridgeback. Rates are $200–250. 1210 Nuns Canyon Road 95442; 707/833-6264; www.relaisdusoleil.com.

Petaluma

Petaluma is a captivating Sunday afternoon stroll, with its tree-lined streets and pocket parks for your dog's pleasure. Victorian buildings, old feed mills, and a riverfront that remains mostly original, but not dilapidated, complete the charming picture. And let's not forget an added canine bonus: Depending on the wind direction, you can often smell fresh cow manure wafting in from the surrounding hills. Dogs thrive on this.

Best of all, dogs get to run leashless during set (if early) hours in a dozen parks, and all day at their very own pooch park! No wonder they call this place PET-aluma.

PARKS, BEACHES, AND RECREATION AREAS

Dogs who live in Petaluma are lucky dogs indeed. A few years back, the enlightened Parks and Recreation Department decided that dogs needed places to run off leash and gave dogs who are under voice control the OK to be leash-free in a dozen parks during certain hours. Most of those hours have increased since then, but you should still watch your off-leash hours like a hawk—the fine for a first offense can be up to $100! Better to invest that money in a good watch. We list most of the parks here.

Dogs also have their very own park, called Rocky Memorial Dog Park. It's not a real looker, but it's one of the largest dog parks in the state. Dogs are singing its praises ("Howl-elujah!").

26 Arroyo Park

🐾🐾🐾🦮 (See Sonoma County map on page 26)

Most of Arroyo Park is very well groomed, with golf course–like green grass and a perfectly paved walking path running through its three acres. However, it seems many dogs prefer the seedier side of the park—the weedier, uncut area on the right as you face the park. We hope that area remains like this for dogs who like to walk a little on the wild side.

Dogs are allowed off leash here 6–11 A.M. weekdays and 6–8 A.M. weekends, and 8–10 P.M. every night. It's just a bone's throw from Wiseman Airport Park, though, which is a much safer place to run a dog, since you can get farther from the road. The park is at Garfield and Village East drives. 707/778-4380.

27 Bond Park

🐾🐾🐾✖️ (See Sonoma County map on page 26)

It's green here, so green that Joe couldn't help but run out of the car and throw himself down on the grass and start wriggling and writhing in ecstasy. I thought for sure he'd found something odorous to roll in, but underneath him was just clean, green grass. He rolled for about 10 minutes, got up, and heaved himself down in another spot, rolling and groaning and making the children in the playground giggle. The park is pleasant, with some shade from medium-sized trees. With six acres, it's a good size for dogs. And it's set in a quiet area, on Banff Way just south of Maria Drive, so traffic is minimal. Dogs are allowed off leash here 6–11 A.M. weekdays and 6–8 A.M. weekends, and 8–10 P.M. every night. 707/778-4380.

28 Del Oro Park

🐾🐾🐾✖️ (See Sonoma County map on page 26)

Del Oro is very suburban. It's got a nice little play area for kids. It's got green grass. It's surrounded by not-too-old suburban homes. It's got soccer goal posts. When we last visited, there were even two old Suburban sport utility vehicles parked in front.

Something not terribly suburban, a fire hydrant in one of the grassy areas, is probably the most coveted part of the park—at least for boy dogs. Well-behaved pooches can be off leash here 6–11 A.M. weekdays and 6–8 A.M. weekends, and 8–10 P.M. every night. The park is at Sartori Drive and Del Oro Circle. 707/778-4380.

29 Glenbrook Park

🐾🐾✖️ (See Sonoma County map on page 26)

Who'd believe it? When we last visited, a great blue heron landed in this narrow park, which is surrounded by newish homes. This was a wonderful sight, because the land around here looks as if it's still in shock from all the development of the past decade.

The park is nearly four acres and is much longer than it is wide. It's directly across the street from Sunrise Park, but it's a little quieter and more attractive, with some medium-sized trees here and there. Its off-leash hours are generous on the hind end: 6–10 A.M. and 6–10 P.M. daily. The park is at Maria Drive and Sunrise Parkway. 707/778-4380.

30 Helen Putnam Regional Park
😼😼😼 (See Sonoma County map on page 26)

This 216-acre county regional park is, and will remain, a minimally developed stretch of converted cow pasture with oak trees. A wide paved trail shared by hikers and bicyclists runs between the main entrance and the Victoria housing development (to enter from that end, go to the end of Oxford Court). Dogs must be leashed. There's no shade from the scrub oaks, and it can get mighty windy. The paved trail has gentle ups and downs. Some other dirt trails give you steeper hill climbs. About 0.25 mile in from the main entrance is an old cattle pond good for a dog swim (if the dog stays on a leash—quite a feat).

Parking is $6. Next to the lot is a kids' playground and a picnic gazebo, set by a creek that's only a gully in summer. Drive south on Western Avenue and turn left on Chileno Valley Road. After a half mile, you'll see the turnoff to the park. 707/565-2041.

31 Lucchesi Park
😼😼😼🐕 (See Sonoma County map on page 26)

This is a well-kept, popular city park with a postmodern community center that impresses people but doesn't stir dogs much. Dogs prefer strolling through empty sports fields, picnicking at shaded tables, lounging under the weepy willows, watching ducks and the spewing fountain at the large pond, and trotting along the paved paths here. No dog swimming is allowed in the pond. It's a rule that makes it impossible to take Jake Dog near the pond, because he can't contain his excitement at the idea of being in the water. We've met other water dogs with the same affliction here.

Dogs are allowed off leash here 6–11 A.M. weekdays and 6–8 A.M. weekends, and 8–10 P.M. every night. Be sure to keep dogs away from the ducks and geese who like to lounge beside their pond, because feathers should not fly as a result of the city's kindly off-leash allowances. The park is at North McDowell Boulevard and Madison Street. 707/778-4380.

32 McNear Park
😼😼😼🐕 (See Sonoma County map on page 26)

McNear is an attractive seven-acre park, with green, green grass, plenty of shade, picnic tables, and a playground. But the part of the park dogs like best is the enclosed athletic field, where they're allowed to romp off leash 6–11 A.M. weekdays and 6–8 A.M. weekends, and 8–10 P.M. every night. The field is usually green and almost entirely fenced, but there are a couple of spots where a clever escape artist could slip out, so heads up. It's at F and 9th Streets. 707/778-4380.

33 Oak Hill Park

🐾🐾🐾🐾 🐕 (See Sonoma County map on page 26)

Dogs love running up and down the gently rolling hills on this five-acre park set in the midst of beautiful old Victorian homes near downtown Petaluma. Oak Hill Park is hilly and oaky (surprise!), qualities dogs enjoy. Some good-sized oaks make their home in various parts of the park, and dogs appreciate their shade-giving arms.

Dogs are permitted to run off leash on the east side of the creek from Sunnyslope to Westridge Drive 6 A.M.–10 P.M. Monday–Friday. That's a lotta hours. But wait, that's not all! They can also visit the park off leash 6–11 A.M. and 5–10 P.M. on weekends. These are magnificent hours. The park is at Howard and Oak Streets. 707/778-4380.

34 Prince Park

🐾🐾🐾🐾 🐕 (See Sonoma County map on page 26)

Dogs are permitted off leash at this attractive 20-acre park during longer hours than they are at most other parks in the city, and they think this is just swell. On a recent visit, a springer-shepherd mix was running around drooling and panting and smiling like a dog in love. His person said when he comes here, he's ecstatic. "Willie loves the grass and the trees. I love the hours for off leash, and I love its safety from traffic," she said. (The park is set back quite far from street traffic.) Off-leash hours are rather confusing at first glance, but they're simple at second glance: 6 A.M.–3 P.M. weekdays September–May, 6–8 A.M. weekdays June–August, 6–8 A.M. weekends, and 8–10 P.M. every night. The park is across East Washington Street from the airport, just a little north of the airport sign. 707/778-4380.

35 Rocky Memorial Dog Park

🐾🐾🐾 🐕 (See Sonoma County map on page 26)

The scenery isn't great, and the land has nary a tree on it, but it's one of the biggest dog parks we've ever encountered. And size does matter, at least when it comes to fenced dog parks.

This flat nine-acre piece of land is the best thing that's happened to Petaluma's dogs since the park system began allowing them off leash at certain parks during limited hours a few years back. Dogs enjoy the smell that can pervade the land; it's beside a marshy area next to the Petaluma River. Fortunately, it's well fenced so dogs can't chase the marsh birds or roll in the marsh muck. The fencing keeps the dogs from escaping to all areas but the parking lot, which leads to the park entrance, which eventually leads a busy road. So if you have a pooch who's prone to running away, be aware the place is safe, but it isn't foolproof.

Because it's so barren here, it can really roast on hot days. Be sure to bring water. A sign at the entrance says No Dogs in Heat, and I thought it was nice

of them to be so concerned about the temperature for dog walking. It took me a few seconds and an eye roll from my husband to realize the sign's true intent.

On our first visit, Joe searched in vain for something to lift a leg on. He found only some garbage cans and a few big weeds, and they were right next to the parking lot. The next visit he just succumbed to the lack of leg-lift targets and took to relieving his bladder like a girl dog. But not, of course, until looking around to make sure no one was watching.

Rocky Park was named after a big-hearted police dog who died at the too-young age of 10 during a narcotics search. It was kidney failure that got him, not the wrong end of a dealer's pistol. Rocky had helped seize a few million dollars of narcotics in his career, but his greatest act came in 1992 when he saved the life of his beloved handler one night. A felon had escaped and the officer chased him to a creek, where the felon got the upper hand and was holding the officer's head underwater. The officer managed to hit a remote control button that opened the windows of the patrol car and released Rocky, who'd seen his friend in trouble. Rocky bolted to the creek and got the upper paw. He saved his friend and helped bag the bad guy. "It was the beginning of the era of Rocky," said Officer Jeff Hasty, a dog handler with the Petaluma Police Department. A bust of Rocky now graces the front lobby of the police department.

This is an easy park to visit if you're on U.S. 101 and your pooch is hankering to stretch his gams. Take the Highway 116 east (*not* west)/Lakeville exit and follow the street just over a half mile to Casa Grande Road, where you'll take a sharp right. Drive a few hundred feet past ugly storage bins and trucks and you'll soon hit the entrance to the park. Unlike most of the other city parks with off-leash times, this one has great hours: 6 A.M.–10 P.M. 707/778-4380.

36 Sunrise Parkway

😊 🐕 (See Sonoma County map on page 26)

If you're a real estate developer, there's a chance you might enjoy this park. It's very, very narrow, squeezed like an old tube of toothpaste by cookie-cutter condos and townhouses. It's too close to traffic. It's not terribly attractive. But in its defense, it does have decent grassy areas and fun (for dogs) weedy patches. Another plus: Dogs can be off leash 6–10 A.M. and 6–10 P.M. daily. Those are some pretty long hours for a pretty slim park. It's at Marina Drive and Sunrise Parkway. 707/778-4380.

37 Westridge Open Space

😊😊😊 🐕 (See Sonoma County map on page 26)

Dogs get to peruse the east side of this three-acre park off leash 6–10 A.M. and 6–10 P.M. daily. The park is long and narrow, with plenty of medium-sized trees, which turn a warm red in autumn. When we visited, a fluffy black cat teased Joe from the middle of the road. Another kitty was there when we more recently sniffed out the park with Jake. Cat-chasers, exercise caution when off leash. The park is on Westridge Drive, near its intersection with Westridge Place. 707/778-4380.

38 Wiseman Airport Park

😊😊😊😊 🐕 (See Sonoma County map on page 26)

Plenty of pooches visit this park, and for good reason. Wiseman is 32 acres of well-kept playing fields, uncut grass, many shade trees, and comfortably wide walking paths. It's also a good place to watch little planes land and take off, because of its proximity to the airport. (They don't call it Airport Park for nothing.) Best of all, dogs can run off leash in the athletic fields during these hours: 6–11 A.M. weekdays and 6–8 A.M. weekends, and 8–10 P.M. every night. The best access is at St. Augustine Circle. 707/778-4380.

PLACES TO EAT

Aram's Cafe: Dine on really good Mediterranean and Armenian food at the five outdoor tables. Aram's is in downtown Petaluma. 131 Kentucky Street; 707/765-9775.

Tres Hombres: The focus here is Mexican, but you'll also taste other Latin influences in the upscale cuisine at this terrific restaurant. Enjoy a tasty meal with your dog at your side at the patio on the square of this "theater district" area. 151 Petaluma Boulevard South; 707/773-4500.

PLACES TO STAY

Motel 6: Rates are $39–80. 1368 North McDowell Boulevard 94954; 707/765-0333.

San Francisco North KOA: This is Jake's kind of camping. Upon arrival at this family camping resort, dogs get a little treat attached to a card that lists the doggy rules. The 60-acre campground is more attractive than most KOAs we've visited. The setting is rural, and there are trees everywhere. Like other KOAs, the campsites are drive-up and pretty doggone close to each other, but it's still a fun place to pitch a tent, especially if you like hot showers and cool pools as part of your camping experience. Better yet, try one of the cute log "Kamping Kabins." They're cozy, with a bunk bed and a queen-size bed. (You provide the bedding.)

Adding to its rural charm, this KOA even has a pen that houses several goats. Visit in the spring to see some adorable furry kids. And now there's a sweet and small fenced-in area for dogs to run around off leash! There's even a little agility equipment. Dogs need to be on leash everywhere else. The rule here, as it is at many KOAs, is no pit bulls. Rates are $30–45 for tent camping. Kamping Kabins are $65–87. 20 Rainsville Road 94952; 707/763-1492 or 800/992-2267; www.sanfranciscokoa.com.

Sheraton Sonoma County: Dogs are welcome to stay at this attractive hotel, as long as they weigh no more than 80 pounds. They're so welcome, in fact, that they'll get use of a big dog bed and doggy bowls. "We like to make their stay nice, too," says a hotelier. One of the more attractive features of this Sheraton is its location: It's close to Rocky Memorial Dog Park. Dogs who need a good run really appreciate the proximity. The hotel has a heated outdoor pool and a hot tub for the humans in your crew. Dogs must stay in first-floor rooms, and they mustn't smoke. (The entire hotel is nonsmoking.) Rates are $139–269. 745 Baywood Drive 94954; 707/283-2888.

Sonoma

Downtown Sonoma is a treat for people, and until the last few years, dogs had been banned from all the good spots—most city parks, Sonoma plaza, and the state historic park. But there's finally something to wag about: a new park just two blocks from the plaza. You can also find some great lodging not too far away.

PARKS, BEACHES, AND RECREATION AREAS

39 Ernest Holman Dog Park/Sonoma Dog Park

🐾🐾🐾 🐕 (See Sonoma County map on page 26)

Ernest was a good dog. So good that his person, Sue Holman, donated enough money for a dog park in his name. (Most of my human friends don't even have such formal-sounding names.) Opened in 1999, Ernest Holman Dog Park—lately known as Sonoma Dog Park—is a real boon to downtown Sonoma. It's small—a little under an acre—and the turf can be mushy in the wet season, but it's incredibly popular. Happy dogs of every ilk tear around this fenced area. When they need to catch their doggy breaths, they repose in the shade of the park's enormous redwood trees. People enjoy sitting on benches and chatting with other dog folks while watching their panting pooches. (There's water for when they—the dogs, not the people—need to wet their whistles.)

The park is two blocks north of the plaza, on First Street West, next to the police station. It's part of the Field of Dreams sporting field complex. 707/938-3681.

⁴⁰ Ernie Smith Dog Park
🐾 🐾 🐾 🐕 (See Sonoma County map on page 26)

It's a little odd that Sonoma's two dog parks are both named after Ernests. This one is named after Ernest Maynard "Ernie" Smith, one of the earliest live-sports announcers, and a beloved figure around here. The dog park is set within Ernie Smith Community Park, and is a half-acre, with water, some shade, and picnic tables. It's a decent place for a little off-leash run. Dogs are allowed in the surrounding parklands, but must be leashed. The park is at the corner of Arnold Drive and Elm Street. Follow the signs to the dog park. 707/539-8092.

PLACES TO EAT

Harmony Lounge: For the best people- and pooch-watching in Sonoma, and some lovely food and drinks to boot, this is *the* place to be. The lounge is set in the gorgeous Ledson Hotel, right on the Sonoma plaza. It's the crown jewel of the plaza, with its ornate architecture and upscale old charm. The lounge's outdoor patio/sidewalk tables are right in front of the hotel, where you can watch the wine-country world float by.

Dogs don't have to be of the little frou-frou genre to eat here. "We've had a couple of Great Danes," says a manager. "There's plenty of room."

The food menu is short, the cuisine is upmarket and light, and the desserts have a decadent flair. Jake recommends the beef tenderloin carpaccio. For a real treat, try the black magic cake with a Sonoma port. Since dogs can't stay at the hotel, you may as well splurge at the lounge. 480 First Street East; 707/996-9779.

Sunflower Café: This is a peaceful haven for dogs and their people. The magnificent garden patio has a fountain that fascinates some dogs and makes others look as if they need to head to the nearest tree fast. Actually, a big, 160-year-old fig tree is in the middle of the patio area, but leg lifts are definitely not permitted.

The café is housed in the historic Captain Salvador Vallejo Adobe, which was built in the late 1830s. He would have loved the coffee here; many say it's the best in Sonoma. And the cuisine is of the delectable high-end-deli genre. Bird dogs appreciate the idea of the smoked duck sandwich, but what sets

Jake to drooling is the Sonoma Cheese Plate. The Sunflower is on the Sonoma Plaza, at 415-421 First Street West; 707/996-6645.

PLACES TO STAY

Best Western Sonoma Valley Inn: If you want to stay close to the town plaza, this hotel is just a little more than a block away. Rates are $149–329. Dogs are $25 extra. 550 Second Street West 95476; 707/938-9200 or 800/334-5784; www.sonomavalleyinn.com.

Casita Carneros: Here's a fabulous first: Dogs are allowed in the private pool here! The pool is huge—about 20 feet by 40 feet—and if your dog is a swimmer, he'll have the time of his life splashing around after a day in wine country. (If he's not a swimmer, the pool can be entirely covered so there's no danger of him becoming a soggy doggy—or worse.) How can a pool be so dog friendly? It's thanks to a heavy-duty sand filter that rids the pool of pet hair. Casita's owner, Cindy, loves dogs and wants them to be able to do the dog paddle in the pool. (For obvious reasons, dogs should stay out of the Jacuzzi.)

The guest cottage is an attractive, air-conditioned, one-bed affair with a fridge and microwave and other amenities of home. Your stay comes with a continental breakfast that comes right to your door, and you'll also get a bottle of Sonoma wine. The property is fenced and on a quiet rural road, on an acre that also has goats and ducks. It's all you need for a vacation in pooch paradise.

We thank Dog Friday and his person, Lori, for pointing us in the direction of the Casita Carneros. Rates are $225, and there's a two-night minimum. Dogs are $25 extra. 21235 Hyde Road 95476; 707/996-0996; www.casitacarneros.com.

The Lodge at Sonoma: This exceptional wine country resort is ripe with gorgeous rooms, top-notch furnishings, and super comfy beds with "clouds of pillows." Many rooms feature a fireplace, balcony, or patio, and all come with plush robes, bath salts, and a fridge. The Lodge also offers signature spa treatments to guests. Private cottages make up the majority of the lodgings here, and they're ideal for a doggy visit because they're large and many open onto a grassy or garden area. They're also on the pricey side, so a lodge room or suite is what dogs on more of a budget opt for.

The lodge, whose surname is "A Renaissance Resort & Spa," is actually in the Marriott bloodline, albeit top-of-the-line Marriott. You don't really say the "M" word around here. On the grounds is a popular tasting room, and a coffee and wine bar, but dogs aren't allowed inside. The humans in your party will also have access to the lodge's pool and decent fitness room.

Rates are $209–719. (The higher room rate is for a cottage in peak season.) There's a two-dog limit, and as with most Marriotts, dogs pay a $75 fee for the length of their stay. 1325 Broadway at Leveroni and Napa Roads 95476; 707/935-6600 or 888/710-8008; www.thelodgeatsonoma.com.

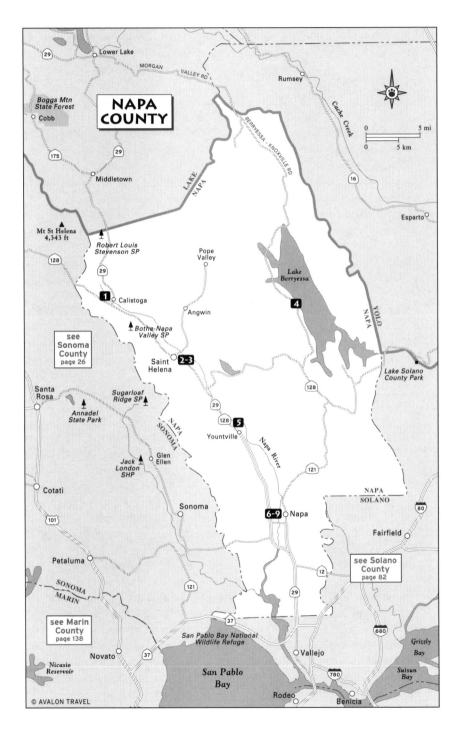

NAPA COUNTY

Lower Lake

MORGAN VALLEY RD

Rumsey

Cache Creek

29

Boggs Mtn
State Forest

Cobb

175

Middletown

29

BERRYESSA – KNOXVILLE RD

16

Esparto

Mt St Helena
4,343 ft

Robert Louis
Stevenson SP

128

29

LAKE
NAPA

Pope
Valley

Lake
Berryessa

1 Calistoga

Angwin

4

Bothe-Napa
Valley SP

see
Sonoma
County
page 26

Santa
Rosa

Saint
Helena

2-3

128

Sugarloaf
Ridge SP

Annadel
State Park

NAPA
SONOMA

29
128 5

Yountville

NAPA

YOLO

Lake Solano
County Park

NAPA

Jack
London
SHP

Glen
Ellen

Napa River

121

Cotati

101

Sonoma

6-9 Napa

NAPA
SOLANO

80

Petaluma

121

Fairfield

SONOMA
MARIN

12

see Solano
County
page 82

see Marin
County
page 138

37

San Pablo Bay National
Wildlife Refuge

29

680

Nicasio
Reservoir

Novato

37

Vallejo

Grizzly
Bay

780

Suisun
Bay

San Pablo
Bay

Rodeo

Benicia

0   5 mi
0   5 km

© AVALON TRAVEL

CHAPTER 2

Napa County

Napa dogs don't whine. They wine. And since there are plenty of dog-friendly restaurants here (and some truly fabulous ones these days), they often wine and dine.

This is the home of the most famous wine-making valley in the United States, and dogs get to experience some of the fringe benefits of this productive area. Several attractive wineries invite well-behaved dogs to relax and sniff around with their owners; find details in the Diversion *Grape Expectations.* Just don't let your dog do leg lifts on inappropriate items, because Bacchus will get you. And your little dog, too.

More top-notch Napa Valley inns than ever before are opening their doors to dogs, but the county's parks still come up a little on the dry side (a unique state of affairs, with all this wine around). With the county's tremendous amount of lush, fertile, and inviting vineyards, you'd think there would also be plenty of parks for dogs to roam. But this isn't the case.

Only about a dozen public parks and a few miscellaneous sites in Napa

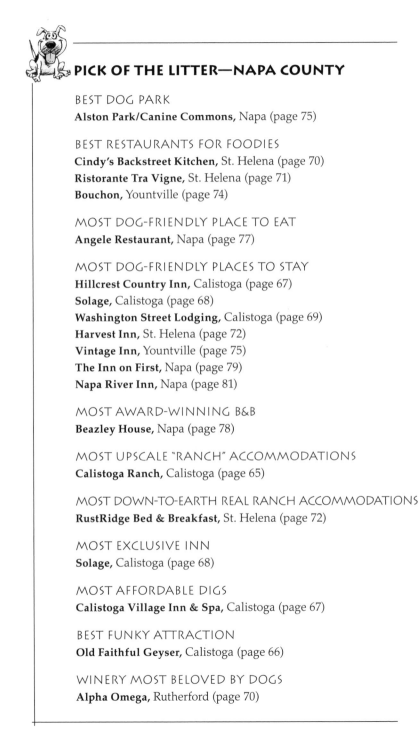

PICK OF THE LITTER—NAPA COUNTY

BEST DOG PARK
Alston Park/Canine Commons, Napa (page 75)

BEST RESTAURANTS FOR FOODIES
Cindy's Backstreet Kitchen, St. Helena (page 70)
Ristorante Tra Vigne, St. Helena (page 71)
Bouchon, Yountville (page 74)

MOST DOG-FRIENDLY PLACE TO EAT
Angele Restaurant, Napa (page 77)

MOST DOG-FRIENDLY PLACES TO STAY
Hillcrest Country Inn, Calistoga (page 67)
Solage, Calistoga (page 68)
Washington Street Lodging, Calistoga (page 69)
Harvest Inn, St. Helena (page 72)
Vintage Inn, Yountville (page 75)
The Inn on First, Napa (page 79)
Napa River Inn, Napa (page 81)

MOST AWARD-WINNING B&B
Beazley House, Napa (page 78)

MOST UPSCALE "RANCH" ACCOMMODATIONS
Calistoga Ranch, Calistoga (page 65)

MOST DOWN-TO-EARTH REAL RANCH ACCOMMODATIONS
RustRidge Bed & Breakfast, St. Helena (page 72)

MOST EXCLUSIVE INN
Solage, Calistoga (page 68)

MOST AFFORDABLE DIGS
Calistoga Village Inn & Spa, Calistoga (page 67)

BEST FUNKY ATTRACTION
Old Faithful Geyser, Calistoga (page 66)

WINERY MOST BELOVED BY DOGS
Alpha Omega, Rutherford (page 70)

County allow dogs. The city of Napa has four parks where dogs are allowed, and all four permit them off leash in certain sections. You may incur the grapes of your dog's wrath if you don't take her to visit one of these leash-free lands next time you're in town.

Calistoga

PARKS, BEACHES, AND RECREATION AREAS

🔟 Pioneer Park

🐾🐾 (See Napa County map on page 62)

This is a small park, but its location, so close to the heart of Calistoga, makes it a great place to stop for a relaxing picnic with your leashed pooch. The two-acre park has plenty of shade trees and enough open area so your canine won't feel claustrophobic.

Going north on Foothill Boulevard, turn right on Lincoln Avenue. In two blocks, turn left on Cedar Street. The park will be on your right within a block. 707/942-2800.

PLACES TO EAT

Barolo: The Italian food is *delizioso,* with small plates, big entrees, and everything in between. The bar is here also popular. Pass by here any given day and you're likely to see at least one or two dogs joining their people at the pretty, covered sidewalk/patio area. Last time we were there, a man was sipping cocktails beside a giant Great Dane, who was a real traffic stopper. 1457 Lincoln Avenue; 707/942-9900.

Scoops & Swirls: This little ice-creamery has all kinds of creative concoctions. Enjoy a cold one beside your dog at the outdoor tables. 1473 Lincoln Avenue; 707/341-3132.

PLACES TO STAY

Calistoga Ranch: When I think of a ranch, I think of horses and dirt and rustic lodgings and good hearty grub. Cowboys, too. Well, that was before I was married. But the Calistoga Ranch, an Auberge Resort, has none of the above. I can only guess that the ranch moniker must come from the 140 acres of secluded canyon land you can enjoy hiking on with your dog. Because it sure doesn't refer to the 46 gorgeous, freestanding, cedar-sided "guest lodges" that make up the place. Nor to the winemaking seminars, spa treatments, beautiful pool, state-of-the-art fitness center, yoga deck, or fine restaurant with artisan foie gras.

The name also couldn't have anything to do with how your "little dawgie" is treated. There's none of that sitting-around-the-campfire-waiting-for-some-vittles-to-drop-off-a-plate nonsense around here! No sir! Dog guests at *this*

DIVERSION

See Old Faithful in Your Own Backyard: You know you're in for a treat when a big sign greets you at the entry to **Old Faithful Geyser:** "Many Notable People Have Come to SEE HEAR AND LEARN the mysteries of this WONDER OF NATURE which captures the imagination. IT'S AMAZING."

And indeed, when dogs see the 350°F plume of water gushing 50 to 70 feet into the air, they generally stare for a few seconds with their mouths agape. But the sight of tourists jumping in front of the geyser for a quick photo before the eruption subsides quickly bores them. Dogs then try to wander to the snack bar and persuade the person on the other end of the leash to buy a couple of hot dogs. But even more fascinating is the scent of goat and pig in nearby pens.

If your dog is the brave sort, don't hesitate to bring him to visit Clow, the fainting goat. Clow butts her head against her fence at first, but she's only playing. After a few minutes, she was calming Joe's fears by licking him on the nose. Soon he was in love. Valentino, the Vietnamese potbellied pig who scared the heck out of Joe, is no longer here. (I hope he didn't go the way of so many of his oversized brethren.)

Old Faithful erupts every 40 minutes, and the eruptions last about two to three minutes. Picnic tables are plentiful, so bring a snack or buy one here between eruptions. A sign at the site warns that dogs aren't allowed in the geyser viewing area, but you can bring your dog—securely leashed—within a safe distance of the geyser and not get scolded or scalded.

The geyser and goats are between Highways 128 and 29 on Tubbs Lane in Calistoga and are open 9 A.M.–6 P.M. in summer, 9 A.M.–5 P.M. in winter. Admission is $10 for adults. 707/942-6463; www.old faithfulgeyser.com.

ranch get a room-service menu and organic dog treats. They also get a nutmeg-brown down-topped velvet dog bed custom-fitted with fine Italian linens by Rivolta Carmignani, a company known for its soft and luxurious sheets. (If you really like the bed, you can go online and buy one.) A housekeeper changes the dog sheets daily. (Please tip her well.) Hmm, nope, the ranch name definitely doesn't have anything to do with a dog's life here.

Maybe it's the fires. Your private lodge comes with a fireplace inside and outside. That's vaguely ranchy, in an upscale sort of way. We're getting warmer. And it's flanked by big trees. OK, that's also kind of ranchy. Warmer! Your lodge also comes with a mini-bar, down duvet, beautiful garden shower, and high-speed Internet access. Cold! Cold!

Is this the kind of place most dogs reading this book can afford? I wouldn't bet the ranch on it. The most basic accommodation is $505–1,450. (Per night.) You can get a super deluxe two-bedroom lodge for $3,850. Dogs pay $125 extra per stay. 580 Lommel Road 94515; 707/254-2888 or 800/942-4220; www .calistogaranch.com.

Calistoga Village Inn & Spa: This could well be the least expensive place to stay with a dog (or without one) in the Napa Valley. It's not fancy. In fact, the rooms are kind of run down and definitely nothing to write home about. But they're clean and spacious. And you know what? The geothermal mineral pools here are pretty darn good! They have a regular-temperature (cool) mineral swimming pool, and a small, warm wading pool, and a large hot tub in a gazebo. I've stayed at fancy places where I haven't enjoyed the pools as much–maybe because they're more crowded. This place isn't a crowd magnet, so sometimes you may be the only one using the pools. A lovely, small garden area surrounds the pool area, giving it a kind of semi-tropical feel. Rates are $75–135. Dogs are $35 extra. 1880 Lincoln Avenue 94515; 707/942-0991; www .greatspa.com.

Hillcrest Country Inn: On the outside it's a good-looking, contemporary house. But on the inside, it's filled with antiques and other family heirlooms of the locally famed Tubbs family. Debbie O'Gorman, owner of Hillcrest, is the last of the Tubbs family to live in the Napa area, and she's tastefully stocked the house with items from the family mansion, which burned down in 1964.

All this is well and good with dog guests, but what they *really* adore is that the house is set on 40 acres where they're allowed to romp on terrific trails without a leash if their humans are well behaved. This is a dog's dream come true, because there just aren't leash-free stomping grounds like these in Napa County, unless you own big property. It's at the base of Mt. St. Helena, and the house is on a hilltop (thus the name), so the views are breathtaking.

Humans enjoy using the gorgeous 40-foot-long pool. Dogs enjoy dipping their paws in the fishing pond. Humans can also use the kitchen and barbecue areas, which is convenient if you don't want to go out to eat every day. A delectable continental breakfast comes with your stay on weekdays, and people who visit on weekends get a delicious home-cooked breakfast.

Debbie, who has two friendly dogs of her own, asks that you bring a bed for your dog, if he sleeps on the floor, or a blanket to place under him if he sleeps on human furniture. She even allows dogs to be left alone in the rooms if they promise to be good dogs. In addition—and better yet for many dogs—Debbie can sometimes pet-sit while you go out. "Whatever makes your dog happy," she says. Rates are $69–165. Dogs are $10 extra. 3225 Lake County Highway 94515; 707/942-6334; www.hillcrestcountryinn.com.

Meadowlark Country House: The simple elegance of this secluded 20-acre estate makes guests feel right at home. The house where dogs with people get to stay has a light and airy feel and attractive decor, but it's really the surrounding property that makes this place so special. Beware, though. Cats and guinea hens also make their home around the house, so if your dog is a chaser, hang on to that leash.

You and your pooch can hike on the estate's trails, past pastured horses, ancient oaks, and fields replete with wildflowers (and meadowlarks, thus the name). It's quiet here—a perfect place for a hilltop picnic with the pooch. If your dog can be trusted off leash, he can hike naked. It's "leashes optional" here, and that's a perfect match for the pool. If it's warm, the humans in your party can cool their heels (and knees and shoulders) in the beautiful swimming pool, which is surrounded by a cobblestone walk. The pool is clothing-optional, so if your dog blushes when he sees tushies, best wear your clothes. If all this isn't enough to fill your day, take a quick drive down the road and spend some time at the Petrified Forest.

Rates are $195–285. A delicious, large breakfast is included in the price, and your dog is welcome to join you (although you'll have to supply his chow). For those who need more paw room, guesthouses are available for $395–425. 601 Petrified Forest Road 94515; 707/942-5651 or 800/942-5651; www.meadow larkinn.com.

Pink Mansion: This enchanting old place is an 1875 Victorian—very picturesque and very pink. It's a frequent recipient of numerous awards for its charm and beauty.

Dogs are allowed in only one room—the Wine Suite (not the Whine Sweet, as some dogs may do to stay here)—so book ahead lest another dog beats you to the phone. It has a fireplace, a private entrance that leads to the garden, and a private sitting room with an extra bed upstairs. Dogs must be of the non-barking, clean, well-behaved variety, and they need to keep off the furniture and the beds.

Bird dogs enjoy the resident doves and parrots. Water dogs like watching their people splash around in the comfy heated indoor pool and adjacent hot tub, but they mustn't set paw in the water. Rates are $245. Pooches are $30 extra. 1415 Foothill Boulevard (Highway 128) 94515; 707/942-0558; www .pinkmansion.com.

Solage: At the other end of the scale from the first accommodations listing in Calistoga–but just a bone's throw away–is this magnificent, world-class resort. It's top-rated by Conde Nast Traveler, Travel & Leisure, and just about any other entity that gives grades to hotels. Solage is a sprawling, gracious, chic, luxurious, relaxing, utterly exquisite resort. Everything is top shelf. The guest studios feature warm woods, polished concrete floors, gorgeous furnishings, organic bath amenities, super high-end bedding, and everything else you could ever want in a sumptuous getaway. If you don't want to get away completely, you'll be happy to know your room has WiFi, flat-screen TV, and an iPod docking station.

You'll get use of fun cruiser bikes during your visit, but dogs prefer it if you stay firmly planted on two feet. The pool here looks like something out of a magazine, flanked as it is by royal palms. Oh, actually it *is* something out of a magazine. The place has been featured in publications all over the world. The spa is also world-renowned, at least in circles that make spas renowned. Dogs have it really great here, too. They're welcome with a plush dog bed, food and water bowls, and treats. And they have 22 acres to explore while here. If you're on a budget, the resort isn't completely out of reach if you visit January through March, when rates are lowest. We haven't stayed here yet, but I'm eyeing a February visit, and Jake promises to remind me. Rates are $295–595. Suites go up to $895. Dogs are $75 per stay. 755 Silverado Trail; 866/942 7442. www.solagecalistoga.com.

Washington Street Lodging: Relax in any of several cabins, each with its own little kitchen. You're just a couple of blocks from Calistoga's main drag here. Joan, the animal-loving owner, has a cat, but she says if the kitty doesn't like your pooch, or vice versa, she'll make herself scarce. Joan also has a happy basset hound who will probably become your fast friend when you visit. Cabins are $105–155, and dogs are charged a $15 fee per visit. 1605 Washington Street 94515; 707/942-6968 or 877/214-3869; www.washingtonstreet lodging.com.

St. Helena

PARKS, BEACHES, AND RECREATION AREAS

🏠 Lyman Park

🐾🐾 (See Napa County map on page 62)

You'll think you're on a movie set for some old-time village scene when you and your dog wander into this small, cozy park on historic Main Street. Leashes are mandatory, but the park has a gazebo, lots of trees and benches, and a lovely flower garden.

The park is nestled snugly between the police station and a funeral home, at 1400 Main Street, and is open dawn–dusk. 707/963-5706.

🏠 Baldwin Park

🐾🐾 (See Napa County map on page 62)

Baldwin Park has everything you could want in a park, except size. But what it lacks in acreage, it makes up for in dog appeal. Set off a small road, it's almost entirely fenced and full of flowering trees, oaks, and big pines. A dirt path winds through green grass from one end of the park to the other, passing by a water fountain and a conveniently placed garbage can.

Unfortunately, dogs must be leashed, but it's still a pleasant place to stretch all your legs after a tour through the wine country. The park is on Spring Street between Stockton Street and North Crane Avenue and is open dawn–dusk. 707/963-5706.

DIVERSIONS

Grape Expectations: What goes great with every type of wine—from chardonnays to cabs to zinfandels—while you're visiting the Napa wine region? Dogs do! More wineries than ever welcome pooches to join their people in some part or another of their operations. Some quietly allow them in the tasting room (since health department officials aren't sure how they feel about this, they don't advertise it), others love them to join you in picnic areas or on winery tours. Many do all of the above, and then some.

You'll find some great ones below. For a more comprehensive list, check out www.napavintners.com/wineries/dog_friendly.asp.

CALISTOGA
Cuvaison, 4550 Silverado Trail North; 707/942-6266; www.cuvaison .com.
Dutch Henry Winery, 4310 Silverado Trail North; 707/942-5771; www.dutchhenry.com. Check out the website for a page dedicated to the winery pets.

NAPA
Clos du Val, 5330 Silverado Trail; 707/261-5200; www.closduval.com.

RUTHERFORD
Alpha Omega, 1155 Mee Lane, at Highway 29; 707/963-9999; www .aowinery.com. This is an exquisite place for real wine connoisseurs

PLACES TO EAT

Cindy's Backstreet Kitchen: Chef, cookbook author, and restaurant entrepreneur Cindy Pawlcyn has another hit on her hands. The owner of the famed Mustard Grill and co-creator of several Bay Area restaurants has created a warm, fun, casual-but-upscale place to gather with friends and eat healthful, delicious, sometimes exotic versions of home-cooked food. As Cindy says on the brochure, this is "a local joint—hip, casual, not fussy. The food we serve is from our hearts, what we make at home and most like to cook."

We like to start with crispy Backstreet flatbread with local cheeses, roasted garlic, caramelized onions, and sun-dried tomatoes. Jake eyed a neighboring table's Mighty Meatloaf and spice-rubbed quails, but darned if they didn't drop a single bite. Your dog can dine with you on the brick patio under a 100-year old fig tree that offers gentle shade. 1327 Railroad Avenue; 707/963-1200.

Go Fish: Chef Cindy Pawlcyn's other local restaurant, Go Fish, is just as dog-who want to make their dogs very happy. Alpha Omega's wines are revered, extremely good, and not cheap. But since dogs don't care about how wine tastes or what awards it gets, here's what's in it for them: they're welcome just about everywhere here, including the big, shaded patio eating/sipping area and the winery's huge, beautiful fountain/pool. A neighbor's dog just wanders over every day for a swim, gets some pats from winery visitors, sniffs out other happy dogs, and heads home. It's a dog's life…

Mumm Napa Valley, 8445 Silverado Trail North; 707/967-7700; www .mummnapa.com. Dogs get royal treatment, with dog treats and water. Mumm Napa Valley even has its own line of logo doggy products.

Peju, 8466 St. Helena Highway; 707/963-3600; www.peju.com.

ST. HELENA
Casa Nuestra, 3451 Silverado Trail North; 707/963-5783; www .casanuestra.com. A most mellow winery where dogs can stare at the resident goats who have a nonvintage table wine named after them. Dogs get tasty biscuits, too.

V. Sattui Winery, 1111 White Lane; 707/963-7774; www.vsattui .com. They've been allowing dogs here since way before it was the thing to do.

YOUNTVILLE
Domaine Chandon, 1 California Drive; 707/944-2280; www.chandon.com.

friendly and delectable as her Backstreet Kitchen. You can't miss the appealing large logo as you drive on Highway 29. It's an old-style print of a fish, holding an umbrella, wearing a hat, and walking. He looks vaguely worried. I would too, if I were a fish around this fabulous restaurant. The fish dishes here are fantastic, from the raw appetizers to the steaming and fresh entrees and pastas. If you're not a fan of fish, there are plenty of other options. Dine al fresco with your dog. 641 Main Street; 707/963-0700.

Pizzeria Tra Vigne: The little sister of the more expensive and upscale Tra Vigne Ristorante, this pizzeria is just what the vet ordered if you have a pooch and a pedigreed palate but a more paltry pocketbook. Lots of families come here. The pastas, pizzas, and salads are delicious. Munch with your dog at the four tables on the patio. Got a thirsty dog? The staff will provide her a bowl of water. 1016 Main Street; 707/967-9999.

Ristorante Tra Vigne: This is one of the most attractive restaurants with some of the best food in the Bay Area. The wood-burning oven gives even the most simple pasta, pizza, and meat dishes a taste that's out of this world. Your dog can dine with you at the 20 tables in the large, gardenlike lower courtyard. (The terrace is out because you have to go through the restaurant to get there, and that's a no-no.) The two of you are sure to drool over the gourmet cuisine. Thirsty dogs get a bowl of water. 1050 Charter Oak Avenue (you'll see the restaurant from Main Street, though); 707/963-4444.

PLACES TO STAY

El Bonita Motel: This little motel provides decent lodging at fairly reasonable prices for this area. Rates are $72–269. Dogs are $15 extra. 195 Main Street 94574; 707/963-3216 or 800/541-3284; www.elbonita.com.

Harvest Inn: This heavenly inn feels so Napa Valley. It's luxurious, but not ostentatious, with beautiful vineyard-culture-inspired grounds and large, tastefully appointed rooms. It's tranquil, romantic, and a place people visit time after time. Most of the dog-friendly rooms come with wood-burning fireplaces and private decks. You'll have views of vineyards or gardens. This place feels like a fine estate, with its magnificent redwoods, pristine gardens, and attention to the most minute detail. And don't forget those pools and hot tubs! (Sorry, no dogs.) Soak away any remaining tensions from "real life," then grab a glass of your favorite vintage.

A delectable breakfast comes with your stay. You'll also have access to fabulous spa treatments, and an onsite wine bar. All rooms come with a small fridge, which is very handy when traveling with a pooch. Speaking of the pooch, the inn's wonderful demeanor extends to dogs, who get use of a comfy dog bed upon arrival. Dogs also get to borrow food and water bowls, so don't bother packing yours. Rates are $299–569. Dogs pay a $100 fee for the length of their stay. 1 Main Street 94574; 707/963-9463 or 800/960-8466; www.harvestinn.com.

RustRidge Bed & Breakfast: If you like wine, horses, or dogs, you need to book a stay at this gracious ranch-style lodging. It's part of the 450-acre RustRidge Ranch & Winery, home of top-notch wine grapes, a great winery, and some mighty nice dogs and thoroughbred horses.

When you get to the ranch, you'll be greeted by dogs Rusty, Charlie, and Holly. "Our three dogs are always so happy to see other dogs," says proprietor Susan Meyer. If you plan to be a guest here, your dog should be a good socializer, because this trio sure is social. Their cat can be curious too, so no cat-killers allowed. Their horses also tend to be very friendly. In fact, Susan says they like to play with her dogs. But you need to keep yours out of their area because their tonnage to your dog's poundage just isn't a fair—or safe—match. (She worries when her dogs get in with them, but so far, so good.)

You and your dogs won't be staying at the main B&B: You'll have your very own, very cool one-bedroom cottage. It's hexagonal, with cathedral ceilings, windows overlooking the vineyards, a full kitchen, wood-burning stove, and a country-contemporary decor. The house is tucked in the trees and is very private. You even have your own Jacuzzi outside.

During your stay you're welcome to hike the land. It's big and beautiful and hilly and ripe with vineyards. You can also play tennis on the property, but most dogs can only be on the receiving end of the game, and that gets old.

Even though your cottage comes with a kitchen, your stay still includes the B&B benefit of a hearty farm-style breakfast of eggs, breads, coffee, and other goodies. In the evening, gather in the B&B's country kitchen to sample RustRidge's wines and enjoy some hors d'oeuvres. The cottage rate is $275. Dogs are $25 extra. 2910 Lower Chiles Valley Road 94574; 707/965-9353 or 800/788-0263; www.rustridge.com.

Lake Berryessa

PARKS, BEACHES, AND RECREATION AREAS

🛂 Lake Berryessa

🐾 🐾 (See Napa County map on page 62)

Lake Berryessa, one of the largest man-made lakes in Northern California, offers 165 miles of shoreline for human and canine enjoyment. Most of the resort areas on the lake allow leashed dogs. Better yet, they allow them off leash to swim. The summer heat is stifling here, so your dog will want to take advantage of the water.

Most resorts rent fishing boats and allow dogs to go along on your angling adventure. The fishing is fantastic, especially for trout in the fall and black bass in the spring. It's cooler then, too, so you won't have to contend with so many folks riding personal watercraft, and your dog won't roast.

If you just want to hike and swim for an afternoon, explore the Smittle Creek Trail. The entrance is just north of the lake's visitors center, on Knoxville Road. The trail takes you up and down the fingers of the lake. In certain times of year, and more arid years, the lake can get so low that the trail is a dusty mile from the water. Grab a trail map or get advice from a concessionaire about best hikes for swimming dogs.

Dogs must be leashed, except when swimming. Plans have been in the works for years to create a 150-mile shoreline trail, which would provide much more romping room for dogs—even some off-leash areas. (See www.berry essatrails.org for more. A link will take you to a page called The Dog Owner's Vision for Lake Berryessa.)

To get to Lake Berryessa from the Rutherford area, take Highway 128 and turn left at the Lake Berryessa/Spanish Flat sign. It's a very curvy route, so take it easy if you or your dog tends toward car sickness. For more information about the lake, call the Bureau of Reclamation Visitor Information Center at

707/966-2111. For questions about lakeside businesses, call the Lake Berryessa Chamber of Commerce at 800/726-1256.

Rutherford

PLACES TO EAT

Rutherford Grill: The outdoor area is *the* place to eat at this wonderful restaurant (and of course, the only place to eat with a dog). It features a wood-burning fireplace, a fountain, and several attractive umbrella-topped tables. Try the "Knife and Fork Baby Back Barbecue Ribs," one of the most requested entrées. (Fear not: If you're not of the carnivorous persuasion, the restaurant offers several tasty dishes without meat.) 1180 Rutherford Road; 707/963-1792.

Yountville

Unlike the bad old days a few years back, dogs are now allowed in all Yountville parks, as long as they're on leash.

PARKS, BEACHES, AND RECREATION AREAS

5 Yountville Park

🐾🐾🐾 (See Napa County map on page 62)

This lush, green, well-manicured park is great for a relaxing walk with your best friend. It's also an excellent spot for a picnic. Just bring your wine, cheese, bread, fruit, and dog treats, and toast to the good life. The park is on Washington Street at Madison Street, in the north end of town. 707/257-9529.

PLACES TO EAT

Restaurants can get mighty crowded around here when tour buses offload, so if you see a bus coming, make sure your pooch is close at hand.

Bouchon: It's only natural that Bouchon would permit pups, because it's a French bistro, and a fabulous one at that. Bouchon, co-owned by renowned chef Thomas Keller (of French Laundry fame), serves absolutely delectable cuisine. If you've never ordered cheese with honeycomb, this is the place to try it. Jake suggests then moving onto a nice big plate of *gigot d'agneau* (roasted leg of lamb, served with a cocoa bean–based ragout), or maybe some *boudin noir,* which I, with all the French prowess I could muster, took to be a dish based on some sort of nice dark sourdough bread. (After all, isn't Boudin a San Francisco bread-baking company? And noir certainly means dark—I learned that in film class.) Upon closer reading, however, I discovered that *boudin noir* means blood sausage. I am grateful the menu was not entirely in French.

Dogs are welcome to join you at the marble-topped tables on the small but fetching patio here. It's set off from the sidewalk by flowers. 6534 Washington Street; 707/944-8037.

Hurley's: The food here is a kind of melding of Mediterranean and California wine country cuisines. You can get everything from spicy vegetarian Moroccan plates to medallions of venison to squash blossom fritters. Enjoy your tasty food with your happy dog at the patio, which offers lots of shade on hot days and heat lamps for chilly nights. Thirsty dogs get water. 6518 Washington Street; 707/944-2345.

PLACES TO STAY

Vintage Inn: Dogs who get to stay here are lucky dogs indeed. This inn ("inn" is an understated description of this place) puts dogs and their people in the lap of luxury, with a perfect blend of old-world charm and new-world design. The airy, beautiful, multilevel villas have fireplaces, and many have views of nearby vineyards. Dogs swoon over the grounds, which have pools, gardens, courtyards, and even a fountain.

This is a great place to stay if you're checking out the wineries on warm days and don't want to bring your dog along. The staff here can arrange for a pet-sitter to watch your pooch so he can keep cool and comfy while you sip your way through wine country. In addition, dogs get a treat bag with their room. I haven't seen the goodies, but I doubt they're Milk-Bones.

Rates are $340–635 and include a California Champagne breakfast and afternoon tea. Dogs pay a $0 fee per visit. 6541 Washington Street 94599; 707/944-1112 or 800/351-1133; www.vintageinn.com.

Napa

PARKS, BEACHES, AND RECREATION AREAS

6 Alston Park/Canine Commons

🐾🐾🐾🐾🐕 (See Napa County map on page 62)

With 157 acres of rolling hills surrounded by vineyards, Alston Park seems to stretch out forever. The lower part of the land used to be a prune orchard, and these prunes are just about the only trees you'll find here.

From there on up, the park is wide-open land with a lone tree here and there. Without shade, dogs and people can fry on hot summer days. But the park is magical during early summer mornings or any cooler time of year.

Miles of trails take you and your dog to places far from the road and the sound of traffic. Dogs are supposed to be off leash only in the lower, flat section of the park, known as Canine Commons. There's now a decent-sized fenced dog park there, complete with poop bags and drinking water.

From Highway 29, take Trower Avenue southwest to the end, at Dry Creek

Road. The parking lot for the park is a short jog to your right on Dry Creek Road and across the street. It's open dawn–dusk. 707/257-9529.

7 Century Oaks Park

(See Napa County map on page 62)

This park is a cruel hoax on canines. Dogs are restricted to a dangerous dog run—a tiny postage stamp of an area without fences, just off a busy street. And as for the park's name, which promises granddaddy oak trees, we're talking saplings here—maybe a dozen in the whole dog-run area. We don't know how many are in the rest of the park, because dogs aren't allowed there even on leash.

The dog-run area (we suggest keeping all but the most highly trained dogs on leash here) is on Brown's Valley Road, just off Westview Drive. Park on Westview Drive and walk around the corner to the dog run. The short walk to the park, with its shade and shrubs, is more enjoyable than the park itself. It's open dawn–dusk. 707/257-9529.

8 John F. Kennedy Memorial Park

(See Napa County map on page 62)

Throw your dog's leash to the wind here and ramble along the Napa River. Dogs are allowed in the undeveloped areas near the park's boat marina. The only spot to avoid is a marshland that's more land than marsh during dry times.

Dogs enjoy chasing each other around the flat, grassy area beside the parking lot. There's also a dirt trail that runs along the river. You can take it from either side of the marina, although as of this writing, the signs designate only the south side as a dog-exercise area. The scenery isn't terrific—radio towers and construction cranes dot the horizon—but dogs without a sense of decor don't seem to mind.

Dogs like to amble by the river, which is down a fair incline from the trail. But be careful if you've got a water dog, because riders of personal watercraft and motorboaters have been known to mow over anything in their path. There's no drinking water in the dog area and it gets mighty hot in the summer, so bring your own.

Take Highway 221 to Streblow Drive, and follow the signs past the Napa Municipal Golf Course and Napa Valley College to the boat marina/launch area. Park in the lot and look for the trail by the river. The park is open dawn–dusk. 707/257-9529.

9 Shurtleff Park

(See Napa County map on page 62)

The farther away from the road you go, the better it is in this long, narrow park. It gets shadier and thicker with large firs and eucalyptus trees. Dogs are allowed off leash as soon as you think they're safe from the road.

The park is almost entirely fenced, but there are a few escape hatches. Two are at the entrance and two others are along the side that lead you into the schoolyard of Phillips Elementary School. This isn't normally a problem, unless your dog runs into the day-care center at lunchtime, as Joe once did. A teacher escorted him out by the scruff of his neck before he could steal someone's peanut butter sandwich.

You'll find the park on Shelter Street at Shurtleff, beside Phillips Elementary School. It's open dawn–dusk. 707/257-9529.

PLACES TO EAT

Angele Restaurant: Doggies who dine at this restaurant's riverfront tables get treats and water! "We love dogs!" says a server. The food is excellent—French with a Napa Valley flair. It can get a little tight here, and as Tera Dog, a rottie pup, wrote me, "Dog biscuits don't cut it when there is the smell of wild salmon and braised duck nearby!" Make sure your dog minds his manners with the neighbors. A big thanks to the aptly named Bacchus, another personable traveling rottie, for sniffing this one out for us. 540 Main Street; 707/252-8115.

Napa General Store: Inside, this is a really fun store featuring all things Napa, and showcasing the works of local artisans. Outside, it's a delightful

café, with a deck right over the Napa River. Dine on tasty salads, sandwiches, pizzas and wraps at the umbrella-topped tables. 540 Main Street (but enter through the back, if you're visiting with a dog); 707/259-0762.

Napa Valley Traditions: Enjoy fresh baked goods and cappuccino at four outside tables shaded by two trees and an awning. Your dog will find as much to enjoy here as you will—inside, the shop usually sells gourmet dog biscuits. 1202 Main Street; 707/226-2044.

Ristorante Allegria: Northern Italy meets California at this delightful find. The menu is seasonally influenced, with flavors that are out of this world. Your taste buds will be really happy here, and if you like wine (which chances are you do, since you're hanging out in Napa Valley), you'll love the wine list. You and your dog can dine together at the 12 umbrella-topped tables on the attractive brick-floor garden patio. 1026 First Street; 707/254-8006.

Uva Trattoria & Bar: Inside, this is a lively, fun, jumping, jazz-infused eatery, with live music Wednesday through Sunday evenings. But dogs can't go in, no matter how hip they are. Fortunately, the restaurant has a few white-tablecloth-covered sidewalk tables in front. Dogs are welcome to join you there for some fresh Italian-Cal cuisine. 1040 Clinton Street; 707/255-6646.

Vintage Sweet Shoppe: This is a darling little, old-fashioned-looking shop, selling top-quality chocolates. It's also a bit of a java shop, featuring some mighty delicious local coffee blends. Sip yours with your dog at your side at the two sidewalk tables. 530 Main Street; 707/224-2986.

PLACES TO STAY

With more choices of dog-friendly lodgings than ever before, Napa is a heavenly place to stay with your furry friend.

Beazley House: This cozy inn, which sits on a half-acre of verdant lawns and gardens, has been voted Napa's Best B&B by listeners of local radio station KVON every year for many years. It makes me wonder: Are dogs the primary listeners of this station?

Dogs are warmly welcomed to the inn's two beautiful buildings by proprietors Jim and Carol Beazley, and sometimes by their friendly golden retriever, Tummy. "I'd rather have dogs than some children," confesses Carol. (Watch out: Your dog may be trying to dial KVON to vote for Beazley House right now…) Tummy, a 12-year-old tripod dog (three legs), loves playing ball, and makes sure there are dog treats around for the canine guests. I hope she's still there when you visit, because she's a love.

The two buildings are imbued with a luxurious-but-casual wine country charm. Rooms have lovely furnishings, plush towels and robes, and even a little nip of chocolate. The Carriage House features rooms with direct garden access—something appreciated by many people with dogs—and The Mansion, circa 1900, sports slightly less expensive, smaller rooms. A scrumptious breakfast buffet comes with your stay, as does an afternoon refreshment hour, with tasty snacks that include Beazley House Chocolate Chip Cookies, beloved by repeat guests.

Rates are $130–330. ("We're a value, not a bargain," says Carol.) Dogs are $30 extra. Check the website for dog specials. 1910 First Street 94559; 707/257-1649 or 800/559-1649; www.beazleyhouse.com.

The Carneros Inn: This gorgeous inn on 27 acres of Carneros grapes is a great place to stay if luxury and relaxation are at the top of your list, and budget concerns are on the bottom. Before reading on, know that you'll be paying a $150 pooch fee for your visit. That's a lot out of the dog-biscuit fund. Stay a while and get your money's worth.

All accommodations here are in the form of elegantly casual cottages. The cottages are grouped into little "neighborhoods," and people with dogs stay in a neighborhood consisting of seven enchanting garden cottages. They all feature wood-burning fireplaces, large windows, French doors, heated slate floors and limestone countertops in the bathrooms, a soaking tub facing your private garden, and a choice of indoor or heavenly alfresco shower.

You're welcome to peruse the property's vineyards and pretty apple orchards with your leashed dog, but no dogs at the patio area of the property's restaurant. Boo hoo! There's always room service.

The inn is a PlumpJack property. The PlumpJack group of wine, resort, and restaurant holdings is co-owned by former San Francisco Mayor Gavin Newsom. So stay here, and you're helping keep him in his spiffy suits. Rates for the dog-friendly cottages are $480–520. Dogs pay that $150 fee per visit. Just one dog is allowed per cottage. 4048 Sonoma Highway 94559; 707/299-4900 or 888/400-9000; www.thecarnerosinn.com.

The Chablis Inn: Don't be fooled by the name of this place: It's not a darling wine country bed-and-breakfast inn. It's simply a decent motel with an enticing moniker. But it's striving to be more innlike, with some rooms offering down comforters and whirlpool tubs. All rooms come with bottled water, too. The motel has a couple of features that most charming inns don't, namely a pool and cable TV. Rates are $79–189. Dogs are $15 extra the first night, $10 the second, and free from the third night on. 3360 Solano Avenue 94558; 707/257-1944 or 800/443-3490; www.chablisinn.com.

Embassy Suites: The rooms are attractive and comfortable, the grounds are lovely, and the made-to-order breakfast that comes with your room is really tasty. Love those omelets! You can eat a bit late and it will last you through mid-afternoon, when you can grab a wine-country snack at a local winery. Adding to the cheer, you'll get free drinks here from 5:30–7:30 P.M. This isn't a normal feature in Embassy Suites. It seems the Napa ambiance has rubbed off on this one. With your room's black-out curtains, you can sleep it off if you need to. Rates are $145–355. Dogs are $50 per stay. 1075 California Boulevard 94559; 707/253-9540; www.embassysuites1.hilton.com.

The Inn on First: This luxurious inn changed hands in 2007 (it was formerly

The Daughter's Inn) and is fast becoming a favorite of pooches touring wine country. At check-in, dog guests get a dog toy, a treat, a souvenir pet tag, and bags for things you tend not to focus on at places like this. In the room your dog will find a custom doggy bed and food and water bowls. What a welcome!

Dogs can stay in three of five garden suites tucked under a 150-year-old oak tree. (Boy dog alert! Boy dog alert!) All three are on the ground floor and have their own private exterior entrances and decks. The suites are spacious and highly comfortable, with large spa tubs not languishing in the bathrooms, but as an integral part of the bedroom/sitting room. A full breakfast and complimentary afternoon snacks are part of your stay.

Rates are $299–345. Dogs are $50 extra per visit. Note: Please don't let your dog sleep on your bed. They had a bad bed-shed experience once with a very nice but extremely sheddy Lab. No, not Jake, thank God. On the subject of cleanliness, they even have a dog shower here, should your dog end up stomping grapes or getting dirty in more normal ways while touring wine country. 1938 First Street 94559; 707/253-1331; www.theinnonfirst.com.

The Meritage Resort at Napa: The Tuscan-inspired architecture and furnishings at the lovely Meritage Resort create a wonderful melding of northern Italian/Napa Valley ambience. Some rooms face vineyards, for a true wine-country experience. The rooms are luxurious, the pampering at the full-service spa exquisite, and the atmosphere decidedly dog friendly. "We appreciate a good dog," a manager told us.

Your dog can't go to the pool or spa, but she'll be able to accompany you to the wonderland that lies outdoors. The vineyard here has walking trails you can peruse with your leashed friend. Our faithful Napa Valley canine correspondent, Bacchus, brings his person, Karen, on a trail that leads to Napa's famed Grape Crusher statue. Try it—you'll like it. In the evening, bring some wine (possibly the free bottle you get at check-in) and head to the outdoor fire

pit for the perfect end to a relaxing day in the Napa Valley. The resort also has an adjacent timeshare counterpart, Vino Bello Resort, should you and your dog want a kitchen, fireplace, living area, and just more space in general.

Rates are $249–700 (the pricier rates are for the timeshares; they're often available on a nightly basis). Dogs are $50 extra (yes, per night). 875 Bordeaux Way 94558; 866/370-6272; www.themeritageresort.com.

The Napa Inn: If Queen Anne–style Victorians are your dog's cup of tea, sniff out this terrific 1899 bed-and-breakfast. Dogs are allowed to stay in one of two pet-friendly rooms. Jake recommends the Garden Cottage, which has a fireplace, mini-kitchen, and French doors that look out on a private flower garden. Dogs mustn't sleep on the beds, so BYOB.

Your stay includes breakfast for two (humans) in the inn's sumptuous dining area. On cooler evenings, the humans in your party can sidle up to a fire in the relaxing parlor. Rates are $195–255. Dogs are $30 per stay. 1137 Warren Street 94559; 707/257-1444 or 800/435-1144; www.napainn.com.

Napa River Inn: This dog-friendly, full-service luxury hotel doesn't just permit pooches: It showers them with goodies and services. You won't believe what this upscale boutique hotel offers dogs. Upon check-in, your dog gets use of a pet blanket embroidered with the inn's logo, a matching placemat, and attractive food and water bowls to put on the placemat. (If you want to buy these items, the gift shop sells them. The ones that come with your room are just loaners.) In addition, dogs get poop bags and locally made gourmet dog biscuits. As you may have guessed, unlike the aforementioned goodies, you don't have to give these items back when you're done with them. If you need a little assistance with dog duties, the bell staff here is often available to take your dog for a little walk along the inn's namesake, the Napa River. Dog-sitting can also be arranged through an outside service, but you'll have to give 72 hours notice. Dogs of any size are now allowed; this is great news for big dogs like Jake, since the old weight limit was just 40 pounds. In fact, the staff hosted a 150-pound mastiff not too long ago!

One of the three buildings that make up the inn dates from 1887. Its rooms are opulent but unpretentious, with fireplaces, clawfoot tubs, and canopy king-size beds. Rooms at the other two lovely buildings feature nautical themes or "contemporary wine country design." Included in your stay is a delicious breakfast at Angele, the dog-friendly restaurant on this 2.5-acre property. Rates are $179–499. Dogs are $25 extra. 500 Main Street 94559; 707/251-8500 or 877/251-8500; www.napariverinn.com.

Redwood Inn: Rates are $67–150. Dogs are $10 extra. 3380 Solano Avenue 94558; 707/257-6111 or 877/872-6272; www.napavalleyredwoodinn.com.

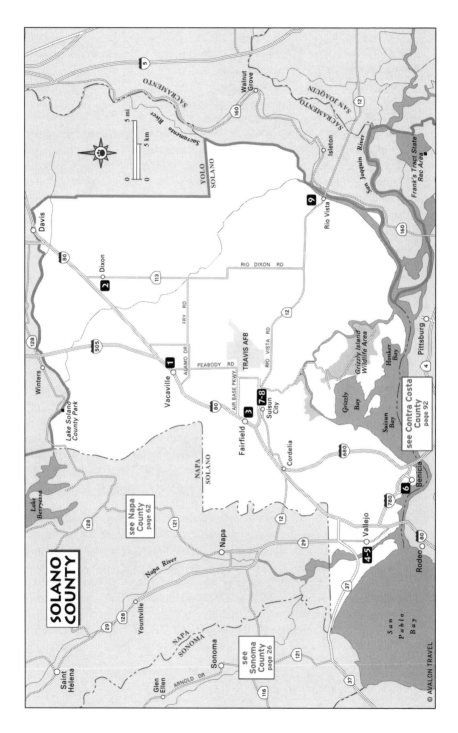

CHAPTER 3

Solano County

Solano County dogs are a happy lot these days, with some decent dog-friendly restaurants to dine in and parks to run around—a far howl better than it used to be here.

The marvelous 2,070-acre Rush Ranch Open Space permits leash-free pooches on a two-mile trail with views that are to drool for. This alone makes it absolutely worth the trip to Solano County. So does the Grizzly Island Wildlife Area, in the thick of the Suisun Marsh. As long as you visit when dogs can be off leash, your pooch will think she's in heaven. Mud heaven. Bring a towel.

If you find yourself at the famed Jelly Belly jelly bean factory in Fairfield, you'll be happy to know that while you wait for the rest of your crew to take the tour inside, you and your dog can have a decent time at the teeny little dog "relief" area beside the parking lot. You'll find some very green grass, some pretty ivy, poop bags, water, and a red fire hydrant ("This hydrant is here for your dog's pleasure," a big sign says. "Not a working hydrant.") If, God forbid, the Jelly Belly factory goes up in flames, at least the firefighters won't be fooled by the doggy decor.) It's not exactly Rush Ranch, but it's better than sitting in your car the whole time watching tired, jelly bean–stuffed children having sugar-induced meltdowns on the asphalt.

PICK OF THE LITTER—SOLANO COUNTY

MOST TEMPTING HYDRANT
Jelly Belly dog "relief" area, Fairfield (page 83)
Janine Jordan Park for Dogs, Vacaville (page 84)

BEST OFF-LEASH HIKING
Rush Ranch Open Space, Suisun City (page 90)

BEST PLACE TO HIKE WITH COWS
Rush Ranch Open Space, Suisun City (page 90)

MOST DOG-FRIENDLY PLACE TO EAT
Valley Cafe, Suisun City (page 90)

BEST GREASY SPOON
Babs Delta Diner, Suisun City (page 90)

MOST DOG-FRIENDLY PLACE TO STAY
Courtyard by Marriott Vallejo Napa Valley, Vallejo
(page 88)

Vacaville

PARKS, BEACHES, AND RECREATION AREAS

🔲 Janine Jordan Park for Dogs
🐾🐾🐾🐕 (See Solano County map on page 82)

Jake gives this park three paws despite its relatively small size of 0.7 acre. That's because it has friendly people, grass (although not always of the green variety), shade trees, and best of all: a golden fire hydrant (most dogs probably only dream of such idols) and a doggy drinking fountain made out of a decommissioned fire hydrant. The golden hydrant is a memorial to Panto, a dearly departed Vacaville Police K-9 partner. The fountain hydrant is an homage to all dogs.

The dog park is within Lagoon Valley Regional Park. If you're going to become a park regular, you should join its organizational group, PAWS (People Aware of the Well-being of the Speechless). The $50 annual membership fee goes toward park upkeep and supplies. (From what a visitor tells us, the park looks as if it's in need of some TLC lately. It wasn't when we saw it, though. Either way, your membership dollars will be put to good use.) Plus your membership will get you into the park without having to pay the $3 entry fee for the regional park. But if you're just passing through and want to check it out, it's worth the $3. (You'll also have to sign a waiver. They're available at the kiosk, or you can download one by going to the dog park's website, www.ourdogpark.org.)

Exit I-80 at Pena Adobe Road/Lagoon Valley Regional Park. Go right at the stop sign (this is Riviera Road), and go left onto Pena Adobe. Follow the signs to Lagoon Valley Regional Park, which will be on your right. Drive 0.2 mile more and you'll come to the dog park. Lagoon Valley's number is 707/449-6122. The number to contact PAWS is 866/510-3681.

PLACES TO EAT

Pure Grain Bakery Cafe: Dine with your dog at the lovely outdoor patio area of this German-style bakery. The rye is to die for. The café's soups, salads, sandwiches, and coffees are tasty, too. And if your dog is like Gracie Autumn (our canine informant in the area), he might enjoy a taste of the café's creamy gelato. (Vanilla is Gracie's choice.) 11 Town Square/Main Street; 707/447-4121.

PLACES TO STAY

Best Western Heritage Inn: Small to medium dogs are allowed here. Don't try to pass your Saint Bernard off as a lapdog, even if he is your lapdog. Rates are $70–100. Dogs require a $50 deposit. If you stay more than three days, it becomes a fee. Huh, that's a new one on me. 1420 East Monte Vista Avenue 95688; 707/448-8453.

Motel 6: If you want to shop at the famous outlet mall in Vacaville and you're traveling with someone who will watch your pooch, this is a convenient place to stay—it's about 1,000 feet from the mall. Shop 'til you drop, then drag yourself back here. Rates are $41–55 for the first adult, $6 for the second. 107 Lawrence Drive 95687; 707/447-5550.

Dixon

PARKS, BEACHES, AND RECREATION AREAS

🐾 Hall Memorial Park

😊😊🐕 (See Solano County map on page 82)

If you have to conduct business with city government and you want your dog to conduct business, too, you couldn't have asked for a better location for a park. It's right behind City Hall.

There's not much in the way of shade here, but on cooler days this park proves a decent stroll for dogs, provided they're leashed or at very firm heel. The park also has a playground, a swimming pool, tennis courts, and picnic areas with barbecues, so it's even better for people. The park is at Hall Park Drive and East Mayes Street. 707/678-7000.

PLACES TO STAY

Best Western Inn: This is a convenient place to stay if you have to attend a University of California event and no rooms are available in Davis. It's just eight miles away, and a swift drive. Rates are $85–119. Dogs are $15 extra. 1345 Commercial Way 95620; 707/678-1400 or 800/528-1234.

Fairfield

If you're here on jelly bean business, you'll be happy to know your dog can do his business too. See the introduction to this chapter for more info on the dog relief area at the Jelly Belly factory.

PARKS, BEACHES, AND RECREATION AREAS

🐾 Rockville Hills Regional Park

🐾🐾🐾 (See Solano County map on page 82)

Hike, fish, and enjoy nature in this 630-acre park filled with trees and trails. The main trail is fairly steep and takes you to the top of the park, where you'll find two small ponds for fishing. After this hike on a summer afternoon, many dogs jump in when they reach the summit. A man told me that a small beagle once disappeared for several seconds and came up with a tiny fish flailing in her mouth. Could this be just another flagrant flailing fish story?

Once you enter the park, you're safe from traffic. But dogs are supposed to be leashed anyway, since the park is officially run by the city of Fairfield, which has a strict leash law. Check out the nature trail that a local Eagle Scout troop has created. A favorite of many dogs is the Mystic Trail. The 25 miles of trails are arranged in sort of stacked loop formations, so it's easy to get lost. Trail maps are available at the entrance. If in doubt, phone the number below for advice.

For the most vigorous workout, try the main trail. It's the one that bends slightly to the left and up a steep hill as you enter from the parking lot. The park is often desolate, so use judgment about hiking alone.

Exit Highway 80 at Suisun Valley Road and drive 1.5 miles (in the opposite direction from the myriad fast-food outlets) to Rockville Road. Go left on Rockville. In about 0.7 mile you'll come to a small brown sign for the park. In 1,500 feet you'll find a small parking area. The entry fee for humans is $3, and dogs are $1. 707/428-7614.

Vallejo

PARKS, BEACHES, AND RECREATION AREAS

4 Dan Foley Park

😺😺 (See Solano County map on page 82)

You won't often see this at Six Flags Marine World—professional water-skiers practicing their acts over sloping jumps, then landing headfirst in the water when everything doesn't work out perfectly.

But you and your dog will be treated to this unpolished spectacle if you visit this park on the right day. The park is directly across Lake Chabot from Marine World, so you get to witness a good chunk of the goings-on there. Since dogs aren't allowed at Marine World, this is an ideal place to walk them if your kids are spending a few hours with more exotic animals. You still get to hear the sound of jazz bands and the roar of amazed crowds.

Dan Foley Park is so well maintained we initially were afraid it was a golf course. Willows and pines on rolling hills provide cooling shade, and there's usually a breeze from the lake. Leashed dogs are invited everywhere but the water. Even humans aren't supposed to swim in it. Picnic tables are right across from the water-ski practice area, so if your dog wants entertainment with his sandwich, this is the place.

The park is on Camino Alto North just east of Tuolumne Street. There is a $4 parking fee, $5 for nonresidents. 707/648-4600.

5 Wardlaw Dog Park

😺😺😺😺 🐾 (See Solano County map on page 82)

Vallejo's first dog park is a testament to how to build a dog park right. It's a decent size, at 2.2 acres, which leaves plenty of room for your galloping dog to gather a good head of steam before having to avoid a fence or bench. Wardlaw has separate sections for large and small/fragile dogs, green grass, little trees that will grow and provide shade one day, attractive landscaping, an interior and exterior walking path, water, and five poop bag dispensers. Even with these dispensers, poop sometimes ends up orphaned. That's where the volunteer "Bark Rangers" step in (and hopefully not on). They help the city keep the park neat and safe and pretty. Bark Rangers are always needed. You can find out how to become one at the park's kiosk.

The non-dog-park area of the surrounding park (Wardlaw Park, to be exact) provides ample parking, a picnic area, bathrooms, and a two-mile walking path that permits leashed pooches. There's even a skate park. The park is fairly convenient from Highway 80, so we'll provide directions from there, should your dog need to stretch her gams on a road trip: Take the Redwood Street East exit and follow it for about a mile. After passing a large-looking park area, turn right on Ascot Parkway. You'll want to stay in the right lane, because you'll be going right again within a block, into Wardlaw. 707/648-4600.

PLACES TO STAY

Courtyard by Marriott Vallejo Napa Valley: While the kids are busy turning upside-down at unnerving speeds at Six Flags Discovery Kingdom, located across the street, you and your dog can curl up, read a book, and enjoy the peace.

The hotel is very dog friendly. It sports an outdoor pet area, allows well-behaved pets to be left in the rooms unattended (if you use the Do Not Disturb sign on the door), and provides old linen "for the use of furniture coverage so that your pet may enjoy the comforts of home," says the pet guideline sheet.

Rates are $99–269. Dogs are charged a $75 fee per visit. 1000 Fairgrounds Drive 94590; 707/644-1200.

Motel 6: This one's a mere two blocks from Six Flags Marine World. Rates are $46–50 for the first adult, $6 for the second. 458 Fairgrounds Drive 94589; 707/642-7781.

Howard Johnson Inn & Suites: Rates are $65–90. Dogs are $15–30 extra, depending on their size. Ninety-something-pound Jake doesn't think that's fair. 44 Admiral Callaghan Lane 94591; 707/643-1061.

Ramada Inn: Rates are $68–150. Dogs are charged a $50 fee per visit. 1000 Admiral Callaghan Lane 94591; 707/643-2700.

Benicia

PARKS, BEACHES, AND RECREATION AREAS

6 Phenix Community Dog Park

😊😊😊😊🐕 (See Solano County map on page 82)

Phenix Community Dog Park, named after a brave retired police dog, is a swell place for dogs. It's got a little more than an acre of grassy leash-free running room, and it's fenced, with water, picnic tables (which little dogs love to dodge under during chase games), poop bags, and small trees that are growing into shade-givers.

The park is in the northwest corner of the 50-acre Benicia Community Park. Enter the parking lot at Rose and Kearny drives and drive to the far west end. Then just follow the wide asphalt path with the painted paw prints to the dog park. Keep in mind that the rest of the park prohibits dogs, so don't let your dog talk you into visiting anywhere but the pooch park. If you enter the park elsewhere, the paw prints will still lead to Phenix. 707/746-4285.

PLACES TO EAT

Java Point: You and the dog of your choice are sure to enjoy the soups, sandwiches, bagels, and jammin' good java served here. This would be a terrific place to bring the pooch even if the food was just so-so. The folks here bring a fresh bowl of water to thirsty dogs. Dine with your smiling, well-quenched dog at the umbrella-topped patios. 366 1st Street; 707/745-1449.

PLACES TO STAY

Best Western Heritage Inn: Rates are $89–120. Dogs pay a $25 fee for the length of their stay. 1955 East 2nd Street 94510; 707/746-0401.

Suisun City

PARKS, BEACHES, AND RECREATION AREAS

7 Grizzly Island Wildlife Area

(See Solano County map on page 82)

This is what dogs have been praying for since they started living in cities: 8,600 acres of wide-open land where they can run—leashless—among the sort of wildlife you see only in PBS specials.

This sprawling wetland, in the heart of the Suisun Marsh, is home to an amazing array of fauna, including tule elk, river otters, waterfowl of every type, jackrabbits, white pelicans, and peregrine falcons.

Of course, walking in marshy areas has its pros and cons. It's muddy, and ticky. But you don't have to get muddy feet here; the landscapes are as varied as the animal life. Dry upland fields are plentiful. You can also canoe down a slough with your steady dog or hike on dozens of dirt trails. Many folks bring dogs here to train them for hunting, which brings us to the unfortunate subject of the park's schedule.

Because of hunting and bird-nesting seasons, Grizzly Island Wildlife Area is closed during fairly large chunks of the year. Be sure to phone first!

If your dog helps you hunt for ducks or pheasant, she's allowed to join you during some of the hunting seasons. Department of Fish and Game staff also occasionally open small sections to people during the off-season, but it's unpredictable from one year to another when and if they'll do it. Even when the park is open, certain sections may be off-limits to dogs. Check with staff when you come in. (Generally, dogs of the nonhunting variety are allowed February, July, and after elk season at the end of September.)

To get to the Grizzly Island Wildlife Area, exit I-80 at Highway 12 heading toward Rio Vista. Turn onto Grizzly Island Road at the stoplight for the Sunset Shopping Center. Drive 10 miles, past farms, sloughs, and marshes, until you get to the headquarters. You'll have to check in here and pay a $2.50 fee unless you have a hunting or fishing license. Then continue driving to the parking lot nearest the area you want to explore (staff can advise you). Don't forget your binoculars. 707/425-3828.

8 Rush Ranch Open Space

🐾🐾🐾🐾 🐕 (See Solano County map on page 82)

From freshwater and saltwater marshes to rolling grass-covered hills and meadowlike pastures, this 2,070-acre open-space parcel is home to some wonderfully diverse landscapes.

The to-wag-for news for dogs is that they're allowed to be off-leash on one of the three trails here if they're under voice control. (They're not allowed to even set paw on the other two.) Suisun Hill Trail is a big hit among canines. The two-mile trail takes you into hills with killer 360-degree views of the Suisun Marsh and the hills and mountains to the north. Rangers tell us that on a clear day, you can see the Sierra Nevada.

Cattle are in these here hills, so if your dog is a chaser, or a herder with an uncontrollable urge to do his job, keep him leashed. (Cattle dogs have been known to try to herd bevies of bovines. The cattle don't think this is cute. Neither do Rush Ranch rangers.) Plenty of wildlife is here, too. If in doubt, leash. (Bikes and horses aren't allowed, so those are two fewer distractions to worry about.)

It can be muddy and mucky here, even in dry season, so be sure to have a towel or two in the car. "It's definitely a three-toweler," warns Jessamy Fisher, who hiked here with dogs Gunther and Savannah. "But it was worth the wet dog/swamp smell in my Honda to see my little angels meet cows for the first time." Aww!

This is a special place, run by the Solano Land Trust. If you'd like to help support the educational and interpretive activities of the Rush Ranch Educational Council, or if you want more information, phone 707/432-0150. For details on Rush Ranch's history, flora and fauna, and other park info, see www.rushranch.org.

From Highway 12, exit at Grizzly Island Road and drive south for a couple of miles. To get to the trail, park near the entrance sign and cross Grizzly Island Road to the gate. Walk to the left and follow the trail markers.

PLACES TO EAT

Babs Delta Diner: Water dogs love Babs Delta Diner because it's right on the Delta waterfront, at the Suisun City Marina. But even landlubbing dogs and their people enjoy Babs' water views. The food is the hearty old-style Americana genre that you'll want to avoid if you're monitoring any of your body's statistics (cholesterol, for instance): Biscuits and gravy, thick-sliced ham, and corned beef hash are featured menu items. You can also get soup and salad, but your hungry, drooling dog will be praying you opt for the goopy meaty fare. Dogs are allowed at the patio seating. Thanks to Gracie Autumn and her person, Deborah, for leading us to Babs. 770 Kellogg Street; 707/421-1926.

Valley Cafe: Your dog will have a hard time forgiving you if you're on your way to Lake Berryessa and you don't stop at this cute eatery. That's because the owner loves dogs and makes 'em feel right at home. Next to the register is a jar of pooch treats that calls dogs from far and wide. If you cock your head just right, you can almost hear it in the breeze. "Oh dogggggyyyyy! Come eat us!!!! We're really yummmmmyyyyyy!!" Dogs also can wet their whistles with bowls of fresh water here. By the way, humans enjoy the café/diner cuisine. The BLT on grainy artisan bread is to drool for. Dine with your dog at the nine umbrella-covered tables outside. (If it's crowded, they'd really appreciate it if you could come back another time.) 4171 Suisun Valley Road; 707/864-2507.

Rio Vista

Humphrey the humpback whale visited this Delta town, and so should your dog. For now, this is a real, dusty Old West town—not one of those cute villages loaded with boutiques and "shoppes." It's refreshing to find a town with more bait shops than banks. However, in the name of "progress," Rio Vista is slowly becoming home to some major housing developments and all the shopping centers and other unsightly amenities that go with them. Get here now, and take some photos on the old streets with your smiling dog. In a few years, they could be collector's items.

Rio Vista isn't bursting with dog amenities. In fact, it's really appropriate to visit with your dog only if you're on a fishing holiday. Then you and your pooch can slip your boat into the water and take off on the Delta for a few hours. Come back with your catch and eat dinner at the county park as the sun goes down on another Delta day.

PARKS, BEACHES, AND RECREATION AREAS

🐾 Sandy Beach County Park

🐾🐾 (See Solano County map on page 82)

Take your dog to the very back of the park for a tolerable little hike, and he can even dip his paws in the Sacramento River! The closer day-use section is completely off-limits to dogs, so be sure you end up in the right area.

Your dog has another chance of getting wet if he follows you into the showers at the campground. Dogs are allowed at the campground. It's not terribly scenic and can get mighty dry at times, but hey, it's a place to stay on the river. There are 42 sites. Fees are $30 a night. Dogs are $1 extra. Half the sites are first-come, first-served. Reservations are recommended during summer.

Take Highway 12 all the way to Rio Vista; follow Main Street to 2nd Street, and go right. When the street bears left and becomes Beach Drive, the park is within a quarter mile. Bring proof of a rabies vaccination. 707/374-2097.

92

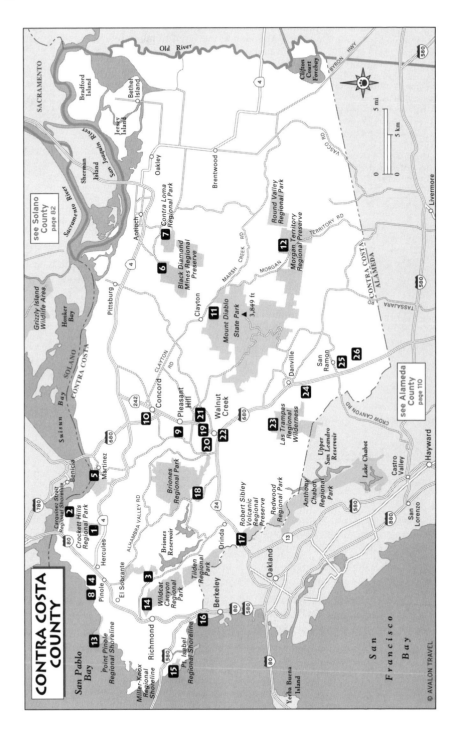

CHAPTER 4

Contra Costa County

Although much of Contra Costa County is considered a sleepy bedroom community for San Francisco, it's a rip-roaring frontierland of fun for dogs. From the renowned off-leash dog haven of the Point Isabel Regional Shoreline to the leash-free inland nirvanas of the East Bay Regional Park District (such as the Morgan Territory, in Clayton), this county enables every dog to have her day, day after day. (For more on the wonders of the East Bay Regional Park District, see the introduction to the *Alameda County* chapter.)

For dogs who like long hikes through highly diverse lands, 10 long regional trails lace Lafayette, Walnut Creek, and the other urban areas of the Diablo Valley. There are 60 miles of trails in all, linking a dozen towns and many beautiful parklands. Dogs must be leashed, but with all the horses and bikes that can visit here, it's a sensible rule.

The Briones to Diablo Regional Trail is one of the more popular trails. It's about 12 miles long and it snakes through some terrific parkland, including the off-leash wonderlands of the Acalanes Ridge Open Space Recreation Area and the Shell Ridge Open Space Recreation Area (both described in the

PICK OF THE LITTER—CONTRA COSTA COUNTY

BEST OFF-LEASH HIKING

Crockett Hills Regional Park, Crockett (page 94)

Sobrante Ridge Regional Preserve, El Sobrante (page 96)

Black Diamond Mines Regional Preserve, Antioch (page 98)

Morgan Territory Regional Preserve, Clayton (page 101)

Briones Regional Park, Lafayette (page 105)

Las Trampas Regional Wilderness, Danville (page 108)

BEST OFF-LEASH BEACH

Point Isabel Regional Shoreline, Richmond (page 104)

BEST CHURCH

First Presbyterian Church of Richmond drive-in church services, Pinole (page 97)

Walnut Creek section). The trail, which is part paved/part dirt, starts at Briones Regional Park's Lafayette Ridge Staging Area, on Pleasant Hill Road just north of Highway 24.

The Contra Costa Canal Regional Trail is a good one for dogs who like to look at water but not set foot in it. We love this 12-mile trail, which follows the (off-limits) canal. For information and a trail map of all 10 regional trails, or for information on all the East Bay Regional Park District parklands, call 888/327-2757, or go to www.ebparks.org.

Crockett

PARKS, BEACHES, AND RECREATION AREAS

🗖 Crockett Hills Regional Park

🐾🐾🐾🐾🐾 🐕 (See Contra Costa County map on page 92)

This 2,000-acre beauty gets less paw traffic than many of the other East Bay Regional Park District lands, but it's probably because it's one of the more recent additions to the district.

Crockett Hills is excellent for well-behaved dogs who enjoy running around the great outdoors naked (without a leash). From shade-giving eucalyptus groves and oak woodland to rolling grasslands to rippling riverfront, the park has something for every dog's taste—unless their taste consists only of shopping at Saks. Late winter is a good time to visit if you like your hills soft and green rather than crunchy brown.

Several miles of trails—mostly fire roads, actually—run through the park. A four-mile segment of the Bay Area Ridge Trail cuts a path through. Views from some points along the way include Mt. Tamalpais, Mt. Diablo, and the Carquinez Strait. Jake likes visiting the staging area, where there's an old barn and a picnic area. Dogs have to be leashed in this section, but if they're under voice control, they don't need leashes in the rest of the park.

From northbound Highway 80, take the Port Costa/Crockett exit (Exit 27), turn left on Pomona Street, drive a few blocks, and go right on Crockett Boulevard, then turn right at the staging area. 888/327-2757.

Port Costa

Port Costa is a sleepy, picturesque town of Victorian cottages. In the 19th century, it was a booming wheat export dock. Of course, if your dog remembers the Frank Norris book *The Octopus,* he already knows this.

PARKS, BEACHES, AND RECREATION AREAS

◻ Carquinez Strait Regional Shoreline

🐾🐾🐾🐾🐾 (See Contra Costa County map on page 92)

This regional shoreline, run by East Bay Regional Parks, lies just east of Crockett. From the Bull Valley Staging Area, on Carquinez Scenic Drive, you can choose one of two leash-free hillside trails. The Carquinez Overlook Loop, to the right, gives better views of Port Costa, the Carquinez Bridge, and Benicia. We once surprised a deer here sleeping in the shade of a clump of eucalyptus.

The eastern part of the park, east of Port Costa, is contiguous with Martinez Regional Shoreline. But beware: You can't get there from here. (Carquinez Scenic Drive is closed at a spot between Port Costa and Martinez. You must turn south on twisty McEwen Road to Highway 4 instead.)

To get to the Carquinez Strait Regional Shoreline from I-80, exit at Crockett and drive east on Pomona Street through town. Pomona turns into Carquinez Scenic Drive, from which you'll see the staging area. 888/327-2757.

El Sobrante

PARKS, BEACHES, AND RECREATION AREAS

3 Sobrante Ridge Regional Preserve

😾😾😾🐕 (See Contra Costa County map on page 92)

This 277-acre preserve brims with deer, coyotes, salamanders, and oodles of birds. Unless your dog is under perfect voice control, it's a good idea to use a leash here. From the Coach Way entrance, follow the dirt trail branching back to the left 100 feet from the entrance. This is the Sobrante Ridge Trail, which will take you through grass, dwarf manzanita, oaks, and coyote brush, up a half mile to views of both Mt. Tam and the top of Mt. Diablo. Branch off on the short loop, Broken Oaks Trail, for a picnic at one of the tables under cool oaks.

This 277-acre preserve is the habitat of the extremely rare Alameda manzanita. So that your dog knows what to watch out for, this manzanita is a gnarled, red-barked shrub that may have sprays of urn-shaped blossoms or clusters of red berries, depending on the time of year. The manzanitas cling to the hillsides. Don't let your boy dog do anything the manzanitas wouldn't want him to do.

From I-80 in Richmond, exit at San Pablo Dam Road and drive south to Castro Ranch Road. Turn left on Castro Ranch, then left at Conestoga Way, going into the Carriage Hills housing development. Take another left on Carriage Drive and a right on Coach Way. Park at the end of Coach and walk into the preserve. 888/327-2757.

Pinole

PARKS, BEACHES, AND RECREATION AREAS

4 Pinole Valley Park

😾😾😾🐕 (See Contra Costa County map on page 92)

This city park is fortunate enough to be contiguous with Sobrante Ridge Regional Preserve. The paved bike path off to the right past the children's playground leads to Alhambra Creek—a good plunge for your dog if he can negotiate the banks wearing a leash. The path then becomes a fire trail and ambles through brush, oaks, and nicely varied deciduous trees. This trail is quite wild and litter-free. It ends at an outlet on Alhambra Road.

And joy of joys! There's a dog park within the park, between the baseball field and the barbecue pits. It's about an acre, with grass, benches, poop bags, water, and a separate section for small dogs. It's fun to mix a little off-leash romp with a leashed walk around the rest of the attractive park.

The entrance to the main park is at Pinole Valley Road and Simas Avenue. 510/724-9002.

DIVERSION

Drive Your Pooch to the Pulpit: Want to take your dog to church? If you don't think he's ready to pray in a pew, you can bring him along to attend a service in the comfort of your car. Since 1975, the **First Presbyterian Church of Richmond** has offered a drive-in service in a shopping mall parking lot. Held 9 A.M.–noon every Sunday outside the Appian 80 shopping center in Pinole, the ceremony attracts a few dozen worshippers every week.

Steve Niccolls, who taught junior high for almost 20 years and is a seminary student, is a popular preacher and "has a heart for the drive-in ministry," says his wife, Emily.

Steve transmits the service over shortwave radio from a mobile pulpit, complete with a sermon and choral music. On the first Sunday of each month, church elders bring communion around to each car on a silver platter. Parishioners honk and flash their headlights at Steve to say "Amen." It's quite a scene—and afterward you can go shopping. Dogs are as welcome to attend as anyone, and three dogs are there almost weekly. (They read about it in a previous edition of this book and dragged their people there.) Other animals are also welcome: Peepers the Duck usually makes a weekly appearance as well.

Exit I-80 at Appian Way. The shopping center is just north of the freeway, on the west side of Appian Way, Pinole. For more information, call 510/234-0954.

Martinez

Martinez has a charming historic district right off the entrance to its regional shoreline park, so spend some time walking with your dog around the Amtrak station and antique shops. You'll see plenty of fellow strollers taking a break from the train.

PARKS, BEACHES, AND RECREATION AREAS

5 Hidden Lakes Open Space

🐾🐾🐾🐾 🐕 (See Contra Costa County map on page 92)

Although the city park called Hidden Valley Park doesn't allow dogs, the open space to the south of it does. It's crossed by one of the East Bay Regional Parks' trails (the California Riding and Hiking Trail) on its way from the Carquinez Strait Regional Shoreline to where it connects with the Contra Costa Canal Trail. Call 888/327-2757 or see www.ebparks.org for maps of the Contra Costa Regional Trails.

One entrance to Hidden Lakes is off Morello Avenue, where it intersects with Chilpancingo Parkway.

Antioch

Antioch is pretty much a desert for dogs, but south of town are two charming spots of relief.

PARKS, BEACHES, AND RECREATION AREAS

6 Black Diamond Mines Regional Preserve

🐾🐾🐾🐾 🐕 (See Contra Costa County map on page 92)

Leash-free dogs, especially leash-free dogs of the male persuasion, think this park is an excellent place to visit. The coal miners who worked and lived here in the 1860s and 1870s planted a variety of drought-tolerant trees not usually found in the East Bay, including something called "trees of heaven." Dogs who sniff these trees seem to know why they're called trees of heaven. Their noses just can't get enough as they press them deep into the bark.

The hills of Black Diamond Mines are jumbled and ragged, looking a lot like the Sierra foothills. From the parking lot, it's a moderate climb to the Rose Hill Cemetery, where Protestant Welsh miners (the tombstones bear the names Davis, Evans, and Jenkins) buried victims of mine accidents and many of their children, who died of diphtheria, typhoid, and scarlet fever.

Plenty of tunnel openings and piles of tailings have been preserved by the park for walkers to examine. A brochure marks mine sites. You should be alert for rattlers during warm seasons, although any rattler not actually snoozing will probably get out of your way before you even know he's near.

You can walk into this East Bay regional preserve from the Contra Loma Regional Park just below it. But from that direction, the trails are too hot and dry for a dog in summer. Instead, enter from the north by car via Somersville Road and park in the last lot, which has some shady trees.

It's $5 to park here. Dogs are $2 extra. Backpack camping is available for $5. From Highway 4 at Antioch, exit at Somersville Road and drive south to the park entrance. Keep driving for a bit more than one mile if you want to park in the lot farthest in. You'll pass wonderful old mining-era houses and barns, now used as park headquarters and offices. 888/327-2757.

7 Contra Loma Regional Park

🐾🐾🐾🐾 🐕 (See Contra Costa County map on page 92)

This 776-acre park is so well hidden amid the barren hills north of Black Diamond Mines that you might not ever know it is here. A few attractive trails, including a trail leading into Black Diamond Mines Regional Preserve, rise into the surrounding hills for you and your leash-free dog to explore. Dogs can be off leash in the backcountry. You'll know it when you see it.

Unfortunately, as in all regional parks, your dog may not accompany you in the swimming area, nor can he take an informal swim in the fishing areas, since park managers want to protect his feet from stray fishhooks. It's probably better not to bring your dog here on a hot day. Instead, save the trip for winter or spring, when the wildflowers burst open.

From Highway 4, take the Lone Tree Way exit. Go south on Lone Tree for a little more than a half mile, then turn right onto Bluerock Drive. Follow Bluerock along the park's east side to the entrance. The fee for parking is $5. The dog fee is $2. 888/327-2757.

Hercules

PARKS, BEACHES, AND RECREATION AREAS

🖪 San Pablo Bay Shoreline Park

😊😊😊 🐕 (See Contra Costa County map on page 92)

This tiny, undeveloped East Bay Regional Park shoreline is just right if you happen to be in Hercules exploring the old Santa Fe Railroad yard. A paved trail runs about 0.12 mile along the tracks. New housing developments and interesting restored Victorian railroad workers' housing surround a small but pretty area of grass, swamp, and eucalyptus trees. Best of all, you and your dog can check it all out without a leash.

If you follow Railroad Avenue to its end, across the line into Pinole, there's a very small and beautifully landscaped city park behind the wastewater treatment plant (which smells fresh as a rose). You must keep your dog on leash here.

From I-80, exit at Pinole Valley Road and travel north. Pinole Valley Road becomes Tennent Avenue, then Railroad Avenue. Park somewhere around the Civic Arts Facility, a cluster of Victorian buildings in a grove of palms and eucalyptus. 888/327-2757.

Pleasant Hill

PARKS, BEACHES, AND RECREATION AREAS

🖲 Paso Nogal Park

😊😊😊😊 🐕 (See Contra Costa County map on page 92)

This large open-space park has the best of both worlds: smooth dirt trails along gentle oak-dotted slopes, where leashed dogs can hike to their hearts' content, and a fenced park where they can throw off their leashes and run like the wind. The dog park has a small-dog section, benches, tables, water, and good parking. It's grassy and surrounded by trees. The trees within the park are nothing but glorified sticks right now, but they'll grow.

The dog park is open dawn to dusk Monday–Friday, 9 A.M.dusk Saturday, and closed Sunday for maintenance. To help preserve the lush grass, it's also closed when it rains, and three days after (This can be weeks at a time during rainy season.) The park is at Morello Avenue and Paso Nogal Road. 925/682-0896.

Concord
PARKS, BEACHES, AND RECREATION AREAS

10 The Paw Patch
🐾🐾🐾🐾🐕 (See Contra Costa County map on page 92)

The grass truly is always greener on the other side of the fence at this wonderful 2.5-acre dog park. It's so green and lush that it has other dog parks green with envy. Dog parks with grass (a.k.a. turf) often struggle in vain against a tide of pounding paws. The grass can end up anything but green and rather downtrodden. But not the grass here—the park district folks work hard to maintain it. In fact, they have won a coveted award for their turf management from the California Parks and Recreation Society.

There's more to this park than grass, though. It's got benches, water, poop bags, a smaller fenced area for small dogs, and lots of toys. The lucky dogs who come here get to sniff through a toy box set out by volunteers, and pick out a favorite toy to play with here, or they find toys scattered around the grass.

The park is within the lovely 126-acre Newhall Community Park. You can take your dog around the park on a leash. From the top of the hill you're rewarded with great views of everything from Mount Diablo to the Carquinez Straits. (This is where you'll also find a Vietnam War memorial.) The park is at Turtle Creek Road and Ayres Road. 925/671-3444.

Clayton
PARKS, BEACHES, AND RECREATION AREAS

11 Clayton Dog Park
🐾🐾🐕 (See Contra Costa County map on page 92)

Big oaks are adjacent to this dog park, but there's very little shade within. A dirt lot has wood chips, but dog people pine for grass. Yet for all its little foibles, this is a perfectly decent place to take a dog for an off-leash romp. It may not be the Ritz, but it's not a dive either. It has a picnic table, two benches, poop bags, and water, and it's along the Creek Trail, which makes for a fine leashed dog walk. The park is on Marsh Creek Road and Regency Drive, across from Clayton Park. 925/673-7300.

12 Morgan Territory Regional Preserve

🐾🐾🐾🐾🐕 (See Contra Costa County map on page 92)

Morgan Territory, named after a farmer who owned the land long before it became part of the East Bay Regional Parks system, is as far away from the Bay Area as you can get while still being in the Bay Area. From its heights, on a rim above the Central Valley, you see the San Joaquin River, the Delta, the valley, and, on a clear day, the peaks of the Sierra. Eagles and hawks soar above as you and your leash-free pooch explore ancient twisted giant oaks and lichen-covered sandstone outcrops below. Morgan Territory is close to the end of the earth and well worth the journey.

As the crow flies, Morgan Territory is equidistant from Clayton, Danville, San Ramon, Livermore, Byron, and Brentwood. And "distant" is the key word.

This 4,147-acre preserve has miles of hiking and riding trails. If you don't want to climb much but want great views of the Central Valley, try the Blue Oak Trail, which starts at the entrance. You'll even see the "back side" of Mt. Diablo. It's an unusual vantage point for Bay Area folks.

Most of the creeks are dry in the summer, though your dog can splash into cattle ponds, if he's so inclined. Watch for wicked foxtails in these grasses. These are the sticky wickets that help make veterinarians a well-off breed.

The easiest access is from Livermore in Alameda County. From I-580, take the North Livermore Avenue exit and drive north on North Livermore Avenue. Shortly after the road curves left (west), turn right, onto Morgan Territory Road, and follow it 10.7 miles to the entrance. From the Walnut Creek/Concord area, take Clayton Road to Marsh Creek Road, then turn right onto Morgan Territory Road. The entrance is 9.4 miles from Marsh Creek Road. 888/327-2757.

Richmond

Point Richmond, the Richmond neighborhood tucked between the Richmond-San Rafael Bridge and Miller-Knox Regional Shoreline, is a cheerful small-town hangout for you and your dog. Consider stopping by for a snack on your way to some of the magical, four-paw shoreline here.

Sit on a bench in the Point Richmond Triangle, the town center. You'll be surrounded by nicely preserved Victorian buildings, the Hotel Mac, and many delis and bakeries, some with outdoor tables. The Santa Fe Railroad rattles past periodically, blowing the first two notes of "Here Comes the Bride."

From I-580, on the Richmond end of the Richmond–San Rafael Bridge, exit at Cutting Boulevard and drive west to town. Bear right on Richmond Avenue. The Triangle is at the intersection of Richmond and Washington avenues and Park Place.

PARKS, BEACHES, AND RECREATION AREAS

🔢 Point Pinole Regional Shoreline

🐾🐾🐾🐾 🐕 (See Contra Costa County map on page 92)

Of all the East Bay Regional Parks' shorelines, this is the farthest from civilization and its discontents, and thus the cleanest and least spoiled. It's also huge and a heavenly walk for dog or owner, with its views of Mt. Tamalpais across San Pablo Bay, and its docks, salt marsh, beaches, eucalyptus groves, and expanses of wild grassland waving in the breeze. Some of the eucalyptus trees are so wind-carved they could be mistaken for cypresses.

The park has fine bike paths, and your dog should be leashed for safety on these, but he's free on the unpaved trails—even on the dirt paths through marshes, such as the Marsh Trail. Just make sure he stays on the trail and doesn't go into the marsh itself. Dogs may not go on the fishing pier or on the shuttle bus to the pier.

From I-80, exit at Hilltop Drive, go west and take a right on San Pablo Avenue, then left on Atlas Road to the park entrance. There's a $5 parking fee and a $2 dog fee. 888/327-2757.

🔢 Wildcat Canyon Regional Park

🐾🐾🐾🐾 🐕 (See Contra Costa County map on page 92)

This is Tilden Regional Park's northern twin. Tilden (see the *Berkeley* section of the *Alameda County* chapter) has its attractive spots, but it's designed for people. Wildcat seems made for dogs, because not much goes on here. Dogs really dig this. Who needs all those human feet passing by anyway? (Unless, of course, they're tracking eau de cow patty or some other savory scent.) Best of all, in many areas you can leave your dog's leash tucked away in your pocket. And you'll get a good dose of nature here: Large coast live oaks, madrones, bay laurels, chaparral, and all kinds of wildflowers thrive in this parkland.

At the main parking lot is Wildcat Creek, which gets low but usually not entirely dry in summer. Then you can follow the Wildcat Creek Trail (actually an abandoned paved road; dogs must be leashed on this trail); it travels gently uphill and then follows the southern ridge of the park. Or follow any of the nameless side trails, which are wonderfully wild and solitary. You can hear train whistles all the way up from Emeryville and the dull roar of civilization below, but somehow it doesn't bother you up here.

Other trails lead through groves of pines or follow Wildcat Creek. The park is roughly three miles long. Dogs are banned—even on leash—from wetlands, marshes, and ponds. And if you come to the boundary with Tilden, remember that dogs aren't allowed in the nature area across the line.

From I-80, southbound, take the McBryde exit and turn left on McBryde Avenue to the park entrance. If you're northbound, take the Amador/Solano

DIVERSION

Foof 'Er Up: Is your pooch starting to smell like a dog? If you go to Point Isabel, you can give your dog both the walk of his life and a bath. **Mudpuppy's Tub and Scrub,** the park's very own dog wash, offers full- or self-service scrubbings in several elevated tubs. The cost is very reasonable, considering it includes shampoo, drying, and someone else to clean the tub afterward. And not only can your dog get unmuddy and downright gorgeous here, he can go home with some pretty doggone nice pooch items, too. Mudpuppy's offers a full line of dog toys, treats, and gifts. Owners Eddie Lundeen and Daniel Bergerac provide a fun, clean atmosphere. Call or stop by before your walk in the park to reserve your tub. (The earlier you do so, the better, especially on weekends.)

And here's some great news for your dog's best friend. (That would be you.) Mudpuppy's has a café next door, **Mudpuppy's Sit and Stay Café.** It has a walk-up window so you and your dog can get some delectable goodies for humans, including espresso, tasty pastries, warming soups (usually featuring one veggie variety and something hearty), chili, great sandwiches, and ice cream. The café makes this area one of the most dog-friendly and dog person–friendly around. Eat, drink, walk, talk, buy, suds, scrub, enjoy.

Mudpuppy's is in the first parking lot inside the park, off Isabel Road, Richmond. 510/559-8899; www.mudpuppys.com.

---

exit. Go three blocks north on Amador Street and turn right (east) on McBryde to the entrance. 888/327-2757.

15 Miller-Knox Regional Shoreline

🐾🐾🐾🐾🦴 (See Contra Costa County map on page 92)

Hooray! Wooooof! Yap! Although your dog must be leashed in developed areas, she can run free on the hillside trails east of Dornan Drive in this 259-acre park.

West of Dornan is a generous expanse of grass, pine, and eucalyptus trees with picnic tables, a lagoon with egrets (so there's no swimming), and Keller Beach (dogs are prohibited). It's breezy here and prettier than most shoreline parks by virtue of its protecting gentle hills, whose trails offer terrific views of the Richmond-San Rafael Bridge, Mt. Tamalpais, Angel Island, and San Francisco. Ground squirrels stand right by their holes and pipe their alarms. Although you can't bring your dog onto Keller Beach, there's a paved path above it along riprap shoreline, where your dog can reach the water if he's so inclined. In the picnic areas, watch for discarded chicken bones!

You can also tour the Richmond Yacht Harbor by continuing on Dornan Drive south to Brickyard Cove Road, a left turn past the railroad tracks. Or, from Garrard Boulevard, drive south till you see the Brickyard Cove housing development. The paved paths lining the harbor offer views of yachts, San Francisco, Oakland, and the Bay Bridge.

From either I-80 or I-580, exit at Cutting Boulevard and go west to Garrard Boulevard. Go left, pass through a tunnel, and park in one of two lots off Dornan Drive. 888/327-2757.

16 Point Isabel Regional Shoreline

🐾 🐾 🐾 🐾 🐕 (See Contra Costa County map on page 92)

With so many Bay Area beaches either outright banning dogs or enforcing unfortunate leash demands, it not easy being a water dog around here these days. Thank goodness for this 21-acre patch of utter water-dog heaven! Dogs are so happy when they come here that some howl as they arrive in their cars. (Some owners do, too, but they're another story.)

Point Isabel is an exception to the East Bay Regional Parks' rule that dogs must be on leash in "developed" areas. This is a decidedly unwild but terrific shoreline park with plenty of grass and paw-friendly paved paths. It's swarming with dogs. In a census by the park district, 558,930 people and 784,370 pooches visited in one year. Fortunately, people here are generally very responsible, and the park looks pretty good, despite being assailed by more than four million feet and paws annually.

The large lawn area is perfect for fetching, Frisbee throwing, and chasing each other around. And the bay and the sand, ahh... these are a water dog's delight. The surf here is usually very tame, making dog paddling a joy.

There are benches, picnic tables, restrooms, a water fountain for people and dogs, and many racks full of bags for scooping. Cinder paths run along the riprap waterfront, where you can watch sailboarders against a backdrop of the Golden Gate and Bay Bridges, San Francisco, the Marin Headlands, and Mt. Tamalpais. On a brisk day, a little surf even splashes against the rocks.

After a wet and wonderful walk, you may want to take your pooch to Mudpuppy's Tub and Scrub, which is right here, for a little cleaning up. And after that, if you've been a very good human, you can treat yourself to a cuppa Joe and some café cuisine at Mudpuppy's Sit and Stay Café. Talk about a people and pooch paradise. (See the Diversion *Foof 'Er Up.*)

From I-80 in Richmond, exit at Central Avenue and go west to the park entrance, next to the U.S. Postal Service Bulk Mail Center. For more info on the park or its wonderful doggy user group, PIDO (Point Isabel Dog Owners and Friends—why isn't it called PIDOF?), see www.pido.org. 888/327-2757.

Orinda

PARKS, BEACHES, AND RECREATION AREAS

🌋 Robert Sibley Volcanic Regional Preserve

🐾🐾🐾🐾🐕 (See Contra Costa County map on page 92)

We're not exactly talking Mt. St. Helens here, but this 371-acre park has some pretty interesting volcanic history. Geologically inclined dogs can wander leashless as you explore volcanic dikes, mudflows, lava flows, and other evidence of extinct volcanoes.

The preserve is actually closer to Oakland than Orinda, but it lies in Contra Costa County. From the entrance on Skyline Boulevard, you can get on the East Bay Skyline National Recreation Trail and walk north to Tilden Regional Park (see the *Berkeley* section of the *Alameda County* chapter) or south to Redwood Regional Park (see the *Oakland* section of the *Alameda County* chapter). Or, for a shorter stroll, take the road to Round Top, the highest peak in the Berkeley Hills, made of volcanic debris left over from a 10-million-year-old volcano.

More attractive and less steep is the road to the quarries. It's partly paved and smooth enough for a wheelchair or stroller, but it becomes smooth dirt about halfway to the quarries. Both trails are labeled for geological features. (Pick up a brochure at the visitors center.) At the quarry pits, there's a good view of Mt. Diablo. This is a dry, scrubby, cattle-grazed area, but in the rainy season your dog may be lucky enough to find swimming in a pit near the quarries. In the spring, look for poppies and lupines.

From Highway 24 east of the Caldecott Tunnel, exit on Fish Ranch Road, drive north to Grizzly Peak Boulevard, and then take a left. Go south on Grizzly Peak to the intersection with Skyline Boulevard. Go left on Skyline. The entrance is just to the east of the intersection. 888/327-2757.

Lafayette

PARKS, BEACHES, AND RECREATION AREAS

🌳 Briones Regional Park

🐾🐾🐾🐾🐕 (See Contra Costa County map on page 92)

From both main entrances to this park, you can walk 0.25 mile and be lost in sunny, rolling hills or cool oak woodlands. Unless you stick to the stream areas, it's not a good park for hot summer days. But with a good supply of your own water, you and your dog, who may run blissfully leashless, can walk gentle ups and downs all day on fire roads or foot trails.

The north entrance requires an immediate uphill climb into the hills, but you're rewarded with a quick view of Mt. Diablo and the piping of ground squirrels, all of whom are long gone safely into their burrows by the time your dog realizes they might be fun to chase. If your dog is a self-starter, this end of the park is fine for you. The Alhambra Creek Trail, which follows Alhambra Creek, does offer water in the rainy season. Stay away from the John Muir Nature Area (shaded on your brochure map), where dogs aren't allowed.

When we're feeling lazy, we prefer the south entrance at Bear Creek, just east of the inaccessible (to dogs) Briones Reservoir. Here you have an immediate choice of open hills or woodsy canyons, and the land is level for a few miles. The Homestead Valley Trail leads gently up and down through cool, sharp-scented bay and oak woodlands.

Watch for deer, horses, and cattle. Some dogs near and dear to me love rolling in fresh cow patties—an additional hazard of the beasts existing in close proximity.

From Highway 24, take the Orinda exit; go north on Camino Pablo, then right on Bear Creek Road to Briones Road, to the park entrance. The parking fee is $5 and the dog fee is $2. 888/327-2757.

Walnut Creek

PARKS, BEACHES, AND RECREATION AREAS

🐾🐾🐾🐾 Wag World Dog Park

🐾🐾🐾 🐕 (See Contra Costa County map on page 92)

What a fun name for a dog park! Dogs who visit Wag World seem to think it deserves the name. They run about with big smiles on their snouts, with nary an altercation (that we've heard about). The grass is green, the drinking water is cool, and the small-dog and large-dog sections are well maintained.

Wag World is within Heather Farm Park. From Ygnacio Valley Road, turn north on North San Carlos Drive and follow it to the back of the park. When the road takes a sharp left, Wag World will be on your right. 925/943-5855.

20 Acalanes Ridge Open Space Recreation Area

🐾🐾🐾🐾🐾 🐕 (See Contra Costa County map on page 92)

In 1974, the city of Walnut Creek set aside a few open spaces for a limited-use "land bank." Dogs must be "under voice or sight command" (translation: off leash if obedient). The trails are open to hikers, dogs, horses, and bicycles, however, so on a fine day, your dog may have some competition.

Acalanes Ridge, close to Briones Regional Park (see the *Lafayette* section of this chapter), is crossed by the Briones to Diablo Regional Trail. Like the others, it lacks water.

A good entry point is from Camino Verde Circle, reached by driving south on Camino Verde from the intersection of Pleasant Hill and Geary Roads. For information on any of the open spaces, call 925/944-5766 or 925/943-5899.

21 San Miguel Park

🐾🐾🐾🐾🐕 (See Contra Costa County map on page 92)

Dogs who are early risers love waking up, throwing on their leashes, coming to this park, and then throwing off their leashes. This grassy four-acre park goes to the dogs 6–9 A.M. daily. It's positively poochy here during the morning canine commute. It's not a fenced area, and that's fine with dogs. Boy dogs and shade-seekers like the park's trees.

The park is a few minutes northeast of the I-680/Highway 24 interchange. From northbound I-680, take the exit toward Ygnacio Valley Road and turn right in 0.5 mile onto Ygnacio Valley Road. In about two miles, turn right on San Carlos Drive and in 0.3 mile, go left at San Jose Court. The park is at San Jose Court, off Los Cerros Avenue. 925/943-5855.

22 Shell Ridge Open Space Recreation Area

🐾🐾🐾🐾🐕 (See Contra Costa County map on page 92)

This huge open space was under the ocean a long, long time ago, and it's home to many marine fossils, thus its moniker. Shell Ridge has 31 miles of trails through oak woodlands and grassy hills. Dogs salivate over this because if they're under "positive voice and sight command" they're allowed to be leash-free everywhere but in the developed areas (parking lots, picnic grounds, and the historic Borges Ranch Site). They also mustn't chase the cattle that graze on the rich grasslands. That's a big no-no. If in doubt, leash.

You can enter by the Sugarloaf-Shell Ridge Trail at the north edge. From I-680, take the Ygnacio Valley Road exit, go east on Ignacio Valley Road to Walnut Avenue (not Boulevard), turn right and right again on Castle Rock Road. Go past the high school, turn right, and follow the signs. 925/942-0225.

PLACES TO EAT

Lark Creek: Enjoy farm-fresh American cuisine with your dog at this popular downtown Walnut Creek gem, co-owned by famed chef Bradley Ogden. The produce, meat, and fish are locally grown/raised/caught when possible. I realize Jake longs for me to order the Yankee pot roast or bacon-wrapped meatloaf, but dishes like English pea risotto or wood-baked flatbread with spring onions, Yukon potatoes, and applewood bacon keep appearing at our table instead. Dine with dog at the sidewalk/patio tables. If it's crowded you'll need to tie your dog to the other side of the fence, but you can still be right beside her. 1360 Locust Street; 925/256-1234.

Stadium Pub: This popular sports pub has 30 TVs, and you can even see some of them from the outside tables where you and your dog get to dine. Jake loves this, because anything with a ball is a ball for him. The staff is friendly, there are 22 beers on tap, and if you order the Chicago-style hot dog and give a bite to your dog, she'll be your best friend forever. (Oh wait, she already is!) 1420 Lincoln Avenue at Main Street; 925/256-7302.

Va de Vi: This downtown Walnut Creek restaurant is a great place to go when your paws need a break from shopping in the area. The food, which is mainly small plates, is superb, and the wine selection is huge. After all, Va de Vi means "It's about wine," in Catalan. Wine and dine with your dog at any of several lovely patio tables. 1511 Mt. Diablo Boulevard; 925/979-0100.

PLACES TO STAY

Holiday Inn Express: This comfy hotel has a pool, which humans enjoy, but what's really special about this place is its proximity to a hiking trail. The staff will tell you about it at the front desk. Alas, only dogs under 20 pounds are permitted, and they're $20 extra. That's a minimum of $1 per pound per night. Ouch! Room rates are $89–179. 2730 North Main Street 94598; 925/932-3332.

Danville

PARKS, BEACHES, AND RECREATION AREAS

🐾🐾🐾🐾🐕 Las Trampas Regional Wilderness

🐾🐾🐾🐾🐕 (See Contra Costa County map on page 92)

This regional wilderness is remarkable for its sense of isolation from the rest of the Bay Area. You can experience utter silence at this 3,298-acre park, and the views from the ridge tops are breathtaking.

Rocky Ridge Trail (from the parking lot at the end of Bollinger Canyon Road) takes you and your leash-free pooch on a fairly steep 0.75-mile ascent to the top of the ridge, where you'll enter the East Bay Municipal Utility District watershed. Since dogs aren't allowed here and permits are required even for humans, it's better to head west on any of several trails climbing the sunny southern flanks of Las Trampas Ridge.

Creeks run low or dry during the summer, so bring plenty of water. Your dog should know how to behave around cattle, deer, and horses.

From I-680 about six miles north of the intersection with I-580, take the Bollinger Canyon Road exit and head north on Bollinger Canyon Road to the entrance. (Go past the entrance to Little Hills Ranch Recreation Area, where dogs aren't allowed.) 888/327-2757.

🐾🐾🐾🐕 Canine Corral Dog Park

🐾🐾🐾🐕 (See Contra Costa County map on page 92)

This 1.5-acre dog park within Hap Magee Ranch Park is a pretty mix of grass and wood chips, with a little shade. It has all the usual dog park accoutrements, including a separate area for small or delicate dogs. From I-680 going north, exit at El Cerro Boulevard and turn right onto El Cerro at the light. At the second light, go right at La Gonda Way. The park is on the left after the stop sign. Park in the paved lot. 925/314-3400.

San Ramon

PARKS, BEACHES, AND RECREATION AREAS

25 Memorial Park Dog Park

🐾🐾🐕 (See Contra Costa County map on page 92)

Once a dog's paws get used to the decomposed granite that's on the surface of this park, it's a decent place for a leash-free romp. It's 1.3 acres, with a separate section within for dogs under 20 pounds. (These are the ones Jake would pick up and carry around a park in his mouth ever so gently when we first adopted him at six months.) There will be shade trees here one day, but until the young trees grow larger, man-made shade structures do the trick. The park has water, poop bags, benches, and picnic tables. It can get very dusty here in the summer.

The park is on the northwest side of town. Exit I-680 at Bollinger Canyon Road and drive west 0.2 mile to San Ramon Valley Boulevard, where you'll find parking straight ahead on the south side of Bollinger. 925/973-3200.

26 Del Mar Dog Park

🐾🐾🐾🐕 (See Contra Costa County map on page 92)

This one-acre fenced park is covered with cedar wood chips. Jake, unfortunately, is content to trot around a little and then settle down to see how many wood chips he can chew to smithereens before I can get him to start acting more like a dog, less like a termite. But normal dogs love gallivanting around here. The park has all the usual amenities, including water, benches, and shade structures (no shade trees yet). The park is on the south side of town, at Del Mar Drive and Pine Valley Road. 925/973-3200.

PLACES TO STAY

San Ramon Marriott at Bishop Ranch: The folks who run this attractive hotel are very friendly to creatures of the doggy persuasion. They always get the name of your dog so they can address her directly. And they provide cute door-hanger signs for people with dogs, to warn the housekeeping that a dog is in the room (never alone, though) and not to enter. Rates are $89–239. Dogs pay a $100 fee for the length of their stay. 2600 Bishop Drive 94583; 925/867-9200.

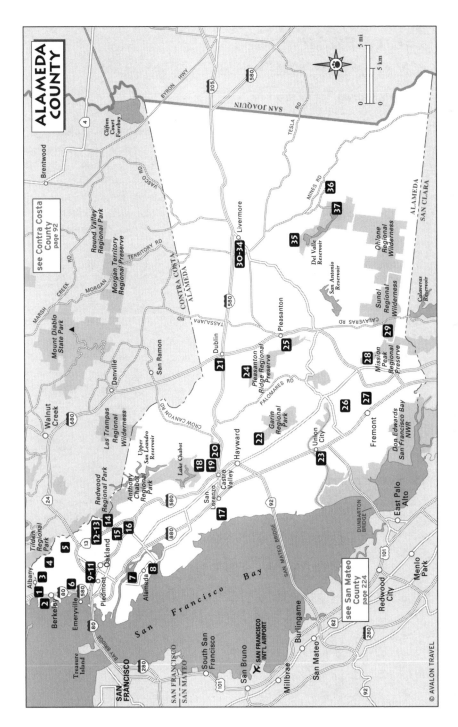

CHAPTER 5

Alameda County

From the hallowed hippie havens of Berkeley's Telegraph Avenue to the pleasing suburban pleasantries of Pleasanton, Alameda County is like California in miniature: It has nearly every level of population density and type, and nearly every temperate natural environment. Somehow, it all works.

Dogs dig it here, whether they're rasta dogs or shaved shih tzus. The county is like the creek it's named after—it's been lined with concrete, filled with trash, and dammed into oblivion, yet it still manages to gush joyfully onward. Some of the wildest country in the Bay Area is in this county, full of hidden gems of nature. So many of these parks are off-leash havens that your dog may think he's dreaming.

The 12-mile Alameda Creek Regional Trail in Fremont is a favorite among dogs. They can run off leash on most of the trail, but where signs say leashes are required, heed the message.

As if all this weren't enough good news, your dog's hair will stand on end when he learns that unless he's a pit bull, he's allowed to run leashless on

PICK OF THE LITTER—ALAMEDA COUNTY

BEST BAYSIDE JUNGLE OF DOGS AND ART
Albany Bulb, Albany (page 113)

MOST MELLOW MUNICIPAL LEASH LAW
Berkeley (page 114)

BEST LEASH-FREE HIKES
Tilden Regional Park, Berkeley (page 116)
Redwood Regional Park, Oakland (page 124)
Chabot Regional Park, Castro Valley (page 128)
Sunol Regional Wilderness, Fremont (page 133)

MOST BONE-A-LICIOUS DOG PARK
Drigon Dog Park, Union City (page 130)

BEST PLACE FOR A DUCK TO EMBARRASS YOUR DOG
San Lorenzo Dog Park, San Lorenzo (page 128)

BEST TIKI BAR
Forbidden Island Tiki Lounge, Alameda (page 122)

MOST DOG-FRIENDLY PLACES TO EAT
Montclair Malt Shop, Montclair district, Oakland (page 126)
Noah's Bagels, Montclair district, Oakland (page 127)

MOST DOG-FRIENDLY PLACES TO STAY
Hotel Durant, Berkeley (page 119)
Waterfront Hotel, Oakland (page 127)

MOST HOUND-HIP BOOKSTORE
Pegasus Books, Berkeley (page 114)

BEST POOCH CHOO CHOO
Tilden Regional Park's miniature train, Berkeley (page 117)

BEST HIKING BUDDIES
Sierra Club's Canine Hike Unit (page 118)

thousands of acres of park land within the East Bay Regional Park District. Some 59 parks and recreation areas and 29 regional interpark trails—95,000 acres in all—fall under the district's jurisdiction. Poop-bag dispensers are installed at the most heavily used areas, such as Point Isabel Regional Shoreline in Richmond (see the *Contra Costa County* chapter).

The only places where dogs must be leashed within the district's parks are in developed areas, parking lots, picnic sites, lawns, and in posted Nature Areas. They aren't permitted on beaches (Point Isabel Regional Shoreline is a major exception), wetlands, marshes, or in the Tilden Nature Area. In addition, dogs have to be leashed along Redwood Regional Park's popular Stream Trail. You can sniff out more details about this magnificent park system by going to www.ebparks.org and looking for the "Dogs" section. (Special rules and permits apply to anyone bringing more than three dogs. This was primarily designed for dog walkers, but if you have a gaggle of dogs yourself, you should check out the info on the site.) Or phone 888/327-2757.

Albany

PARKS, BEACHES, AND RECREATION AREAS

1 Albany Bulb

🐾🐾🐾🐕 (See Alameda County map on page 110)

By the time you read this, this wild bayside jungle of crazy public art and leash-free dogs may be on its way to becoming an environmentally correct habitat with no tolerance for off-leash dogs or outdoor sculpture or paintings that aren't government-approved. Your best bet is to run here as fast as your paws will take you if you want to see this spit of land in its current fun, anarchic, freewheeling style.

This bulb-shaped peninsula used to be a dump, which was covered over and eventually became a home to the homeless. After most of the homeless were swept out in 1999, art and leash-free dogs flourished. The windy beach is a hit with dogs, who are by far the majority species on the beach. You'll drool over the million-dollar views of San Francisco Bay and the Golden Gate Bridge. The trails through the grasslands are also fun for a good romp, although it can feel a bit post-apocalyptic if the Bulb doesn't have many visitors when you're there.

Along your explorations you'll find unique works of art—most of it from found scraps of metal and construction material and flotsam in the vicinity. ("Trash art" is what some of the artists call it.) Some is quite awful, but much is truly enchanting, made by talented artists. Among the pieces: Life-sized people made of flotation foam, driftwood art of all forms, a striped concrete abode, a huge fertility goddess, a metal and wood arch featuring a dog and happy people, and a mixed media dragon.

DIVERSION

Stroll down Solano: A portion of Solano Avenue that runs through a bit of North Berkeley and Albany is a very friendly place to take your dog. People here truly enjoy pooches, and a few stores will let your leashed dog come in with you to browse.

Pegasus Books, 1855 Solano Avenue, is a wonderful independent bookstore. (It has a sister bookstore on Shattuck Avenue in Berkeley, and a close cousin, Pendragon, in Oakland. We're not talking a major national chain here.) When you and your dog come in to look for books, the staff will give your pooch a biscuit. "We welcome dogs!" said a staffer. Canine correspondent Whomper, who told us about this place, has spent very agreeable nights here awaiting Harry Potter releases (back when Harry Potters were still being released).

Many staffers have their own pets, as you can see on the pet page of the website: www.pegasusbookstore.com. They're an understanding group, but please, no leg-lifts on the literature. 510/649-1320.

There's been an ongoing rift pitting park users and artists against environmentalists and others who want to see this become part of the adjacent Eastshore State Park. Right now it's owned by the city of Albany and managed in part by the East Bay Regional Parks District. It's a messy legal stew I won't get into here. Our paws are crossed for art and dogs, but the way the situation is going you'll definitely want to make sure leash-free is OK when you visit. (Thank you to Charlie and his person, Patti, for helping us sniff out this unbucolic gem.)

Exit Highway 80/580 or the Eastshore Freeway at Buchanan Street and head west. Park along the road at the far western end of Buchanan, and walk toward the bay. The road will turn into a trail, which you'll follow out to the Bulb. If in doubt, look for other dog walkers. 510/528-5710.

Berkeley

You'll see a lot more unleashed dogs in Berkeley than in any other Bay Area city. That's because Berkeley, well known for its tolerance of eccentricity, has a fittingly liberal leash law: If your dog isn't wearing a leash but stays within

six feet of you and is obedience trained, she'll be considered leashed! It's there in black and white in the city code. It's a very forward-thinking law, and it's been around for ages. Jake and I can't take advantage of this. (I can just picture myself explaining to the animal control officer: "Oh, six FEET. I thought it was six METERS!")

You also have to carry a poop bag at all times when your dog is out and about with you, leashed or not.

PARKS, BEACHES, AND RECREATION AREAS

🅱 César Chávez Park

🐾🐾🐾🐾 🐕 (See Alameda County map on page 110)

Urban pooch paradise doesn't get much better than this. Dogs who come here get to feel the bay breeze blowing through their fur as they frolic with their friends on 17 acres of prime land on the San Francisco Bay. Trails meander up and down the rolling hills and wind through a couple of quiet meadows. There's grass, grass everywhere.

The views of San Francisco, the Golden Gate Bridge, and the Bay Bridge are some of the best around. The park is equipped with plenty of poop-bag stations crammed to the gills. Use them. In fact, while you're at it, pick up an "orphan" poop if you see one lying around. Many people worked very hard for

DIVERSION

Go Shopping in 1969: You and your dog can shop in the autumn of love when you stroll through the sidewalks of **Telegraph Avenue** near the UC Berkeley campus. Street vendors sell tie-dyed clothes, crystals, pottery, and T-shirts airbrushed with clouds. Street performers sing, juggle, beg for money, or do whatever else comes naturally. Incense and other herbaceous odors waft through the air, but dogs prefer the scents of all the nondeodorized humans.

Dogs who reminisce about the 1960s really dig it here. They're perceived as totally cool dudes and given major amounts of love from people who like to hug dogs hard. When we last visited, Jake was wearing his favorite psychedelic bandana, and he received a few "duuuudes" per block.

Some dogs—and humans—may find the weekend crowds a sensory overload. If your schedule allows, try a cool afternoon. From I-80, take the Ashby exit, go about two miles east to Telegraph Avenue, and turn left (north). The street-merchant part begins around the intersection of Dwight Way.

a very long time to get this park established, and the goal is to keep it beautiful and dog friendly.

This is also a great place to fly a kite, and there are plenty of instructions posted on how to do it safely around here.

Take University Avenue west past the I-80 interchange and follow the signs to the Berkeley Marina and César Chávez Park. 510/981-5150.

₃ Ohlone Dog Park

😈😈🐕 (See Alameda County map on page 110)

For years after it opened as the first leash-free dog park in America in 1979, Ohlone provided a model for other cities considering opening a dog park. But sadly, the park is often in pretty bad shape these days, with mud happening before rainy season and in winter overtaking everything, including the mulch and woodchips used for covering the mud.

Still, it's a decent place for an off-leash romp in a safely fenced area. You'll find a water faucet, complete with a dog bowl set in concrete, and two picnic tables for owners who want to relax while their dogs socialize. The grass isn't always green here, but it's definitely better than what's on the other side of the fence. The park is at Martin Luther King Jr. Way and Hearst Street. 510/981-5150.

₄ Tilden Regional Park

😈😈😈😈🐕 (See Alameda County map on page 110)

Humans and dogs alike give Tilden a big thumbs-up (dewclaws-up). Leash-free dogs find the scents from its western ridge delectable and humans find the ridge's breathtaking views of the entire San Francisco Bay equally enticing.

Escapes from civilization are everywhere in this 2,078-acre park. Try the trails leading east from South Park Drive. They connect with the East Bay Skyline National Recreation Trail.

You can pick up the Arroyo Trail at the Big Springs sign and take it all the way to the ridge top. There's a great stream at the trailhead that you can follow through laurel, pine, toyon, and scrub on your low-grade ascent. Your dog may want to take a dip in the stream for refreshment.

After the trail veers from the stream, it steepens and leads into cypress-studded meadows and eucalyptus groves. Eventually it feeds into the Skyline National Recreation Trail, also known as the Sea View Trail, offering vistas over the bay along the way.

Dogs aren't allowed in the large nature area at the northern end or in the Lake Anza swimming area. Leashes are required in all the developed areas, including picnic grounds and ball fields. Remember to watch your step in the areas frequented by dogs, as some owners neglect to clean up after their furry friends. There's nothing like stepping in a steaming pile of dog dung to put a damper on a day of exploring nature.

DIVERSION

Ride a Dog-Sized Train: If your dog's not an escape artist or the nervous type, he's welcome to ride with you on **Tilden Regional Park's miniature train.** The open-car train takes you for a 12-minute ride through woods and past stunning views of the surrounding area. Adventurous dogs like it when the train toots its whistle as it rumbles past a miniature water tower, a car barn, and other such train accessories. When Joe Dog appeared on KRON-TV's *Bay Area Backroads* riding the train, he was fine until we hit the little tunnel—then he decided he wanted to go home. He was relieved that part ended up on the cutting-room floor.

The Redwood Valley Railway Company runs trains 11 A.M.–dusk weekends and holidays (not Thanksgiving or Christmas) only, except during spring and summer school vacations, when it runs from 11 A.M.–5 P.M. weekdays and until 6 P.M. weekends. Tickets are $2; kids under two and dogs ride free. You must keep the dog on a tight leash and make sure he doesn't jump out. It's in the southeast corner of Tilden Regional Park in Berkeley. From the intersection of Grizzly Peak Boulevard and Lomas Cantadas, follow the signs. 510/548-6100. www.redwoodvalleyrailway.com.

Speaking of steaming, be sure to check out Tilden's miniature steam train for a riveting good time. (See the Diversion *Ride a Dog-Sized Train.*)

From Highway 24, take the Fish Ranch Road exit north (at the eastern end of the Caldecott Tunnel). At the intersection of Fish Ranch, Grizzly Peak Boulevard, and Claremont Avenue, take a right on Grizzly Peak and continue north to South Park Drive. One more mile north brings you to Big Springs Trail. During peak season, continue on Grizzly Peak to the Shasta Gate. 888/327-2757.

5 Claremont Canyon Regional Preserve

😊 😊 😊 😊 🐾 (See Alameda County map on page 110)

This large park is full of steep hillside trails that lead to crests with stunning views of the university and the surrounding hills and valleys. If your dog likes eucalyptus trees and doesn't like leashes, take him here. It's one of those tree-filled, leashes-optional parks.

From Highway 13 (Ashby Avenue), drive north on College Avenue. Turn right on Derby Street, past the Clark Kerr Campus of UC Berkeley. The trailhead is at the southeast corner of the school grounds, near the beginning of Stonewall Road. 888/327-2757.

DIVERSION

Take a Hike! East Bay dogs who enjoy the great outdoors are very lucky indeed. Berkeley is the home base for the San Francisco Bay chapter of the Sierra Club. The club holds several fun hikes for dogs each year, via its **Canine Hike Unit,** and most of the hikes are in the East Bay. Dogs get to hike and play off leash, as long as they're well behaved and under voice control. Hikes are of varying difficulties and lengths. Some involve easy swimming (Jake is drooling), some involve camping, some even involve meeting the love of your life (when Sierra singles and their dogs come out to play). The folks who participate in the canine hikes are almost as friendly and fun-loving as their dogs. Phone 510/848-0800 for info on the dog hikes, or to find out how to join the Sierra Club. You don't have to be a member to do the hikes, but one of the benefits of membership is that you'll receive a schedule of all Sierra Club events—including doggy hikes—every two months. www.sanfranciscobay.sierraclub.org.

PLACES TO EAT

So many restaurants here have outdoor tables where dogs are welcome. Because of space, we list just a few.

French Hotel Cafe: Any café with "French" in the name is bound to be a winner for dogs, as long as it has outdoor seating. And this funky little café has several sidewalk tables where dogs are welcome. The coffee is really good here. It's the perfect antidote to chain coffee restaurants, and the people-watching is splendid. So is the free Wi-Fi. 1540 Shattuck Avenue; 510/548-9930.

La Mediterranée: This delicious and inexpensive Middle Eastern restaurant has built up quite a following; there's usually a line on weekends when Cal is mid-semester. The folks here will let your dog sit quietly at your feet at the outdoor tables, which have the added benefit of an outdoor heater on cool nights. You might want to tie your dog up on the sidewalk outside the fence separating the tables if it's especially crowded. 2936 College Avenue; 510/540-7773.

Rick and Ann's Restaurant: Dogs feel really at home here, because Rick and Ann and their staff love dogs. And dogs love that the food is delicious and all-American. Joe's favorites were meatloaf and creamy macaroni and cheese, and Jake feels the same way. It may take you a while to choose something from the imaginative menu, but just about anything you select will be great. Dine at the outdoor tables with your friendly dog, and please make sure she doesn't block the aisle, because it's easy for people to trip on dogs strewn hither and thither here. 2922 Domingo Avenue; 510/649-8538.

Sea Breeze Market and Deli: Smack in the middle of the I-80 interchange, you won't even notice the traffic as you and your dog bask at sunny picnic tables, where crab claws crunch underfoot and begging is outstanding. Dogs are perfectly welcome so long as they don't wander into the store itself. You can buy groceries, beer, wine, classy ice cream, or a meal from the deli, including fresh fish and chips, calamari, prawns, scallops, chicken, and quiche. The deli serves croissants and coffee early; if you live in the East Bay, you can zip in for a quick croissant and a dog walk at César Chávez Park before work. It's at the foot of University Avenue, past the I-80 entrance. 598 University Avenue; 510/486-0802.

PLACES TO STAY

Beau Sky: This 1911 Victorian inn near the UC campus has a friendly staff and makes for a cozy stay for you and the dog in your life. It's a combination of boutique and Bohemian—and a fun place to spend a night with your dog. Humans get a free continental breakfast. Rates are $109–159. Dogs are $10 extra. 2520 Durant Avenue 94704; 510/540-7688; www.beausky.com.

Claremont Hotel Club & Spa: Yes, dogs are allowed to stay in this exquisite hillside hotel that's a stunning and beloved part of the landscape of the Berkeley hills. But they have to be under 20 pounds. Because all other dogs will be weeping if I go into detail about this place, I won't ooh and ahh about the well-appointed luxurious rooms that come with plush spa robes and top-end amenities. I'll just stop here. Ninety-pound Jake is visibly relieved not to have to sit through the mouth-watering description. We both hope that by the book's next edition this silly size limit is gone. Rates are $179–399. Dogs pay a $99 fee per stay, and must stay on the first floor. 41 Tunnel Road 94705; 510/843-3000 or 800/551-7266; www.claremontresort.com.

Doubletree Hotel, Berkeley Marina: What's better than staying in San Francisco during a visit to the Bay Area? Looking at San Francisco during a visit to the Bay Area! Many of the nearly 400 guest rooms here look toward the city. If it's foggy in San Francisco, you may never see the city, but that's OK, because the hotel is a fine place to stay with a dog. (And you can request Marina or hillside or courtyard views, if city sights aren't for you.)

It's clean and quiet, with comfy rooms. A respectable breakfast comes with your stay. Management preers dogs under 50 pounds, but they do make exceptions. Dogs feel welcome here, because they get use of a dog bed/pillow and dog bowls during their visit. Rates are $99–299. Dogs are $75 per stay. 200 Marina Boulevard 94710; 510/548-7920; www.doubletree1.com.

Golden Bear Inn: Rates are $77–100. Dogs are $10 extra. 1620 San Pablo Avenue 94702; 510/525-6770; www.goldenbearinn.com.

Hotel Durant: This beautiful, four-star boutique hotel is super conveniently located next to the university, but in a world of its own. The rooms are a study in understated elegance, with blues and golds intermingling to make your stay feel royal and relaxing. Rooms come with free WiFi, flat-screen TVs, iPod docking stations, little fridges, and—get this—100 percent certified organic bathrobes. Get used to organic here, because upon arrival, dogs get organic dog treats. They sometimes also get a plush football of their very own. (Jake's would be destroyed in minutes.) If your dog would like use of a hotel dog bed, you can arrange that when you make your reservation.

The hotel is part of the dog-friendly Joie de Vivre top-notch hotel chain. Rates are $99–230. 2600 Durant Avenue 94704; 510/845-8981 or 800/738-7477; www.jdvhotels.com.

Emeryville

PARKS, BEACHES, AND RECREATION AREAS

6 Emeryville Marina Park

🐾🐾 (See Alameda County map on page 110)

If you're a human, this is a fine park. If you're a leashed dog, it's just so-so. A concrete path follows the riprap shoreline past cypress trees and through manicured grass. A quick and scenic stroll down the north side will give you a fine view of the marina and a miniature bird refuge where egrets, sandpipers, blackbirds, and doves inhabit a tiny marsh. Dogs who like to bird-watch think it's cool here.

Dogs who like to fish don't have it so easy. Pooches aren't allowed on the fishing pier. But if you console them with an offer to picnic at tables with grand views of the Bay Bridge, they usually snap out of their funk.

From I-80, take the Powell Street exit at Emeryville and go west on Powell to the end of the marina. It has lots of free parking. 510/596-4330.

PLACES TO EAT

Kitty's: Your dog will want to bring you to this busy bar for the name alone. The food is pretty good, and you can eat it alongside your requisite drinks at the shaded patio area. 6702 Hollis Street; 510/601-9300.

Townhouse Bar & Grill: The exterior looks like a rustic old cabin a couple of grizzled miners might walk out of gripping their suspenders and carrying a flask of something strong and homemade. In fact, this place, built in 1926, was once home to a profitable bootlegging business and has been through many incarnations since. The current owners chose to keep the exterior charm of bygone days, but the rest of the Townhouse has been updated and glossed up a great deal.

Dogs are welcome to join you at the old wooden side patio. Some tables are shaded by umbrellas, so nab one of those on a hot day. The food is an eclectic blend of casual, somewhat upscale American specialties. 5862 Doyle Street; 510/652-6151.

Wally's: Eat really good, garlicky Greek food at outside tables tucked into a narrow area beside the restaurant. If you like vivacious Mediterranean food, this is a great choice. 3900 San Pablo Avenue; 510/597-1303.

Alameda

PARKS, BEACHES, AND RECREATION AREAS

7 Alameda Point Dog Run

(See Alameda County map on page 110)

While this fenced park encompasses two acres along the Oakland Estuary, it's not much to look at—or to be in, for that matter. There are no trees. The ground is pretty much rock-hard, having baked in the sun and weathered through the years. Being just 100 feet back from this part of the estuary does provide a breeze, but the wind tends to be a bit strong here. Your dog's ears may flap in the breeze, but more likely they'll just stream straight back. There's no water, either. It's a good place to take a dog if you're near the ferry terminal, because it's on Main Street, adjacent to the terminal. It's better than nothing. 510/747-7529.

8 Alameda Dog Exercise Area

(See Alameda County map on page 110)

Wahoo! This is one of the bigger fenced-in dog parks we've encountered. It's nearly six acres, shaded here and there by some wonderful big cypress and pine trees. The ground wants to be grass, but it's pretty much packed dirt at this point. Dogs have a howling good time chasing each other around big brush patches here and there. Among the amenities: benches, a separate section for small dogs, water, and poop bags. But the best amenity here is a natural one: a fresh bay breeze. The park is right off the bay. You can see the masts of the boats in the harbor from the dog park.

The park is set beside Crown Memorial Beach, which bans dogs. The dog park is actually part of Alameda's largest park, Washington Park. That park has lots of great amenities for people, including wonderful playgrounds and ball fields. Leashed dogs enjoy the wide green expanses, the bike path, picnic area, and the edge of the marsh here. The dog park is at 8th Street and Central Avenue. It's to the left of Washington Park's tennis courts. 510/747-7529.

PLACES TO EAT

Aroma Restaurant: Any restaurant that has something about smell in its name is a sure-fire winner in a dog's book. And this places smells pretty good, with the scent of the basic Italianesque cuisine wafting out. (Must be the garlic.) It's right on a narrow bit of the Oakland Estuary, just a bone's throw from the Park Street Bridge. Dine with dog at the awning-topped outdoor tables. 2237 Blanding Avenue; 510/337-0333.

Forbidden Island Tiki Lounge: Humans have to be 21 or older to come here, but well-behaved dogs of any age can join you at the patio for a drink (or two or three or four, as it often goes here) at this fun, kitschy tiki bar. The drinks are tropical, large, and strong, and bear names like Suffering Bastard, Fugu for Two, the Combover, and Missionary's Downfall.

The lounge operates under a one-strike dog policy: "The first dog to fight with another dog or attack a patron will cause dogs to be permanently banned from Forbidden Island," warns lounge literature. My guess is that there's a reason this policy is so well defined. Well-behaved dogs and people only, please. 1304 Lincoln Avenue; 510/749-0332.

Piedmont

Piedmont is almost entirely residential, and very proper and clean. This means you won't be able to find a stray scrap of paper to scoop with, so be prepared. Its quiet streets are delightful for walking, offering views from the hills.

The parks below allow dogs off leash—but only if they have a permit from the city's police department. Licensed dogs from any city can get one, but it'll cost you more if you don't live in Piedmont, and more still if your dog is not spayed or neutered. The police department's animal services division issues these permits during limited hours on Wednesdays only. Phone 510/420-3006 for permit details.

PARKS, BEACHES, AND RECREATION AREAS

9 Linda Off-Leash Area
🐾 🐕 (See Alameda County map on page 110)

This is just a strip of pavement running down a dirt area (formerly grass) about the length of one city block. There's some shade. The "park" is set along a hill, but it's too close to a couple of roads for true off-leash comfort as far as my dogs are concerned. For some reason it gets tremendous use.

Beach Park is across from Beach School, at Linda and Lake avenues. You'll see the little doggy signs. A permit is required for your off-leash use; phone 510/420-3006 for permit details. 510/420-3070.

10 Dracena Park
🐾 🐾 🐾 🐾 🐕 (See Alameda County map on page 110)

Parts of this park are grassy, with tall shade trees here and there. But the part dogs long for is the off-leash section. It's a lovely area, with a paved path up and down a wooded, secluded hill. Tall firs and eucalyptus provide plenty of shade, and sometimes it's so quiet here you can hear several kinds of birds.

The area isn't fenced, and at the top and bottom there's potential for escape artists to run into the road, so be careful and leash up at these points if you have any doggy doubts.

Poop bags are provided. The trail takes about 15 minutes round-trip, if you assume a very leisurely pace. We like to enter on Artuna Avenue at Ricardo Avenue, because it's safest from traffic and parking's plentiful on the park side of the street. But lots of folks enter at Blair and Dracena avenues. A permit is required for your off-leash use; phone 510/420-3006 for permit details. 510/420-3070.

11 Piedmont Park

🐾🐾🐾🐾 🐕 (See Alameda County map on page 110)

The huge off-leash section (allowed with permit only; phone 510/420-3000 for details) of this beautiful park is one of the best examples of a leash-free dog area in the state. A few salmon-pink concrete pathways lead you and your happy dog alongside a gurgling stream and up and down the hills around the stream. It's absolutely gorgeous and serene back here. (On our last visit, a hummingbird greeted us at the entrance and was back again when we left.) The park smells like heaven, with eucalyptus, redwood, acacia, pine, and deep, earthy scents wafting around everywhere. It reminds me of a serene Japanese garden, minus the Japanese plants.

The stream is fed year-round by a spring higher in the hills. This is pure bliss for dogs during the summer. The trails for dogs and their people run on the cooler side anyway, with all the tall trees. Almost the entire leash-free section is set in a deep canyon, so it's very safe from traffic. A leisurely round-trip stroll will take you about an hour, if you want it to. Poop bags are supplied at a few strategically located stations along the paths. Use them.

To get to the leash-free section of this elegant park, come in through the main entrance at Highland and Magnolia Avenues. You'll see a willow tree just as you enter. Continue on the path past the willow tree and follow it down to the left side of the stream. You'll see signs for the dog area. Be sure to leash up in other parts of the park, should you explore beyond the stream area. 510/420-3070.

Oakland

Oakland is slowly going to the dogs. While most of the city's parks ban dogs outright, the city now has a few leash-free parks, and one in the planning stages. To find out what you can do to get the much-needed Lake Merritt Dog Park up and running, go to www.odogparks.org.

If you're looking for a super dog-friendly neighborhood, look no further than Montclair. The bookstore, the florist, the pet store, and the hardware store have all been very kind to four-legged friends. In addition, a couple of dog-friendly Montclair eateries listed in this section really go all out for dogs.

PARKS, BEACHES, AND RECREATION AREAS

12 Joaquin Miller Dog Park

🐾🐾🐾🐆 (See Alameda County map on page 110)

What a refreshing change from Oakland's more well-used dog parks. This park is a pretty good size, and is surrounded not by concrete, but by big redwoods, thanks to its location in beautiful Joaquin Miller Park. It's an excellent spot if you and your best friend want to bring a little Mother Nature into your lives. The park has two separate sections—one for large dogs, one for small dogs—and all the usual dog-park amenities. The ground cover is wood chips. When fresh, they smell good, but they're a little tough on pooch paws.

The park doesn't seem to be that well known. Some days you may have the park nearly to yourself. That can be a blessing or a curse, depending on what kind of mood you and your dog are in. Exit Highway 13 at Joaquin Miller Road. Follow it east so Sanborn Drive, and go left into Joaquin Miller Park. You'll see signs for the dog park. 510/238-7275.

13 Redwood Regional Park

🐾🐾🐾🐾🐆 (See Alameda County map on page 110)

Although it's just a few miles over the ridge from downtown Oakland, Redwood Regional Park is about as far as you can get from urbanity while still within the scope of the Bay Area. Dogs who love nature at its best, and love it even more off leash, adore the 1,836-acre park. People who need to get far from the madding crowd also go gaga over the place.

The park is delectable year-round, but it's a particularly wonderful spot to visit when you need to cool off from hot summer weather. Much of the park is a majestic forest of 150-foot coast redwoods (known to those with scientific tongues as *Sequoia sempervirens*). The redwoods provide drippy cool shade most of the time, which is a real boon for dogs with hefty coats. Back in the mid-1800s, this area was heavily logged for building supplies for San Francisco, and it wasn't a pretty sight. But fortunately, sometimes progress progresses backward, and the fallen trees have some splendid replacements.

There's something for every dog's tastes here. In addition to the redwoods, the park is also home to pine, eucalyptus, madrone, flowering fruit trees, chaparral, and grasslands. Wild critters like the park, too, so leash up immediately if there's any hint of deer, rabbits, or other woodland creatures around. Many dogs, even "good" dogs, aren't able to withstand the temptation to chase.

Dogs have to leash up along the beautiful Stream Trail, which runs along the environmentally sensitive stream. Mud is inevitable if you follow the

Stream Trail, so be sure to keep a towel in the car. Water dogs may try to dip their paws in Redwood Creek, which runs through the park. But please don't let them. This is a very sensitive area. Rainbow trout spawn here after migrating from a reservoir downstream, and it's not an easy trip for them. If you and your dog need to splash around somewhere, try the ocean, the bay, or your bathtub.

No parking fee is charged at Skyline Gate at the north end (in Contra Costa County—the park straddles Contra Costa and Alameda counties). Entering here also lets you avoid the tempting smells of picnic tables at the south end. The Stream Trail leads steadily downhill, and then takes a steep plunge to the canyon bottom. It's uphill all the way back, but it's worth it. From Highway 13, exit at Joaquin Miller Road and head east to Skyline Boulevard. Turn left on Skyline and go four miles to the Skyline Gate.

If you prefer to go to the main entrance on Redwood Road, exit Highway 13 at Carson/Redwood Road and drive east on Redwood Road. Once you pass Skyline Boulevard, continue two miles on Redwood. The park and parking will be on your left. The Redwood Road entrance charges a $5 parking fee and a $2 dog fee. 888/327-2757.

14 Hardy Dog Park

🐾🐾🐕 (See Alameda County map on page 110)

This two-acre park in the Rockridge district has easy freeway access and plenty of shade. That's because it's under the freeway. Still, it's a huge improvement from its previous incarnation as a fenced quarter-acre patch of dirt. Now it's big and grassy, with benches, water, and poop bags.

It can get rather loud and busy here, so now that there are other choices for parks in town, you might wish to take your dog elsewhere.

To get to the park from Highway 24, take the Claremont exit and follow Claremont Avenue back under the freeway. The park is under the freeway, at Claremont and Hudson Street. 510/238-7275.

15 Mosswood Dog Park

🐾🐕 (See Alameda County map on page 110)

There's nothing like having a dog park right next to a tennis court. Ball dogs delight in stray tennis balls that find there way over here. The park has decent shade in the form of trees that edge it, and while quite small, manages to squeeze in room for separate sections for small and large dogs. The problem with this park is that it's kind of isolated, an in area that others have described as "sketchy." Don't come here by yourself when it's getting late. The trees aren't the only things that can be a bit shady around here. Dogs aren't allowed anywhere else in Mosswood Park except the dog park. You can access it from the parking lot on Webster Street, near 36th Street. 510/238-7275.

16 Leona Heights Regional Open Space

🐾🐾🐾🐕 (See Alameda County map on page 110)

Unmarked on most maps, and devoid of most amenities (water and restrooms, for instance), this 271-acre open space is good for dogs who like to get away from the crowd. You won't find many bikes or horses here. Since it's part of the East Bay Regional Park District, your dog need not be on leash.

The open space stretches from Merritt College south to Oak Knoll, and from I-580 east to Chabot Regional Park. A bumpy fire trail goes from Merritt College downhill to the southern entrance, just north of Oak Knoll. The best way to enter is to park at a lot off Canyon Oaks Drive, next to a condominium parking lot. Right at this entrance is a pond, but you won't see any more water as you ascend. It's a dry hike in warm weather.

The 2.7-mile fire trail leads gently uphill all the way to Merritt, through coyote brush and oak woodland. In spring, it's full of wildflowers and abuzz with the loud hum of bees. Watch out for poison oak.

From I-580, exit at Keller Avenue and drive east to Campus Drive. Take a left (north), then a left on Canyon Oaks Drive. 888/327-2757.

PLACES TO EAT

Oakland's College Avenue, in the Rockridge district, has a tolerant family atmosphere. Lawyers with briefcases buy flowers on the way home from the BART station, and students flirt over ice cream. I've never seen anyone in this neighborhood who didn't love dogs.

The avenue is known to be a food lover's paradise, and among the attractions are a string of restaurants with outdoor tables, several of which follow. The Montclair district also has a couple of hits with the dog crowd.

Cafe Rustica: The pizza here is elegant. Eat it at the outdoor tables with your drooling dog. 5422 College Avenue; 510/654-1601.

Cole Coffee: This is a cheery and popular place with very good coffee (in the bean or in the cup), tea, and supplies. On weekend mornings, it's dog central. 307 63rd Street at College Avenue; 510/653-5458.

Montclair Malt Shop: Don'tcha just hate it when you go to an ice cream parlor and your dog's eyes almost tear up with the anticipation of a single drop of yummy cold cream falling from your cone to the ground so he can lap it off the sidewalk? You won't have to deal with those pleading eyes if you visit this delightful ice creamery: Dogs can order their very own special brew of pooch-friendly ice cream, known as Frosty Paws. Then you can dine together at the bench outside, or just stand around and talk with other dog people while your dog inhales his frozen treat. The place is known for its dog business; on a recent hot summer afternoon, 17 dogs were outside, downing their ice creams with delight. "We love dogs here," says super-friendly Diane, who makes the best malt this side of the bay. (She will be the first to tell you this, and she speaks the truth.) 2066 Mountain Boulevard; 510/339-1886.

Noah's Bagels: Not only do dogs get water in doggy bowls here, but they also get "floor bagels" when available. These are bagels that have been dropped on the floor, either by customers or employees. Do dogs care that their bagel has taken a little roll on terra firma? No! A little dirt only makes them more delectable. Dine with your dog at several outdoor tables here. 2060 Mountain Boulevard; 510/339-6663.

PLACES TO STAY

Waterfront Hotel: Ahoy! Do you and your dog love the nautical life? This is the place to stay next time you're in town. Many of the rooms of this fun, recently upgraded 143-room hotel look out at the boats in the marina at Jack London Square. The entire hotel, from stem to stern, has a maritime theme. You may feel as if you've set sail in your blue and gold guest room with nautical-inspired décor. There's an airy, open feel here that's hard to find in these climes.

Free Wi-Fi comes with your room, as does a large plasma-screen TV and an iPod docking station. But don't waste your time on tech. Enjoy the tranquility and vibrance you'll find all around you at this dog-friendly Joie de Vivre hotel. Dogs love it here, in part because of the briny breeze, but also because they feel very welcome here. Dogs get use of a comfy doggy bed during their stay. They also get yummy treats, and bowls for food and water. As with all Joie de Vivre hotels, there's no extra fee for dogs, even with all these goodies! 10 Washington Street 94607; 510/836-3800 or 888/842-5333; www.jdvhotels.com.

San Lorenzo

PARKS, BEACHES, AND RECREATION AREAS

17 San Lorenzo Dog Park

🐾🐾🐾🐕 (See Alameda County map on page 110)

It's just ducky with your dog if you want to take him to this pretty dog park: Part of it curves around a duck pond. The quackers sometimes waddle right by, somehow knowing that their canine friends can't get to them through the fence. It's almost like a cartoon at times, with a duck strutting his stuff while a dog looks on with almost embarrassed disbelief that there's no way on dog's green earth that he'll be having duck for dinner that night.

The dog park is only a half acre, but it has all the good pooch-park amenities, including water, benches, and poop bags. It's grassy with some decomposed granite. There's not much shade, although the back end has some big trees on the outside perimeter, which can provide shade at times.

The dog park is toward the back of San Lorenzo Community Park, at the very west end of Via Buena Vista. The address is 1970 Via Buena Vista. 510/881-6700.

Castro Valley

PARKS, BEACHES, AND RECREATION AREAS

18 Chabot Regional Park

🐾🐾🐾🐾🐕 (See Alameda County map on page 110)

You and your leash-free dog can throw your urban cares to the wind when you visit this 4,972-acre park filled with magnificent trails and enchanting woodlands. Except for the occasional sounds of gunfire, you'll scarcely believe you're in the hills east of metropolitan Oakland. But fear not—the guns you'll hear are merely being used for target practice at the park's marksmanship range.

The trails at Chabot (sha-BO) are so secluded that if no one is firing a gun, the only sounds you may hear are those of your panting dog and the singing birds. Adventure-loving dogs like to take the Goldenrod Trail, starting at the southern terminus of Skyline Boulevard and Grass Valley Road. It connects with the East Bay Skyline National Recreation Trail, which winds through Grass Valley and climbs through eucalyptus forests. Lucky dogs can be off leash everywhere but in developed areas.

Campsites are $20–28. Dogs are $2 extra. Reserve by phoning 888/327-2757. No reservations are taken October 1–March 31, when the 23 sites are first-come, first-served.

From the intersection of Redwood Road and Castro Valley Boulevard in Castro Valley, go north on Redwood about 4.5 miles to Marciel Gate. (The campground is about two miles inside the gate.) From Oakland at the intersection of Redwood Road and Skyline Boulevard, go about 6.5 miles east on Redwood to Marciel Gate. For general park info, call 888/327-2757.

19 Castro Valley Dog Park

🐾🐾🐾🐕 (See Alameda County map on page 110)

This is a fun place to take a dog for some leash-free exercise. It's about 0.6 acre and has water, poop bags, and benches. It's set within the beautiful Earl Warren Park, whose walking path is worth sniffing out despite the on-leash requirement. The park is at 4660 Crow Canyon Road. Exit I-580 at Crow Canyon Road and head north several blocks. 510/881-6700.

20 Cull Canyon Regional Recreation Area

🐾🐾🐾🐕 (See Alameda County map on page 110)

Dogs may be off leash up on the grassy slopes laced with eucalyptus stands, but they have to wear their leashes in the areas designed for human fun. It's not such a bad fate, considering that there are plenty of grassy slopes away from developed areas.

In summer, fishing and swimming are popular here. But pooches may not go near the swimming complex, which includes an attractive pavilion and sandy beach. Leashed dogs may visit picnic areas, the Cull Creek area, and the willow-lined reservoir that sports a wooden bridge and a handful of ducks and coots.

From I-580, take the Center Street/Crow Canyon Road exit. Go left on Center Street and take a right on Castro Valley Boulevard. Follow it to Crow Canyon Road and take a left. Take another left on Cull Canyon Road. It's a half mile to the park entrance. 888/327-2757.

Dublin

PARKS, BEACHES, AND RECREATION AREAS

21 Dougherty Hills Dog Park

🐾🐾🐾🐾🐕 (See Alameda County map on page 110)

Do you or your dog appreciate fun art? If so, a visit to Dougherty Hills Dog Park should be a priority. The spacious park features a permanent art installation by artist Michele Alcantara, with whimsical sculptures of dogs and the things they like, like fire hydrants. In addition, the park is home to a fun agility course. These two extras are really unique in the land of dog parks. The park itself is set on a gentle slope, and is a pleasant, grassy romp, with separate sections for small and large dogs, and some decent shade provided by trees. The park is at Stagecoach Road and Amador Valley Boulevard. 925/833-6645.

Hayward

PARKS, BEACHES, AND RECREATION AREAS

22 Garin Regional Park and Dry Creek Regional Park

🐾🐾🐾🐾🐕 (See Alameda County map on page 110)

Garin Regional Park is about one mile and one century away from one of the busiest streets in Hayward. It's a fascinating place for you and your dog to learn about Alameda County farming and ranching. The parking lot next to Garin Barn—an actual barn, blacksmith's shop, and tool shed that is also Garin's visitors center—is strewn with antique farm machinery.

A total of 20 miles of trails, looping among the sweeps of grassy hills, beckon you and your dog. Off-leash dogs are fine on the trails once you've left the visitors center. Dogs seem to like to think they're on their own farm here, looking for all the world as if they're strutting down their very own property and watching out for evil feline intruders.

Dry Creek, which runs near the visitors center, was a delightful small torrent one day when we were there after a March storm. There isn't much shade on hot days, though. That's when you might want to try cooling your paws at tiny Jordan Pond. It's stocked with catfish, should your dog care to join you on his kind of fishing excursion.

From Highway 238 (Mission Boulevard), Tamarack Drive takes you quickly up the hill to Dry Creek Regional Park. Garin Avenue takes you to Garin, or you can enter Garin from the California State University, Hayward campus. The parking fee is $5. Dogs are $2 extra. 888/327-2757.

Union City

PARKS, BEACHES, AND RECREATION AREAS

23 Drigon Dog Park

🐾🐾🐾🐾🐕 (See Alameda County map on page 110)

A dogbone-shaped walkway dotted with pawprints? Doggy tunnels, hoops, jumps, and other fun agility toys? Fire hydrants galore? A gated entrance featuring a giant dog bone and big concrete pillars with huge paw prints? What is this—dog heaven or something?

Yes! Drigon (DRY-ghin) Dog Park is pooch paradise that happens to be firmly planted on grassy terra firma. Its unique design is the brainchild of two dog-loving parks district planners—a $300,000 shining gem that's utterly to drool for. You drive by, you see it, you can't help but smile, even if you don't have a dog. It's real-world-meets-cartoon-fantasy—something you could find around the corner if you lived in Toontown.

The park is 1.5 acres, with a small section for wee dogs. It has water, poop bags, nicely designed benches, and shade in the form of a permanent awning. Everything here is doggy: The concrete around the newly planted trees has embedded paw prints. The hydrants are concrete (they can't rust or corrode from boy dog bladder activities) and have drainage. This helps keep the grassy area pretty green.

The park, named for a heroic police dog who is in a more ethereal dog heaven now, is closed Mondays for maintenance, and for 48 hours after inclement weather to keep it from becoming mud soup. It's in the middle of a residential suburban neighborhood, at 7th Street and Mission Boulevard. 510/471-3232.

Pleasanton

PARKS, BEACHES, AND RECREATION AREAS

24 Pleasanton Ridge Regional Park

(See Alameda County map on page 110)

This fairly recent and beautiful addition to the East Bay Regional Parks system is an isolated treat. Dogs may run off leash on all the secluded trails here as soon as you leave the staging area.

You can reach Pleasanton Ridge from either Foothill or Golden Eagle Roads. At the Foothill Staging Area, there are fine picnic sites at the trailhead. Climb up on the Oak Tree fire trail to the ridgeline, where a looping set of trails goes off to the right. The incline is gentle, through pasture (you share this park with cattle) dotted with oak and—careful—poison oak. Wildflowers riot in spring. It's a hot place in summer. At the bottom of the park, however, is a beautiful streamside stretch along Arroyo de la Laguna. There's no water above the entrance, so be sure to carry plenty.

From I-680, take the Castlewood Drive exit and go left (west) on Foothill Road to the staging area. 888/327-2757.

25 Muirwood Park Dog Exercise Area

(See Alameda County map on page 110)

Dogs enjoy galloping around this very long, narrow park in part because it's so easy on their paws. The ground cover is affectionately known as "forest floor material," which is basically degraded wood chips mixed with leaf and branch litter. Much as you'd find in the real Muir Woods in Marin, the stuff makes for cushy walks and runs—it's great for the joints of older dogs.

If your dog likes chasing far-flung balls, this is a perfect place for it. The park is about 300 feet long by 40 feet wide, which means there's plenty of room to use your tennis ball launcher to its full capacity. The park has all the usual dog-park amenities, including benches, separate sections for small and large dogs, water, and poop-bag dispensers. There's ample shade from evergreen acacias—a popular food with giraffes. (You won't likely see any giraffes wandering through the dog park, but park workers have been known to collect leaves and branches for the giraffes at the Oakland Zoo.)

The park is at 4701 Muirwood Drive. The cross street is Las Positas Boulevard. 925/931-5340.

PLACES TO STAY

Marriott Pleasanton: This hotel has a very hip, chic style in the lobby and lounge, and sumptuous comfort in the rooms. Rates are $69–159. Dogs pay a $100 fee for length of their stay. 11950 Dublin Canyon Road 94588; 925/847-6000; www.marriottpleasanton.com.

Fremont

PARKS, BEACHES, AND RECREATION AREAS

26 Alameda Creek Regional Trail

🐾🐾🐾 🐕 (See Alameda County map on page 110)

This 12.4-mile trail runs from the bayshore to the East Bay hills. The trail is actually two trails: The one on the southern levee of the Alameda Creek is paved, and leashes are the law here (understandably, with all the bikes passing by). The one on the northern levee is unpaved and permits dogs off leash for the entire length of the creek!

Dogs are sometimes disappointed to discover that 1) the creek is lined with concrete and 2) the trail doesn't just pass through farmland and greenbelt areas. It also runs alongside rail yards, industrial lots, and quarries. Junkyard dogs like it. Wilderness dogs just shrug their hairy shoulders.

A scenic stretch of trail is at the Niles Canyon end. Dogs find it especially interesting in winter after a storm, when there's actually water in the concrete-lined creek and ducks and coots splash around. Shinn Pond in Niles, and the Alameda Creek Stables in Union City are popular canine congregation sites.

You may enter this trail at many points near the creek's mouth—in the salt flats of the bay by Coyote Hills Regional Park. The trail officially begins in Fremont's Niles district, at the intersection of Mission Boulevard (Highway 238) and Niles Canyon Road (Highway 84). You can find an excellent map and more detailed info on the trail at www.ebparks.org. 888/327-2757.

27 BART Dog Park

🐾 🐾 🐾 🐕 (See Alameda County map on page 110)

Many years ago, the dog park within Central Park was called Fremont Dog Park. Then it became Central Park Dog Park. And in its latest incarnation—and a move to the west side of the park—it's called BART Dog Park. And it's green, green, green! That's thanks to the soft artificial turf that blankets the park. It looks better than it used to when it was balding grass, although cleaning the poo can be a bit of a challenge at times. It can also get pretty toasty on warm days. There's a separate section for small dogs. The park has benches, poop bags, lighting, a nice gazebo, and water.

The park is within the beautiful, 450-acre Central Park, which leashed dogs are welcome to explore. The dog park is on the west side of the park at 1110 Stevenson Boulevard, between Mission Boulevard and Paseo Padre Parkway. 510/790-5541.

28 Mission Peak Regional Preserve

🐾 🐾 🐾 🐾 🐕 (See Alameda County map on page 110)

Smart Fremont dwellers take their dogs to this 2,596-acre park. It's a huge expanse of grass, dotted with occasional oak groves and scrub. Unfortunately for humans who get short of breath, the foot trails head straight up. Trails to the top rise 2,500 feet in three miles. (Pant, pant.)

Leash-free dogs love this place. The entrance at Stanford Avenue offers a gentler climb than the entrance from the Ohlone College campus. You'll pass Caliente Creek if you take the Peak Meadow Trail, but in hot weather, there won't be much relief from the sun. Be sure to carry water for yourself and your dog. The main point of puffing up Mission Peak is the renowned view stretching from Mt. Tamalpais to Mt. Hamilton. (On very clear days, you can see to the Sierra's snowy crest.) Your dog may not care much for the scenery, but she'll probably appreciate the complete freedom of the expanse of pasture here.

There's a $3 fee to park here. From I-680, take the southern Mission Boulevard exit in Fremont (there are two exits; the one you want is in the Warm Springs district). Go east on Mission to Stanford Avenue, turn right (east), and in less than a mile, you'll be at the entrance. 888/327-2757.

29 Sunol Regional Wilderness

🐾 🐾 🐾 🐾 🐕 (See Alameda County map on page 110)

You and your leash-free dog will howl for joy when you visit this large and deserted wilderness treasure. It's like going to a national park without having to leave your poor pooch behind.

One of the best treats for canines and their companions is a hike along the Camp Ohlone Trail, which you reach via the main park entrance, on Geary Road. The trail takes you to an area called Little Yosemite. Like its namesake,

Little Yosemite is magnificent. It's a steep-sided gorge with a creek at the bottom, lofty crags, and outcrops of greenstone and basalt that reveal a turbulent geological history. Its huge boulders throw Alameda Creek into gurgling eddies and falls. There's no swimming allowed here, much to Jake's dismay.

You can return via the higher Canyon View Trail or head for several other destinations: wooded canyons, grassy slopes, peaks with peeks of Calaveras Reservoir or Mt. Diablo. The park brochure offers useful descriptions of each trail. Dogs may run leashless on trails except for on the Backpack Loop.

Dogs are allowed only at the Family Campground site at headquarters and not at the backpacking campsites farther in. Sites are $14. The dog fee is $1. Dogs must be leashed in the campground or confined to your tent. (Anyone whose dog has ever chased off after a wild boar in the middle of the night understands the reason for this rule, and this park has plenty of boars.) Call 510/636-1684 to reserve. Reserved sites are held until 5 P.M. The day-use parking fee is $5, plus $2 extra for your dog.

From I-680, take the Calaveras Road exit, then go left (east) on Geary Road to the park entrance. The park may be closed or restricted during fire season, June–October. 888/327-2757.

PLACES TO STAY

Best Western Garden Court: Rates are $69–119. Dogs are $15 extra. 5400 Mowry Avenue 94538; 510/792-4300.

Livermore

PARKS, BEACHES, AND RECREATION AREAS

Livermore is barking up the right tree: It now has seven city dog parks. Add that to the regional parks and wilderness areas, and this city has become a real slice of dog heaven!

30 Martin Pound Dog Park

🐾🐾🐕 (See Alameda County map on page 110)

We visited on a rainy day, and it was more of a mud pit than anything else. Between the rain and the paws, the park had taken a pounding. Thus the park's name? We hear that on drier days it can be a decent, grassy, delightful affair. The folks here are really friendly, which always makes the sun shine. Large and small dogs have separate areas. The park is at Bluebell Drive and Shetland Road; 925/373-5700.

31 May Nissen Dog Park

🐾🐾🐕 (See Alameda County map on page 110)

At one-third of an acre, this is the smallest of Livermore's dog parks. But there's still enough room for dogs to have a decent time. There's water, some grass, and shade-providing trees. A double-gated entry helps prevent escape artist pooches from bolting when someone leaves or enters the park.

The dog park is set within May Nissen Park. It's on Rincon Avenue, just south of Pine Street. 925/373-5700.

32 Vista Meadows Park

🐾🐾🐾🐕 (See Alameda County map on page 110)

Your dog can't quite live out a favorite nursery rhyme and go 'round the mulberry bush here, but he can go under a mulberry tree (or do a leg lift on it, which is a popular pastime with some dogs here). This 0.75-acre fenced park has some mulberry trees on its back end. There's even a bench under them, should you feel like relaxing in their shade. The grass here is pretty worn down, but it can come back again with the help of the wonderful parks department. Amenities include water, poop bags, and a double-gated entry. The park is at Westminster Way and Lambeth Road. 925/373-5700.

33 Bruno Canziani Dog Park

🐾🐾🐾🐕 (See Alameda County map on page 110)

This pleasant, grassy park has lots of room for dogs to run around. Even though it's just over an acre, there's nothing to get in the way, for better or worse.

There's no separate small-dog section, and no real trees to speak of. That means dogs can charge around without having to put on the brakes or power steering too much. It's not fancy, but it does the trick. At South Charlotte Way, between Flagg Lane and Stockton Loop; 916/373-5700.

34 Max Baer Dog Park

🐾🐾🐾🐕 (See Alameda County map on page 110)

This 0.6-acre, fenced-in dog park is level and grassy, with lots of shady trees. It's double-gated, for your dog's safety. Inside the park are poop bags, a water fountain and bowls, and chairs where people can hang out while their dogs romp. On summer evenings, as many as 25–30 dogs enjoy the park. "Everybody loves it," says veterinarian Martin Plone, who was behind the park's birth in 1993. "It's become a meeting place for people. While their dogs are playing, people form friendships."

The dog park is part of the popular Max Baer Park. It's at Murdell Lane and Stanley Boulevard. 925/373-5700.

35 Del Valle Regional Park

🐾🐾🐾🐾🐕 (See Alameda County map on page 110)

This popular reservoir is best known for swimming, boating, fishing, and camping. Like Chabot Regional Park in Castro Valley, it's primarily a manicured and popular human recreation area, with neat lawns and picnic tables (where dogs must be leashed).

But, glory be to dog, the park sports several unspoiled trails for leash-free hiking in the surrounding hills. And, unlike at Lake Chabot, here you're permitted to take a dog on a rented boat. Every dog can have his day here.

From this recreation area, you can enter the Ohlone Wilderness Trail—29 miles of gorgeous trail through four regional parks.

The 150 sites at Family Camp allow dogs, but only on leash or confined to your tent. Sites are $20–25. Reserve by calling 888/327-2757.

From I-580, take North Livermore Avenue from downtown Livermore. It will become South Livermore Avenue, then Tesla Road. Take a right (south) on Mines Road, and then turn right on Del Valle Road. The parking fee is $6. The dog fee is $2. 888/327-2757.

36 Ohlone Wilderness Trail

🐾🐾🐾🐾🐕 (See Alameda County map on page 110)

Some of the area's most remote and peaceful wilderness areas are accessible only by way of this 29-mile trail. The trail stretches from Mission Peak, east of Fremont, through Sunol Regional Wilderness and Ohlone Regional Wilderness to Del Valle Regional Park, south of Livermore. You and your occasionally leash-free dog (signs tell you when it's allowed) will hike through oak and bay woods and grassy uplands that are carpeted with wildflowers in spring.

You'll also see abundant wildlife—if you're quiet and lucky, you might even see an endangered bald eagle. If your dog can't take the pressure of merely watching as tule elk and deer pass by, you should keep him leashed.

Because of some restrictions, you won't be able to do all 29 miles at once with your dog. That's OK. In fact, that's probably just fine with your dog.

A permit is required. Pick it up for $2 at the visitors center, East Bay Regional Park District headquarters, or the Del Valle or Sunol kiosks. 888/327-2757.

37 Ohlone Regional Wilderness

🐾🐾🐾🐾 🐕 (See Alameda County map on page 110)

The centerpiece of this magnificent parkland is the 3,817-foot Rose Peak—only 32 feet lower than Mt. Diablo. Leash-free dogs are in heaven on earth as they explore the surrounding 6,758 acres of grassy ridges. Wildlife is abundant, so if your dog isn't obedient, it's best to keep her leashed. The tule elk appreciate it, and your dog will appreciate it, too, should you run into a mountain lion.

The regional parks system shares the wilderness with the San Francisco Water District, which wants to limit the human presence here. Dogs may not stay overnight in the campgrounds.

To enter this wild and breathtaking area east of Sunol Regional Wilderness, you must pick up a permit (which includes a detailed trail map and camping information) for $2 at the visitors center, East Bay Regional Park District headquarters, or at the Del Valle and Sunol kiosks. 888/327-2757.

PLACES TO STAY

Residence Inn Livermore: These are convenient little apartments/suites if you need more than just a room. Rates are $149–204, and there's a $75 fee per doggy visit, so you might want to stay a while. 1000 Airway Boulevard 94550; 925/373-1800.

138

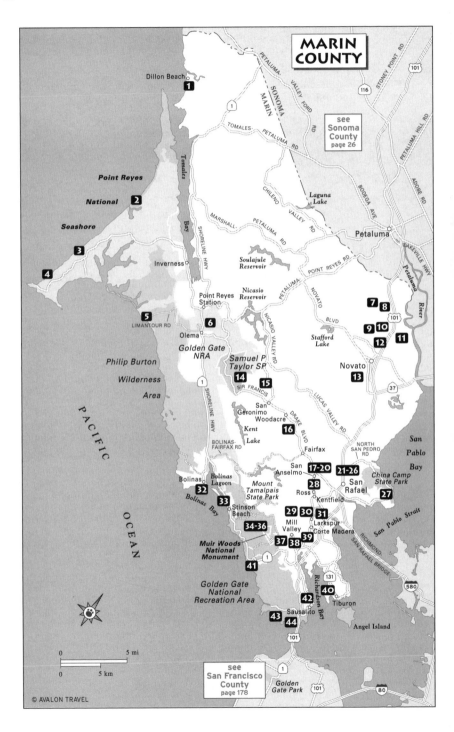

CHAPTER 6

Marin County

This is a good place to be a dog or a well-heeled human. For four-legged friends, it's got it all, from the bay to the ocean to the redwoods and hilly parklands in between. Throw in some dog-friendly restaurants, inns, and cottages, and you've got the makings of a pooch paradise.

Dogs need only be under voice control on certain Golden Gate National Recreation Area (GGNRA) trails in the Marin Headlands, and at Muir Beach and Rodeo Beach! At this time, no leashes are necessary for well-behaved dogs. At press time, the GGNRA was considering restrictions on dog access to its beaches and parklands, ranging from banning dogs completely to greatly curtailing off-leash areas. Please call ahead or look for signage before throwing your leash to the wind. Marin County operates many dog-friendly Open Space District lands. The landscapes include grassy expanses, wooded trails, redwood groves, marshes, and steep mountainsides. The idea is to set aside bits of land so that Marin never ends up looking like Santa Clara Valley. The Open Space parks are free and undeveloped.

PICK OF THE LITTER—MARIN COUNTY

BEST OFF-LEASH HIKE
Marin Headlands Trails, Sausalito (page 175)

BEST SOCIAL HOUR
Remington Dog Park, Sausalito (page 173)

BEST REMOTE BEACH
Kehoe Beach, Inverness (page 142)

BEST OFF-LEASH BEACHES
Muir Beach, Muir Beach (page 173)
Rodeo Beach and Lagoon, Sausalito (page 174)

PLACE TO HIKE OFF LEASH IN THE HEAT
Baltimore Canyon Open Space Preserve, Larkspur (page 160)

BEST PLACE TO PAY HOMAGE
TO THIS BOOK'S ILLUSTRATOR
Farley Bar, Sausalito (page 176)

BEST BREAD
Bovine Bakery, Point Reyes Station (page 145)

BEST SMELLS
Sol Food Restaurant, San Rafael (page 159)

MOST DOG-FRIENDLY PLACES TO EAT
Mojay's Cafe, San Rafael (page 159)
Mama's Royal Cafe, Mill Valley (page 168)
Fish, Sausalito (page 176)

INN WITH MOST DOG-FRIENDLY ACCOUTREMENTS
Ocean Song Retreat, Bolinas (page 163)

INN WITH ITS OWN DOG RUN—AND A LLAMA AND ALPACA
Inverness Valley Inn, Inverness (page 144)

MOST HISTORIC, AMAZINGLY BEAUTIFUL PLACE TO STAY
Cavallo Point–The Lodge at the Golden Gate, Sausalito (page 177)

BEST RIDE FOR SALTY SEA DOGS
**Ferry rides and sunset cruises with the Angel Island Tiburon
Ferry company,** Tiburon (page 171)

Dogs can run leash-free are on designated fire roads in the more dog-friendly parks. They must be leashed on trails. Most dogs don't mind the wide berth. Speaking of wide berth, you're not allowed to bring more than three dogs at a time to Open Space lands. This rule keeps commercial dog walking at bay. Also, we've been told that too many people are parking illegally to use these lands. There are many complaints from neighbors on adjacent roads. Be sure to park legally. See www.marinopenspace.org for more park info, or phone 415/499-6387.

Life on a leash isn't the same as the untethered life. But it's not always a drag. Marin offers some real gems to leashed pooches. Most dogs are surprised to discover that if they wear a leash, they're even permitted to explore a bit of beautiful Mt. Tamalpais. Dogs' mouths also tend to drop open when you mention they can visit parts of the 65,000-acre Point Reyes National Seashore, home to 350 species of birds and 72 species of mammals, not including dogs. Because it's a delicate ecosystem and a national treasure, dogs are banned from campgrounds, most trails, and several beaches. But there are still some great places to explore. Where dogs are permitted, they must be on leash. It's a small price to pay to be able to peruse the place with the pooch at all. Kehoe Beach, Point Reyes Beach South, and Point Reyes Beach North are the seashore's most dog-friendly areas.

Coastal Marin is a fantastic place for a great getaway with your dog. In this edition, we're thrilled to bring you several new waterfront or near-waterfront lodgings that are super dog friendly. And be sure to check out the Farley Bar, in Sausalito. There's a direct tie between it and this book. I'll leave you to find out more, below.

Dillon Beach

PARKS, BEACHES, AND RECREATION AREAS

🄁 Dillon Beach Resort

😺 😺 😺 😺 🐾 (See Marin County map on page 138)

Don't let the name fool you: This is a beach, not a high-end hotel with dozens of spa treatments. What really gets dogs excited is that not only are they allowed on the beach, but at a certain point that seems to confuse everyone we've spoken with there, they can throw their leashes to the wind. The rule says something to the effect that from the parking lot to the high tide line, dogs must be leashed, and from the tide line and into the water, dogs can be leash free. Check with the person at the kiosk when you drive in. Please make super-sure your dog is truly under voice control before letting her go, because this a rare privilege these days. (The next leash-free beach to the north is in Humboldt County; to the south it's in Pacifica.)

The beach is privately run and very well maintained. If you notice broken glass or anything that's not in keeping with a clean, safe beach, the staff asks you to report it.

There's a $5 fee per vehicle. It's worth the price. The beach is the northernmost beach in Marin County. So far north, in fact, that it has the Sonoma County area code. The address is One Beach Avenue; 707/878-2696.

PLACES TO STAY

Lawson's Landing and Resort: When you camp here, you camp in a grassy meadow along the sand dunes. There are no set campsites, just the open meadow. That's great, because sometimes you can have the whole place to yourself. Other times you have to share the meadow with lots of other outdoorsy sorts of folks. Day use is $8. Camping is $26–31. Weekly rates are available. Lawson's Landing is easy to find once you're in Dillon Beach. The address is 137 Marine View Drive, P.O. Box 67, Dillon Beach, CA 94929; 707/878-2443; www.lawsonslanding.com.

Inverness

This sweet, quiet village on Tomales Bay is one of the most attractive in Marin. The dog-friendly beaches, cafés, and lodgings are to drool for. What's not to love about this place?

PARKS, BEACHES, AND RECREATION AREAS

🐾 Kehoe Beach

🐾 🐾 🐾 🐾 (See Marin County map on page 138)

This is our favorite of the Point Reyes National Seashore beaches that allow dogs, since it's both the most beautiful and the least accessible. The only parking is at roadside. You take a half-mile cinder path through wildflowers and thistles, with marsh on one side and hill on the other. In the morning, you may see some mule deer. Then, you come out on medium-brown sand that stretches forever. Since the water is shallow, the surf repeats its crests in multiple white rows, as in Hawaii. Behind you are limestone cliffs. Scattered rocks offer tidepools filled with mussels, crabs, anemones, barnacles, snails, and sea flora.

In such a paradise of shore life, the leash rule makes sense. The chief reasons for leashing dogs (or banning them altogether) at the Point Reyes National Seashore beaches are the harbor seals that haul out onto the beaches. They're in no position to get away fast from a charging dog. The snowy plover, a threatened shorebird that nests on the ground, also appreciates your dog obeying the leash law. In fact, sections of this beach and the other Point Reyes beaches may become closed long-term because of these birds. Restricted areas will be posted so tell your dog to keep her eyes peeled.

From Inverness, follow Sir Francis Drake Boulevard to the fork. Bear right on Pierce Point Road and go about four miles; park beside the road where you see the sign and walk about a half mile to the beach. 415/464-5100.

🐾 Point Reyes Beach North
🐾🐾🐾🐾 (See Marin County map on page 138)

Point Reyes Beach North is a generous, functional beach. There's no long trail from the parking lot, no special tidepools or rocks, just a long, clean, beautiful running beach for the two of you. Officially, however, dogs must be leashed.

From Inverness, take Sir Francis Drake Boulevard. Follow signs for the lighthouse. Go about 10 miles. The turnoff for the beach is well marked. 415/464-5100.

🐾 Point Reyes Beach South
🐾🐾🐾 (See Marin County map on page 138)

Point Reyes Beach South is a little narrower and steeper than Point Reyes Beach North, and it has a few interesting sandstone outcrops with wind-carved holes. It has a bit less of that wide-open feeling. Leash the dog, and steer clear of dog-restricted areas.

Follow the directions for Point Reyes Beach North; it's the next beach southward. 415/464-5100.

PLACES TO EAT

Inverness Store: Lots of dogs visit this little grocery store, which has been around for more than 80 years. The folks here are kind to doggies and welcome them to munch a lunch at the picnic table at the dike here. They even invite dogs and their people to bring a blanket and make it a real picnic. (No ants, though.) 12784 Sir Francis Drake Boulevard; 415/669-1041.

PLACES TO STAY

Dancing Coyote Beach Bed & Breakfast Cottages: Do you like the fantasy of two-story, airy, pretty cottages with cathedral ceilings, fireplaces, decks, skylights, and attractive, comfy décor? Do you dream of such a cottage–a dog friendly one, no less–just steps from a beach? Does such a place even exist? Yes it does! The cottages at Dancing Coyote Beach provide the kind of coastal getaway many of us dream of but few of us ever imagined could be anywhere but the pages of an old book or a scene in a movie.

They should have called these the Dancing Dog Beach cottages, because they make dogs (and their people) dance for joy. Good dogs are welcome to be off leash here. The private Tomales Bay beach (private for land access at least) is calm and sandy. Bring a kayak, or if your dog is a swimmer, pack a good tennis ball or two. At least prepare to dip your toes so you can soak in the coastal ambiance all the way.

Your stay here will be utterly serene if you want it to be. Enjoy the provided breakfast on your private deck, stroll the beach, explore the gardens, curl up by the fire with a good book and a great dog, cook a romantic dinner in your cottage's kitchen. Or head to dinner at one of the wonderful restaurants nearby. Staff can even arrange an in-room massage. Ahhh…

Rates are $175–300. Dogs are $50 per stay. The cleaning fee is extremely understandable here. Sand and wet dogs tend to make a place more challenging to clean. 12794 Sir Francis Drake Boulevard 94937; 415/669-7200 or 800/210-1692; www.dancingcoyotecottages.com.

Inverness Valley Inn: Feel like going on a farmy getaway with your dog, but want to keep it bright, attractive, and free of herds of annoyed-looking cows? Look no further than the Inverness Valley Inn, where the rooms and suites are airy and pretty, the 15 acres are beautiful, and the farm animal population just right for the tastes of a city or suburban dog. Here's a list of the inn's menagerie, according to Alden, who runs the place with his wife, Leslie: Four dogs, one llama, one alpaca, goats, geese, and about 2,000 gophers. (Jake has submitted an offer to eradicate about 1,000 of them if he can stay for free for a weekend.)

The inn's rooms and suites come with kitchenettes, which is very appealing when traveling with a dog. Just between us, it can get tiring seeking out dog-friendly restaurants for every meal. And it definitely saves money to bring at least some of your own food along. All units have a fireplace, most have a deck or patio. And how about this for a fantastic and unusual feature? The inn has its very own grassy little dog run! It's not big, but it's a fenced area where you can let your dog enjoy a little off-leash time. That is a brilliant idea! Applause!

As if guest dogs here aren't lucky enough, they get a dog bed upon check-in, and towels and poop bags to help keep everything spic and span. And Alden and Leslie will tell you about some secret favorite dog-friendly spots nearby. Rates are $149–219. You can bring as many dogs as you like here–another unique aspect of this inn–and your whole pack will cost you only $25 for the first night, $10 for each night thereafter. 13275 Sir Francis Drake Boulevard 94937; 415/669-7250 or 800/416-0405; www.invernessvalleyinn.com.

Manka's Inverness Lodge: Often, humans and their dogs spend the night here, eat breakfast, and decide never to return home. It's an old hunting lodge and cabins, surrounded by woods and the beaches and mudflats of Tomales Bay—and the owners love dogs.

The lodgings are super-cozy, fun, luxurious, and unique. Features vary from one to the other and include fireplaces, huge tubs, antiques, and a variety of surprising decorative touches. Views are either of Tomales Bay or the surrounding woods.

Dogs can stay in any of the six cabins or the four rooms. The two-bedroom Boathouse is the largest and would be Jake's favorite, but water dogs aren't allowed there because it's right on the water and swimming dogs tend to make the place soggy—not really something the Boathouse needs. Rates for the cabins are $495–795. Dogs are $100 extra for the length of their cabin stay. Rates for the rooms in the lodge are $215–335, and dogs are $50 extra per stay.

Look for the uphill turn off Sir Francis Drake Boulevard and take Argyle Way about 400 yards to the lodge. P.O. Box 1110, Inverness, CA 94937; 415/669-1034; www.mankas.com.

Rosemary Cottages: The two gorgeous cottages that share this spacious, wooded property are the kind of places you and your dog will not leave easily. The Fir Tree Inn and The Rosemary Cottage are set in a secluded spot, each with a wall of windows looking out at the stunning forest scenery of the Point Reyes National Seashore. A deck overlooks a sweet-smelling herb garden. Inside the cottages are cozy and beautifully crafted, with a full kitchen and many homey details. Snuggle up near the wood-burning stove on chilly evenings after a day of whale-watching and dog-walking at nearby beaches. Hearth-type dogs love it here.

There's plenty of privacy: Although the cottages share the garden and hot tub (which uses milder chemicals than chlorine and its harsh brethren), many guests spend their vacation here and never even know just where the other cottage is.

Owner Suzanne Storch wants your stay to be as restful and healthful as possible. She provides a "green" environment (only more-natural cleansers are used) and has been switching over to organic sheets and towels. Best of all, she provides the most delectable organic breakfast fixings, including a basket of oranges and other fruit, granola, yogurt, organic locally made bread and muffins, homemade jam, and eggs from her chickens. Even the coffee, tea, milk, and sugar are organic! The cost for these amazing breakfast baskets is $12 per person.

The Rosemary Cottage is $255 for up to two people, and The Fir Tree is $295. Extra people are $25 each. If you have one dog, you'll pay a $40 flat fee. For two dogs you'll pay a $50 flat fee. Directions are available online, and the mailing address is P.O. Box 273, Inverness, CA 94937; 415/663-9338 or 800/808-9338; www.rosemarybb.com.

Point Reyes Station

This community is the commercial hub of West Marin. But that's not saying much, because it's not exactly Development Central out here. In fact, there are probably more cows than people. You'll find some terrific places to eat (two of them with names relating to cows, in fact) and to spend the night with your dog.

PLACES TO EAT
Bovine Bakery: The bread here will make you drool, which will make your

dog embarrassed. Dine on bread or pizza or "killer monster cookies" at the bench in front. 11315 Highway 1; 415/663-9420.

Cafe Reyes: The patio on the café's side is big and very attractive, with excellent views of local scenery. Even dogs seem to enjoy its ambience. The food is great, too. Tasty wood-fired pizzas are the stars here. Bring yours to the 15 umbrella-topped tables and wolf it down with your pooch at your side. There's not really a street address. It's on Highway 1 and is big and wooden. You can't miss it. 415/663-9493.

Cowgirl Creamery at Tomales Bay Foods: No, this isn't related to the nearby Bovine Bakery, although they do sound good together. Cowgirl Creamery cheeses are so delectable they're worth the drive out to this end of the world. Sure, you can get these organic artisan cheeses around the Bay Area, but this is where they're born. On Fridays you can take a short tour of the cheese-making operation, still housed in an old barn.

Buy cheese, upscale deli items, organic produce, and baked goods inside (without your dog) and enjoy a restful meal together at the courtyard picnic tables. Note that the outside of the barn/store bears the name Tomales Bay Foods. 80 Fourth Street; 415/663-9335.

PLACES TO STAY

The Berry Patch Cottage: This garden cottage is surrounded by trees and has a private yard with plenty of berries (thus the name), fruit trees, and nut trees. The cottage's pleasant owners live next door, and they invite guests to share their vegetable garden. The cottage is basic, with furniture and appliances a couple of readers have said are a little run-down. If you expect luxury, you should probably look elsewhere. Rates are $100–150. Dogs are $5 extra.

There's also a newer, smaller unit available now, and it has an enclosed patio with French doors. The mailing address is P.O. Box 712 94956. You'll get the physical address when you make a reservation. 415/663-1942 or 888/663-1942; www.berrypatchcottage.com.

Point Reyes Schoolhouse Compound: The three glorious getaway cottages that make up the old schoolhouse area are the cat's meow for dogs and their people. On a serene stretch of rolling pastureland in Point Reyes Station, the cottages have a sweet country theme and seem perfectly at home in their surroundings. Dogs love it here, because each cottage is adorned with its own private enclosed patio. They're wonderful places to relax outside with your pooch.

The cottages have fully equipped kitchens that come with a real bonus: a lovely picnic basket and all the gear that goes with it (excluding the food). Now there's no excuse for not taking your pooch on a picnic. In addition, each cottage has a fireplace, as well as access to a secluded garden, hot tub, outdoor fireplace, and hammock.

Rates are $185–245. Dogs are $75 extra for the length of their stay. The cottages are on the historic Old Point Reyes Schoolhouse Compound. The mailing address is P.O. Box 56, Point Reyes Station, CA 94956; 415/663-1166; www .pointreyesschoolhouse.com.

Point Reyes Station Inn: Dogs are welcome to stay in two rooms at this romantic, beautiful country inn. They're furnished with sweet antiques, and have fireplaces and access to a private garden. A delectable, huge continental breakfast features organic eggs from the inn's very own chickens, and homegrown

DIVERSION

If Only Dogs Could Read: Point Reyes Books once sent me a letter that ended like this: "We welcome genteel canines, whether a reading rover or a browsing bowser—or just a patiently waiting companion. *Se habla* milkbone." So of course, next time we found ourselves pawing around for a good book, Joe hounded me to drive with him to this wonderful little bookstore. He immediately fell in love with the place. Dogs get lots of loving and a crunchy biscuit. After a recent visit, his protégé, Jake, decided that instead of chewing books, he'd simply make dog-eared pages. Anything to go back.

This store really is a treat—for dogs and humans. It has a big selection of new and used books, with a strong outdoor book section. Combine a visit here with a hike and a lunch, and you've got yourselves a doggone great day. 11315 Highway 1, Point Reyes Station; 415/663-1542; www.ptreyesbooks.com.

organic seasonal produce. Rates for the pet-friendly rooms are $125–195. 11591 Highway 1 94956; 415/663-9372; www.pointreyesstationinn.com.

Seven Grey Foxes: These two plainly furnished apartments are tucked away on a quiet country road in a cozy neighborhood just outside the village. It's very peaceful here. The two-room apartment (a.k.a. the cottage) has views of attractive gardens, a kitchenette, and a Franklin fireplace. The one-room apartment is just a smaller version of the other except with no kitchenette. Dogs are a big part of Seven Grey Foxes, accounting for 80 percent of their business. Rates are $95–115 for the smaller and $150 for the larger. You'll get the address when you make your reservation. 415/663-1089; www.seven greyfoxes.com.

Olema

PARKS, BEACHES, AND RECREATION AREAS

5 Limantour Beach
🐾🐾🐾🐾 (See Marin County map on page 138)

This bountiful beach at Point Reyes National Seashore is most people's favorite, so it's often crowded. From the main parking lot, walk 0.25 mile through tule marsh, grasses and brush, and scattered pines, past Limantour Estero. Dogs are not permitted at the northwest end of the beach and must be leashed everywhere else.

Rules for leashed dogs are clearly marked—a refreshing exception to the obscure and contradictory rules in so many parks. For example, approaching Limantour Beach on the path, you'll see a sign that says dogs are prohibited to your right, allowed to your left. This beach is plenty big, so it's an excellent arrangement that keeps dog owners and dog avoiders equally happy. You may walk with your dog to Santa Maria Beach.

From Highway 1, look for the turnoff to Bear Valley Road, which runs between Olema and Inverness Park. Take Bear Valley from either direction to Limantour Road; turn south on Limantour all the way to the beach. 415/464-5100.

6 Bolinas Ridge Trail
🐾🐾🐾🐾 (See Marin County map on page 138)

This Golden Gate National Recreation Area trail, part of the Bay Area Ridge Trail, is not for sissies—canine or human. It climbs steadily for 11 miles from the Olema end, giving you gorgeous views of Tomales Bay, Bolinas, and the ocean, and ends up at the Bolinas-Fairfax Road below Alpine Lake. The GGNRA website proudly states that this is "the best trail in the area for walking a dog."

You must keep your dog leashed. One good reason for this is that there are cattle roaming unfenced along the trail. And the trail is very popular with non-sissy mountain bikers. (The trail is wide, but made of dirt and rock.) From the western end, you'll walk through rolling grassland with cypress clumps. Rock outcrops sport crowns of poison oak, so watch it.

You may be able to cope with 11 miles of this, but remember your dog's bare pads and don't overdo it. Also, it isn't much fun for man or beast to walk 11 miles attached by a leash.

Unfortunately, only the Bolinas Ridge Trail is open to dogs; you can't take any of the spur trails going south.

The western end begins about one mile north of Olema on Sir Francis Drake Boulevard. There's roadside parking only. 415/556-0560 or 415/663-1092.

PLACES TO STAY

The Olema Inn: This absolutely enchanting inn is exactly 100 years younger than our nation. It opened on July 4, 1876. That's a long, long time ago by California standards. The inn has obviously been revamped a bit since then, but it still retains the elegant charm of the era. The six beautiful rooms feature antique furniture mingling with up-to-date luxuries such as super-comfortable European Sleepworks mattresses topped with down comforters. (No dogs on the bedding, please.) A fresh breakfast of croissants, local artisan cheeses, fruit, and beverages comes with your stay. Eat it in the dining room or enjoy it in the pretty garden, the lush green grounds, or the big patio out front. Dogs can join you on the patio for lunch and dinner, too. Rates are $174–222. 10,000 Sir Francis Drake Boulevard 94950; 415/663-9559; www.the olemainn.com.

Novato

PARKS, BEACHES, AND RECREATION AREAS

7 Mount Burdell Open Space Preserve

😊😊😊😊🐕 (See Marin County map on page 138)

Mount Burdell is the largest of Marin's Open Space preserves. You'll share it with cattle, but there's plenty of room. There are several miles of trails, including part of the Bay Area Ridge Trail, that wind through its oak-dotted grasslands. Dogs have to be leashed on trails but are permitted to run leashless on fire roads here. Be sure to heed signs: Parts of the Open Space are off-limits to dogs because they're sensitive wildlife areas, and dogs aren't usually terribly sensitive to wildlife.

A creek is 0.15 mile up the trail starting at San Andreas Drive, but it's dry in summer. In winter, you might find the preserve's Hidden Lake. In summer, there are lots of foxtails and fire danger is high. No fires are ever allowed. Camping is allowed by permit, but there are no facilities.

From San Marin Drive, turn north on San Andreas Drive. Park on the street. 415/499-6387.

8 Miwok Park

🐾 🐾 🐾 (See Marin County map on page 138)

This is one of the best city parks we've visited. Dogs must be on leash, but it offers a great combination of dog pleasures and human amenities. Paved paths, good for strollers, wind through pine trees. You will find boccie ball courts, horseshoes, a kids' gym, and a lovely shaded picnic area with grills.

Outside the Museum of the American Indian in this park is an intriguing display of California native plants that the coastal Miwuk used for food, clothing, and shelter.

Best of all for canines, Novato Creek flows deep and 30–40 feet wide (even in summer). A woman we encountered with a golden retriever told us that the muddy bottom can sometimes be soft and treacherous, so keep a close eye on your dog if he goes swimming. The park is at Novato Boulevard and San Miguel Drive. 415/899-8200.

9 Indian Tree Open Space Preserve

🐾 🐾 🐾 🐾 🦮 (See Marin County map on page 138)

This is a great choice for a hike if the weather is hot: Your ascent to the top (and to terrific views) takes you through cool, shaded woodlands of oak, madrone, and bay. You'll also encounter redwoods and ferns along the way. At the top, the open area isn't parched and sun-baked like so many areas around here in summer: It's often cool and drippy with fog. Jake the dog, who lives in a foggy area of the city and can't take the heat, is very happy here. You needn't leash on fire roads here, but watch out for horses. Leashes are the law on the preserve's trails.

From U.S. 101, exit at San Marin Drive/Atherton Avenue; drive west on San Marin. After San Marin turns into Sutro Avenue, take a right onto Vineyard Road. Park along the dirt county road that begins at the trailhead. 415/499-6387.

10 Dogbone Meadows

🐾 🐾 🐾 🐾 🦮 (See Marin County map on page 138)

Lucky dogs who visit here have two fenced acres of off-leash running room and all the "playground equipment" they could want. The park sports tunnels, ramps, jumps, hanging tires, and other fun agility equipment. Big dogs have big toys, and little dogs have littler toys. Everyone's happy here.

The park is a pretty combination of grass and landscaping bark, with the rolling hills of O'Hair Park in the background. (You can walk your dog on leash in this 100-acre city park.) The volunteers who worked so hard to make this park a reality have planted 35 trees, but it will take many years before they're shade-giving. Until then, people gather under shade structures on hot, sunny days. If your dog is dirty from all the romping around, you can use the dog-wash station near the entrance/exit. The park is at San Marin Drive and Novato Boulevard, on the left as you're heading west. 415/899-8200.

11 Deer Island Open Space Preserve

🐾🐾🐾🐾 (See Marin County map on page 138)

This preserve is called an island because it's a high point in the floodplain of the Petaluma River, an oak-crowned hill surrounded by miles of dock and tules. You can easily imagine it surrounded by shallow-water Miwuk canoes slipping through rafts of ducks. The trail is a 1.8-mile loop of gentle ups and downs above ponds and marshy fields. There are some sturdy old oaks among the mixed deciduous groves, and lots of laurels. The trail is partly shaded and bans bikes. Dogs must be leashed.

From U.S. 101, exit at San Marin Drive/Atherton Avenue; drive east about 1.5 miles and take a right on Olive Avenue, then a left on Deer Island Lane. Park in a small lot at the trailhead, by a small engineering company building. 415/499-6387.

12 Indian Valley Open Space Preserve

🐾🐾🐾🐾🐕 (See Marin County map on page 138)

Lots of dogs come here to trot around in leashless ecstasy on the fire road. On hiking trails, they have to trot around in leashed ecstasy. The hiking trails and fire roads are partly sunny, partly shaded by laurels, and much revered by canines. Take the Waterfall Trail if you love waterfalls and don't mind leashes. You'll be rewarded at the end, unless of course it's dry season.

From U.S. 101, exit at DeLong Avenue and go west on DeLong, which becomes Diablo Avenue. Take a left on Hill Road and a right on Indian Valley Road. Drive all the way to the end; park on this road before you walk left at the spur road marked Not a Through Street, just south of Old Ranch Road. Cross Arroyo Avichi Creek right at the entrance (dry in summer). 415/499-6387.

13 Loma Verde Open Space Preserve

🐾🐾🐾🐕 (See Marin County map on page 138)

This rugged Open Space connects to a couple of others, which makes for a vigorous hike if you and your dog aren't fair of paw. There are two access points to this Open Space, where dogs are allowed off leash on fire roads. One, south of the Marin Country Club, is a waterless, tree-covered hillside with a fire road. Bikes are allowed, so be sure to keep your leash-free dog under voice control. It's a good road if you like easily reachable high spots; there are fine views of San Pablo Bay. Exit U.S. 101 at Ignacio Boulevard. Go west to Fairway Drive and turn left (south), then left on Alameda de la Loma, then right on Pebble Beach Drive. Access is at the end of Pebble Beach.

The second access point is through the Posada West housing development.

From Alameda del Prado, turn south on Posada del Sol. The trail opening is at the end of this street. 415/499-6387.

PLACES TO STAY

Inn Marin: Any lodging that boasts three "dog pot stations" on the property has got to be doggone dog-friendly (and doggone clean, too). These stations are actually just waste cans coupled with plastic bag dispensers, but we appreciate the inn's discreet name for them. The 70-room inn is stylish, clean, and convenient to U.S. 101. It features excellent amenities for people traveling on business (data ports, two-line speaker phones, large desks) and people with disabilities (seven rooms have special features for wheelchairs, and for sight- or hearing-impaired guests). Rates are $99–269. Dogs are $20 total for the first six days, and then $20 per week after. (And get this: You can have up to four per room!) 250 Entrada Drive 94949; 415/883-5952 or 800/652-6565; www.innmarin.com.

TraveLodge: Rates are $55–99. Dogs are $10 extra. 7600 Redwood Boulevard 94945; 415/892-7500.

Lagunitas

PARKS, BEACHES, AND RECREATION AREAS

🐾 Samuel P. Taylor State Park

🐾🐾🐾 (See Marin County map on page 138)

An exception among the state parks: Dog access isn't too bad. You can take a dog into the picnic areas, and that's worth doing here. The main picnic area right off Sir Francis Drake Boulevard is cool and often lively with the grinding call of jays. It's an easy place to bring out-of-state visitors who may just want to eat a sandwich, hug a redwood, and go home. The park has hollow trees stretching 20 feet across that you can actually stand inside.

But best of all, you and your dog can peruse the beautiful Cross Marin Trail, which runs through the park. This is a paved trail popular with bikers, but it makes for a scenic, shady hike for you and your leashed friend. You can pick up the trail at the Redwood Grove Picnic Area.

The park has 60 campsites. Sites are $35. From April through October, call for reservations: 800/444-7275. The park's day-use fee is $8. The entrance is on Sir Francis Drake Boulevard about two miles west of Lagunitas. 415/488-9897.

PLACES TO EAT

Lagunitas Grocery: Grab a sandwich at the deli inside and feast on it at the outdoor tables with your dog. Thirsty dogs can ask for a bowl of water. 7890 Sir Francis Drake Boulevard; 415/488-4844.

Woodacre

PARKS, BEACHES, AND RECREATION AREAS

15 Gary Giacomini Open Space Preserve

🐾🐾🐾🐾 🐕 (See Marin County map on page 138)

The most recent addition to Marin's Open Space lands is this 1,600-acre gem. The preserve stretches for seven miles along the southern edge of the San Geronimo Valley. Stands of old-growth redwoods shade the ferny lower regions of the park. The higher you go, the more grassy it gets. Dogs such as Jake (i.e., male) prefer the trees, but they can get the best of both worlds by following one of the wide fire trails and sniffing out various areas along the way.

Pooches may go leashless on the fire roads but not on the more narrow hiking trails. Come visit before the rest of the doggone world finds out about this hidden treasure.

From U.S. 101, take Sir Francis Drake Boulevard west to San Geronimo Valley Drive and turn left. You can park at the intersection of Redwood Canyon Drive, just west of Woodacre, and begin your hike at the nearby trailhead. This is a fun route to take with your dog, since it brings you from thick forest to the top of the ridge. 415/499-6387.

Fairfax

This small, friendly, progressive town is known as the birthplace of the mountain bike. That's not news that will put a wag in your dog's tail, but this will: Secret Agent Dog, a pooch with impeccable taste, had his person write to tell me that "Fairfax is… one of the most dog-friendly places we've ever lived." Mutt Mitt dispensers are placed strategically through town, and there are two drinking fountains (one by the baseball field, one by town hall) for both humans and dogs. People here love to see dogs with their people; some stores will welcome your dog if it's not busy, but we'll leave that on a case-by-case basis.

PARKS, BEACHES, AND RECREATION AREAS

16 Cascade Canyon Open Space Preserve

🐾🐾🐾 (See Marin County map on page 138)

Doggone it. Dogs are no longer legally allowed to be leash-free on the fire road here. Jake doesn't like this slowly encroaching leashes-only rules at Marin Open Space lands, and neither does his human fellow hiker. Still, the fire road makes for a pleasant walk that leads all the way into the Marin Municipal Water District lands of Mt. Tamalpais (where leashes are the law, too).

The hiking trails at Cascade Canyon are even more enjoyable. The main trail sticks close to San Anselmo Creek, which is reduced to a dry creek bed in summer. A no-bicycles trail branches off to the right and disappears into the creek; the left branch fords the creek. When the water's high, you may be stopped right here. But in summer, you can walk a long way. Side trails lead you into shady glens of laurel and other deciduous trees, but there's lots of poison oak, too.

The park is at the end of Cascade Drive. The Town of Fairfax sign says Elliott Nature Preserve, but it's official Open Space. Please don't park at the end of Cascade. Spread out so the folks who live at the end of Cascade don't get so inundated with dogs. Pooches have been a problem for some residents, whose beautiful flowers and lawns have succumbed to dog feet and pooch poop. Be courteous, and think how you'd feel if the shoe were on the other paw. 415/499-6387.

San Anselmo

San Anselmo Avenue provides you and your mellow pooch a laid-back stroll, and you can both cool your paws in San Anselmo Creek, which runs through town. Your well-behaved pooch can even be off leash, provided she's under voice control.

PARKS, BEACHES, AND RECREATION AREAS

17 Red Hill Dog Park

🐾🐾🐾🐕 (See Marin County map on page 138)

The defacto dog park that was used by so many dogs for so many years has finally become a real dog park! It's the recreational version of Pinocchio, who wished he could be a real boy so badly that one day he became one. (Jake asks forgiveness for my analogy.)

The park is now fenced, with grass, a walking path, benches, tables, water, and some baby trees that will be toddler's by this book's next edition. Jiminy Cricket, that'll be swell! The park is between Shaw Drive and Sunny Hills Drive, behind the Red Hill Shopping Center in the Ross Valley area. 415/258-4601.

18 Loma Alta Open Space Preserve

🐾🐾🐾🐾🐕 (See Marin County map on page 138)

A little canyon amid bare hills, lined with oaks, bay laurel, and buckeye, this is an exceptional Open Space preserve. Shade is plentiful. The trail follows White Hill Creek, which is dry in the summer. Leashes are required on the trails, but obedient dogs can throw their leashes to the wind on the fire road.

You can park at the trailhead at the end of Glen Avenue, a turn north off Sir Francis Drake Boulevard. 415/499-6387.

19 Memorial Park

🐾🐾🐾🐕 (See Marin County map on page 138)

This pleasant and popular city park has tennis courts, three baseball diamonds, and a children's play area. Next to the diamonds is an area where leash-free dogs romp joyfully, fetching, chasing Frisbees, or socializing. Even a creek runs nearby. There's a hitch—dogs can be off leash only before 8 A.M. and from one hour before sunset to, well, sunset. The park is at Veterans Place, a quick jog east from San Francisco Boulevard. 415/258-4640.

20 Sorich Ranch Park

🐾🐾🐾🐾🐕 (See Marin County map on page 138)

The biggest and by far the wildest city park in San Anselmo is Sorich Ranch Park, an undeveloped open space soaring to a ridge top from which you can see a distant make-believe San Francisco skyline across the bay. From the very top of the ridge, you also can see Mt. Tamalpais and most of San Rafael, including the one-of-a-kind turquoise and salmon Marin County Civic Center, designed by Frank Lloyd Wright. (Some Marinites are glad there's only one.)

The entrance from the San Anselmo side is at the end of San Francisco Boulevard, and the path is pretty much straight up. But if you aren't up to a 10-minute puffing ascent, you can just stroll in the meadows at the bottom. No leash is required, and the park is uncrowded and often pleasantly breezy. No water is available, and it can be scorching in summer. 415/258-4640.

PLACES TO EAT

Bubba's Diner: If you found an eatery by this name in many other towns, you might be inclined to stride by with nary a glance, lest you absorb grease and saturated fat just by looking at it. But being that this Bubba's Diner is in San Anselmo, grease is not the main ingredient of most dishes, and the saturated fat is at least upscale saturated fat.

Bubba's is a really fun, unpretentious place to bring a dog for some extra-tasty American-style eats. The cheery owner, Beth, likes to see well-behaved dogs dining at the two awning-shaded tables and benches in front of the restaurant. But she warns people not to tie dogs to the benches, lest the dog drag away the bench. (One small pooch actually went exploring the neighborhood, pulling the hefty pine bench behind him!) Take Beth's advice and hook your dog to the pay phone if you're dining alone and need to run in to place your order.

Choose from dozens of yummy dishes here. The food varies from health-ful and delicious (oyster salad, grilled salmon with asparagus and sautéed spinach) to decadent and delicious (pot roast, fried chicken, burgers, mashed potato pancakes). If you're pining for some fried green tomatoes, look no further: Bubba's is famous for them. Thirsty doggies can get water here. 566 San Anselmo Avenue; 415/459-6862.

San Rafael

PARKS, BEACHES, AND RECREATION AREAS

21 Lucas Valley Open Space Preserve

🐾🐾🐾🐾 🐕 (See Marin County map on page 138)

This space of rolling, oak-dotted hills affords great views of Novato and Lucas Valley developments. The summit here is 1,825 feet—the second-highest in Marin. We like to take the scenic Big Rock Trail up to the Big Rock Fire Road. It's a gentle grade for beasts and their people.

The preserve has a dozen access points, most from Lucas Valley and Marinwood. One access point is reached by turning left (north) off Lucas Valley Road on Mount Shasta Drive, followed by a brief right turn on Vogelsang Drive. Park near this dead end and walk in. Keep in mind that all Marin Open Space Preserves require pooches to be on leash except on fire roads. (Thanks to giant local golden retriever Duke, who set us straight on the preserve's exact location.) 415/499-6387.

22 Terra Linda–Sleepy Hollow Divide Open Space Preserve

🐾🐾🐾🐾 🐕 (See Marin County map on page 138)

This ridgeline preserve has many entrances, but generally the best are the highest on the ridge. We'll describe the one that starts you at a good high point, so that you don't have to climb. From the entrance at the end of Ridgewood Drive, you can walk into Sorich Ranch Park in San Anselmo.

From this ridge, you can see the city of San Rafael, U.S. 101, the wonderful turquoise-roofed Marin County Civic Center, the bay, and the hills of Solano County. No leash is necessary on fire roads, unless you're worried about your dog's tangling with deer. But pooches must be leashed on trails.

Park near the very end of Ridgewood Drive. The entrance is unmarked, and you have to step over a low locked gate. 415/499-6387.

23 Field of Dogs

🐾🐾🐾🐾 🐕 (See Marin County map on page 138)

We love the name, love the park. The people behind Field of Dogs worked really hard to make the park a reality. It took about six years. It's not only real now, but it's a great place to take a dog for off-leash exercise.

The one-acre park has little trees, big trees, a double-gated entry, benches, picnic tables, poop bags, and very nice park-goers—of both the pooch and people variety. Some trees are in the middle of the park, and we've heard about more than one head-on canine collision with a tree during chase games. After the swirling stars and tweeting birds wear off, the dogs are just fine.

The park is behind the civic center, at 3540 Civic Center Drive. It's an easy jaunt from U.S. 101. Exit U.S. 101 and continue east to Civic Center Drive, which is the first light. Turn left and the park will be on your right just past the post office and firehouse. 415/499-6405.

24 John F. McInnis County Park

🐾🐾🐾🐕 (See Marin County map on page 138)

This is an all-around, got-everything park for people. Among its riches are two softball fields, two soccer fields, tennis courts, a picnic area, a scale-model car track, a nine-hole golf course, miniature golf, batting cages, and a dirt creekside nature trail.

Best of all for trustworthy dogs, they can be off leash, so long as they're under verbal command and out of the golf course. This park isn't particularly pretty, but it's very utilitarian. From U.S. 101, exit at Smith Ranch Road. 415/507-4045.

25 San Pedro Mountain Open Space Preserve

🐾🐾🐾 (See Marin County map on page 138)

A narrow footpath rises moderately but inexorably upward through a madrone forest. But if you make it up far enough, you'll be rewarded with terrific views of the bay and Marin's peaks. Unlike most other Open Space lands in Marin, this one doesn't permit pooches off leash on fire roads because the fire roads at the top are city property. This means dogs have to be leashed here. It's probably just as well since so many deer call this park home.

Park at the entrance at the end of Woodoaks Drive, a short street off North Point San Pedro Road just north of the Jewish Community Center of Marin. 415/499-6387.

26 Santa Venetia Marsh Open Space Preserve

🐾🐾🐾🐾 (See Marin County map on page 138)

Dogs are very lucky to be able to visit this saltwater marsh. Only leashed pooches on their best behavior should come here, because the preserve is home to an endangered bird, the California clapper rail. Keep your eyes peeled: It looks like a chicken (and apparently tastes something like one, too—it was heavily hunted during the Gold Rush, when its meat was considered a delightful delicacy), but it has a long beak.

Mmm, doggy, the scents can be mighty strong here sometimes. They're so doggone nose-flaring good your dog may not even notice he's wearing a leash. You may not feel the same about the odor, but, hey, just keep saying to yourself, "it's a natural smell."

It's cool and breezy here, but gentler than any San Francisco Bay shore park.

The grasses and pickleweed make a pretty mixture of colors, and swallows dart above the ground hunting insects. Be sure to keep on the trails because this is sensitive marsh habitat. And rangers tell us that even though there are fire roads here, dogs can't do their usual leash-free thing because of the endangered wannabe chicken. Understandable.

From U.S. 101, take the North San Pedro Road exit. Drive east on North San Pedro Road about two miles, then turn left on Vendola Drive. Go about 0.1 mile on Vendola and park near the open space gate on the left. 415/499-6387.

27 China Camp State Park
🐾🐾🐾 (See Marin County map on page 138)

You shouldn't miss a drive through this lovely park, although it's not terribly hospitable to dogs except at Village Beach, the site of the 1890s Chinese fishing village for which the park is named. As you drive in, you'll see a rare piece of bay, marsh, and oak-covered hills as the Miwuks saw it. The hills, like islands, rise from salt-marsh seas of pickleweed and cordgrass. You'll see the No Dogs symbol at every trailhead, in case you're tempted. However, with your dog you may visit any of three picnic grounds on the way, via North Point San Pedro Road. Buckeye Point and Weber Point both have tables in shade or sun overlooking San Pablo Bay, mudflats at low tide, and the hills beyond the bay. Bullhead Flat lets you get right next to the water, but there's no shade at the tables.

Watch for the sign to China Camp Village, a left turn into a lot, where there's some shade. You'll see the rickety old pier and the wood-and-tin village. Park, leash your dog, and walk down to the village and the beach. On weekdays, this park is much less crowded. There are more picnic tables overlooking the water by the parking lot, an interpretive exhibit and, on weekends, a refreshment stand serving shrimp, crab, and beer. You can eat at picnic tables right on the beach—small, but pleasantly sheltered by hillsides, with gentle surf.

Swimming is encouraged here, and it's often warm enough. Derelict fishing boats and shacks are preserved on the beach. You can walk all the way to a rocky point at the south end, but watch out for the luxuriant poison oak in the brush along the beach. You may occasionally find broken glass.

There are 31 primitive walk-in campsites here. As in all state parks, dogs must always be leashed or confined to your tent. Sites are $35. To reserve (recommended April–October), call 800/444-7275. From U.S. 101, take the North Point San Pedro Road exit and follow it all the way into the park. (Don't go near McNears Beach County Park just south of China Camp. Dogs are strictly forbidden.) There's a $5 parking fee. 415/456-0766.

PLACES TO EAT
Le Chalet Basque: If you've never had Basque cuisine, this is a great place to try it. The portions are ample, tasty, and affordable, and your good dog can

join you on the patio. The restaurant is well off the beaten path, in San Rafael's San Venetia neighborhood, but there's usually a good crowd. 405 North San Pedro Road; 415/479-1070.

Le Croissant Restaurant: With a name like this you'd expect California/French café cuisine, but don't let the name fool you: The food here is of the good old-fashioned 1960s diner genre. Breakfasts are heavy and delicious, or try the soups, salads, and sandwiches later in the day. Your dog can join you on the tree-shaded patio. Le Croissant is in the canal area of San Rafael, at 150 Bellam Boulevard; 415/456-0164.

Mojay's Cafe: The coffee is very good here, but if coffee isn't your cup of tea, you can order pastries, smoothies, soups, salads, and sandwiches. Dogs not only get water, but they're treated to treats here, too! 1800 4th Street; 415/256-2420.

Ristorante La Toscana: The Italian food here is basic and good. Enjoy pasta or several meaty dishes, including broiled lamb chops or New York minute steak, with your dog at the outside tables. The restaurant is across from the Civic Center and gets crowded when evening events take place. 3751 Redwood Highway; 415/492-9100.

Sol Food Restaurant: I dare you to walk by this Puerto Rican restaurant and not stop in for a bite. Those little scent tendrils so familiar on old cartoons reside here. They wake up early and entice people inside all day. You'll be drooling before you sit down at one of the few oft-busy outdoor tables. The flavors are vibrant, alive, complex, yet distinct. Every bit of every dish melts in the mouth. A lot of people get hooked, so Sol Food has developed a really fun website for people who want to order their food online. Check it out at www .solfoodrestaurant.com. Sometimes when I'm slogging along in some writing task at my desk in my house in a foggy San Francisco neighborhood, I click on the "enter" page and let the background music and restaurant noise take me away to sunny Puerto Rico as I continue to write. It works! I'm in Puerto Rico as I write this. Really. Just ask Jake. He's with me. 732 4th Street; 415/451-4756.

PLACES TO STAY

Panama Hotel: Dogs are welcome to stay in three attractive rooms at this charming, funky, circa-1910 inn. These dog-friendly rooms are on the ground floor, have private sitting porches or patios, and tile or slate floors. In other words, they're easy maintenance and roomy enough for people with pets.

Pets feel welcome here. "We enjoy having dog guests," says one of the owners. To the point: Dogs get a couple of treats, two bowls, and pet towels upon check in. A continental breakfast comes with your room. Rates for the dog-friendly rooms are $165–175. Dogs are $15 extra, and there's a two-dog limit per room. 4 Bayview Street 94901; 415/457-3993 or 800/899-3993; www .panamahotel.com.

Villa Inn: This is a pleasant and affordable place to spend the night with your dog. Rates are $69–125. 1600 Lincoln Avenue 94901; 415/456-4975; www.villainn.com.

Ross

PARKS, BEACHES, AND RECREATION AREAS

28 Natalie Coffin Greene Park

😸 😸 😸 (See Marin County map on page 138)

Leashed dogs are welcome at this enchanted mixed forest of redwood and deciduous trees. The picnic area has an old-fashioned shelter built of logs and stone.

The park borders generic Marin Municipal Water District land, and from the park, you can pick up the wide cinder fire road leading to Phoenix Lake, a five-minute walk. Bikers, hikers, and leashed dogs are all welcome on this road, but the lake is a reservoir, so no body contact is allowed—for human or beast.

The road continues, depending how far you want to walk, to Lagunitas Lake, Bon Tempe Lake, Alpine Lake, and Kent Lake (no swimming in any of them—sorry, dogs). Combined, the water district offers 94 miles of road and 44 miles of trail in this area, meandering through hillsides densely forested with pine, oak, madrone, and a variety of other trees. For a trail map, send a self-addressed, stamped envelope to Sky Oaks Ranger Station, P.O. Box 865, Fairfax, CA 94978, Attention: Trail Map.

At the corner of Sir Francis Drake Boulevard and Lagunitas Road, go west on Lagunitas all the way to the end, past the country club. You'll find a parking lot and some portable toilets. 415/453-1453.

Larkspur

PARKS, BEACHES, AND RECREATION AREAS

29 Baltimore Canyon Open Space Preserve

😸 😸 😸 😸 🐕 (See Marin County map on page 138)

If you don't like heat, this 175-acre Open Space is a fine place to come for a summer stroll. You have less chance of getting roasty-toasty here than at many other nearby parks: The big oaks, madrones, bays, firs, and even redwoods tend to keep things cool in the canyon. It even has a year-round creek and a seasonal 30-foot waterfall, Dawn Falls. It's worth the hike to the end of the canyon to see this cascade. It's about 2.2 miles round trip and has only a 300-foot elevation change—something most healthy dogs and people can easily manage.

Since it's a trail, not a fire road, dogs need to be leashed, as per Open Space District rules. Leashes aren't required on the fire roads, but bikes are also allowed on these trails, so be careful.

In the spring the place is verdant, lush, and full of wildflowers. That's our favorite time to visit. And unlike so many Bay Area locales, fall provides some real, live autumn colors, thanks to the maples here. When I'm missing the change of seasons, Baltimore Canyon beckons. On crisp, dewy mornings, I'm tempted to belt out the *Hairspray!* tune "Good Morning Baltimore," but for Jake's sake, I refrain.

From this Open Space you have good access to a lot of fire roads through the ridges connecting with Mt. Tamalpais (remember, though—no dogs at Mt. Tam State Park trails) and water-district lands.

Exit U.S. 101 at Paradise/Tamalpais Drive, and go west on Tamalpais Drive for about 0.8 mile. At the stop sign for Magnolia Avenue, turn right, and drive 0.6 mile. Turn left onto Madrone Avenue, just past the Lark Creek Inn. The road will be narrow and will eventually turn into Valley Way. In 0.8 mile, you'll find a small turnaround at the end of the road. Park only at the white-outlined roadside spaces, about 30 feet from the trailhead. 415/499-6387.

30 Blithedale Summit Open Space Preserve
🐾🐾🐾🐾🐕 (See Marin County map on page 138)

The access point at the end of Madrone Avenue—the north end of this Open Space—is a delightful walk in hot weather, through cool redwoods that let some light filter through. This isn't one of those really dark, drippy canyons; you're at a medium-high altitude on the slopes of Mt. Tamalpais. The trail follows Larkspur Creek, which retains some pools in summer. Cross the foot-bridge and follow the slightly rough foot trail. Unfortunately, leashes are now the law on these trails, but you can let your dog off his leash once you hit the fire road.

The drive up narrow Madrone Avenue is an adventure in itself; redwoods grow right in the street. According to a sign at the entrance, the part of this space belonging to the city of Larkspur requires dogs to be leashed. 415/499-6387.

31 Canine Commons
🐾🐾🐾🐕 (See Marin County map on page 138)

Canine Commons is popular with common canines. It isn't a very big dog park, but it was the first in Marin, opening its doggy gates in 1989. That's ancient history in the annals of dog parkdom. It's a basic dog park, with water, poop bags, and tennis balls.

Canine Commons is set within Piper Park, where you can play or watch softball, volleyball, tennis, and even cricket. Outside Canine Commons, dogs must be leashed. The park is between Doherty Drive and Corte Madera Creek. Canine Commons is at the west end of the park. 415/927-5110.

PLACES TO EAT

The Left Bank: Your dog doesn't have to be a poodle to enjoy dining at this terrific French restaurant. Because it's a French place, management knows that dogs and restaurants really do mix. But because they're in America, they have to abide by local health regulations and keep doggies from dining inside. That's OK, though, because there are plenty of outside tables. When it's crowded, managers ask that you tie your dog to the railing that surrounds the outdoor area. You can still dine right beside your pooch. Thirsty pooches can get a bowl of water. 507 Magnolia Avenue; 415/927-3331.

Table Cafe: You'd never guess such an amazing restaurant (formerly Tabla Cafe, until an upscale Manhattan restaurant with the same name threatened a lawsuit) could be tucked away in a shopping center known for its hardware store. But here it is. Table Cafe's food is extremely delicious, organic, and mostly locally grown or raised. The cuisine is best described as California-India fusion. Table is known for its *dosa*, a kind of Indian crepe filled with your choice of flavorful ingredients. Dogs are welcome to join you at the umbrella-topped outdoor tables. 1167 Magnolia Avenue; 415/461-6787.

Bolinas

Bolinas is famous for trying to hide from curious visitors—thereby drawing hordes of them. They keep coming, even though town citizens regularly take down the turnoff sign on Highway 1. So if you're coming from the east (San Francisco area), turn left at the unmarked road where Bolinas Lagoon ends. If you're coming from the west, turn right where the lagoon begins. Don't worry—if you succeed in finding the place, people are friendly.

Sometimes it seems as if half the inhabitants of Bolinas are dogs, most of them black. They stand guard outside bars, curl at shop owners' feet, snooze in the middle of the road. You'll find no city hall in Bolinas, an unincorporated area, and no chamber of commerce. Dogs are always welcome here, but cars, horses, bicycles, and too many unleashed dogs compete for space. Be thoughtful and keep your pooch leashed in town.

PARKS, BEACHES, AND RECREATION AREAS

Alas, dogs are no longer officially allowed on beautiful Agate Beach.

32 Bolinas Beach

🐾🐾🐾 🐕 (See Marin County map on page 138)

At the end of the main street, Wharf Road, is a sand-and-pebble beach at the foot of a bluff. Dogs are free to run off leash. But watch for horses—with riders and without—thundering past without warning. It's animal anarchy here, and it's not the cleanest beach in Marin. We give it points for fun, though. 415/499-6387.

PLACES TO EAT

Coast Cafe: This is a very dog-friendly spot for breakfast, lunch, dinner, beer, wine, and ice cream. "Dogs are great!" has been the mantra of more than one waiter we've met here through the years. Dogs can dine with you at the street tables and sometimes the patio tables (ask first). A bowl of water is available on request, and in the morning, a coffee kiosk sells dog biscuits. Yum! 46 Wharf Road; 415/868-2298.

PLACES TO STAY

Ocean Song Retreat: Welcome to dog heaven. Your stay at this enchanting 1924 Craftsman-style cottage includes no worries about doggy in-and-out privileges: The cottage is set on a beautiful and completely fenced acre. Your dog will be safe from traffic as you enjoy the scenic seaside country life. The property overlooks the ocean. It's vastly relaxing, especially if you take advantage of the cottage's full spa, which comes with a sauna (an unbelievably cute little free-standing structure), hot tub, and cold plunge. Yes, a full spa right in your own backyard! Want a massage? Just call Creta, the cottage's dog-loving owner, and she'll arrange one. Don't feel like cooking in the cottage's kitchen or going out? Just call Creta again, and she'll make sure you get the catered meal of your dreams.

Creta has thought of everything that a dog or a dog's person could want in a getaway. She'll even give you access to a canine agility field/playground, right next door. And your dog will know he's in dog heaven when he samples the treats Creta provides. Creta—among her many talents—is a dog-treat baker. She owns the Bolinas Barkery. She knows what dogs like. They like her, they like her treats, they like her style of canine hospitality. And they appreciate the dog bed that comes with the cottage, too. No need for your dog to haul around his own clunker when you stay here. Rates re $250–325. 105 Kate Road 94924; 415/868-2064; www.oceansongretreat.com.

Smiley's Schooner Saloon & Hotel: No, you can't stay at the saloon (much as you might want to after a night of revelry with the fun-loving crowd here—besides, dogs can't go in the saloon, no matter how old they are in dog years). But you can stay with your dog at the Smiley's hotel. It's a very cool, funky, historic place, with rooms that are actually pretty decent for the price. (A friend told me her room was a little musty, but pleasant.) Smiley's really encapsulates the feel of Bolinas.

How old is Smiley's? I'll let a Smiley's ditty tell you: "Before Lincoln was president… Before baseball was a game… Before Jingle Bells was a song… There was Smiley's." Smiley's was established in 1851. That's Gold Rush–old. But don't let that stop you from bringing your laptop: Smiley's has free Wi-Fi. Rates are $100–115. Dogs are $15 extra. 41 Wharf Road 94924; 415/868-1311; www.coastalpost.com/smileys.

Stinson Beach

It's fun to poke around the town of Stinson Beach, which is swarming with surfers and tourists on beautiful days. You'll find a relaxed attitude toward dogs at the outdoor snack-shop tables. Bolinas Lagoon, stretching along Highway 1 between Stinson Beach and Bolinas, is tempting but environmentally fragile, so you should picnic along the water only if your dog is controllable. You'll also be taking a chance with muddy paws in your car. Don't go near Audubon Canyon Ranch, where herons and egrets nest.

PARKS, BEACHES, AND RECREATION AREAS

33 Upton Beach ("Dog Beach")

🐾 🐾 🐾 🐾 (See Marin County map on page 138)

Highway 1 to Stinson and Bolinas is worth the curves you'll negotiate. Don't be in a hurry. On sunny weekends, traffic will be heavy. Try it on a foggy day—it's otherworldly. Anyway, dogs often don't care whether or not the sun is shining.

The Stinson Beach area abounds with happy dogs, but the part of the beach that's run by the National Park Service bans the critters. They're allowed only at the picnic areas and parking lot there. Ooh, fun!

Fortunately, Upton Beach, the county-managed stretch of beach where private houses are built at the north end, does allow dogs on leash. This is itself a bit of a contradiction, because as you walk along with your obediently leashed dog, dogs who live in the houses lining the county stretch, and who don't have to wear leashes, come prancing out like the local law enforcement to check out the new kid.

Take the beach turnoff from Highway 1. Turn right at the parking lot and park at the far north end. Walk right by the sign that says, "No Pets on Beach"—you can't avoid it—and turn right. Where the houses start is the county beach. You'll see a sign dividing the two jurisdictions saying, "End of Guarded Beach." 415/507-4045.

PLACES TO EAT

Parkside: Dogs love dining at the patio tables with their people. The atmosphere is relaxed and thoroughly enjoyable. The food is tasty American-California cuisine. Sure, you can get yummy burgers and salads, but items like oven-roasted lemon-thyme polenta share the menu, and will make you glad you drove the extra distance to get here. *The San Francisco Chronicle* once wrote that Parkside's food "is some of the best in all of coastal Marin and Sonoma counties." 43 Arsenal Avenue; 415/868-1272.

PLACES TO STAY

Redwoods Haus Bed and Breakfast: It's hard to categorize this place. It's funky, it's a little odd, it's clean, it's super-friendly, it's comfy, and it's cheap compared to most other West Marin lodgings. A very masculine boxer friend of Jake (a boxer dog, not the Muhammad Ali variety) stayed in what's called The Pink Room. With its pink bedspread, pink floral curtains, pink lamp, and other pink decorative touches and white girly furniture, it looks rather dollhouse-y. He didn't mind a bit, mostly because his people promised not to let anyone know that he stayed there. "Fergus would be so embarrassed," says Denise, his person. (Oops... Sorry, Fergus.)

Jake's favorite of the four guest rooms is The Crows Nest, which has soft but more masculine hues than The Pink Room and sports excellent ocean views. It's the biggest room, too, with a queen-size bed, a day bed, and a queen-size futon.

Here's an example of the funky nature of the Redwoods Haus: "All rooms come with... access to our piano, acoustic guitars, video library, charcoal barbecue, biergarten, and buffet area," its literature announces. That's quite a combination of amenities. It continues, "Cats are OK—purrr. Dogs are OK—wooof."

Rooms come with breakfast. It's not gourmet, but with eggs, ham, cereal, fruit, bread, and beverages, it hits the spot. Rates are $55–165. The Redwood Haus is at 1 Belvedere Street (at Highway 1) 94970; 415/868-9828; www .stinson-beach.com.

Mill Valley

PARKS, BEACHES, AND RECREATION AREAS

34 Mount Tamalpais State Park

😺😺😺 (See Marin County map on page 138)

Generally, dogs are restricted to paved roads here. But dogs may stay in the campground, and there are also a few spots near the summit where you can take your dog (via the Marin Municipal Water District lands). The views from here are something you'll certainly appreciate on a clear day.

Stop for lunch at the Bootjack Picnic Area, west of the Mountain Home Inn on Panoramic Highway and about a quarter mile east of the turnoff to the summit, Pan Toll Road. The tables are attractively sited on the hillside under oak trees. The nearby Old Stage Fire Road is a water district road going almost the whole distance to the summit. You can also enter the Old Stage Fire Road right across from the Pan Toll Ranger Station, at the intersection of Panoramic Highway and Pan Toll Road. Pooches have special permission to cross the 100 feet or so of state park trail approaching water district trail.

The Bootjack Picnic Area parking lot charges $8 to park. (Once you pay in any state park lot, your receipt is good for any other spot you hit that day.) The park has 16 developed walk-in campsites that allow dogs. They're at the Pan Toll Station Campground. Sites are $25. All sites are first-come, first-served. 415/388-2070.

35 Mount Tamalpais Summit
😺 😺 😺 (See Marin County map on page 138)

The summit of Mt. Tam is worth the $6 fee that you're charged merely to drive here. But in addition to appreciating the magnificent views, you may also take your dog on one trail up here.

You'll find a small refreshment stand, restrooms, a visitors center, and viewing platforms. On clear days, you can see nine counties, whether you want to or not. In summer, white fingers of fog obscure a good part of your view as they creep between the "knuckles" of Marin's ridges.

It's too bad if your leashed dog doesn't care about views. But he will take eagerly to the smoothly paved Verna Dunshee Trail, about one mile long, running almost level around the summit. About three-quarters of this trail is also wheelchair-accessible.

From U.S. 101, take the Stinson Beach/Highway 1 exit. Follow Highway 1 to Panoramic Highway, which will be a right turn. Continue on Panoramic to the right turnoff to Pantoll Road; Pantoll soon becomes East Ridgecrest Road and goes to the summit, and then loops back for your trip down. 415/945-1455 or 415/388-2070.

36 Mount Tamalpais–Marin Municipal Water District Land
😺 😺 😺 (See Marin County map on page 138)

Your very best bet for a dog walk high on the mountain is to find one of the water district fire roads near the summit. Your dog must be leashed, but at least she can go on the trails with you, and you both can experience the greenness of this wonderful mountain. At this elevation, the green comes from chaparral, pine, and madrone.

Just below the summit on East Ridgecrest Boulevard, watch for the water district's gate and sign. This is the Old Railroad Grade Fire Road, which descends 1,785 feet from the entry point just west of the summit. On the way it intersects Old Stage Fire Road, then emerges at the Bootjack Picnic Area. En route, you'll cross three creeks. For obvious reasons, you'll be happier in warm weather taking this road down, not up; get someone to meet you in a car at the Bootjack Picnic Area.

Another spot to pick up a water district trail is off Panoramic Highway just west of the Mountain Home Inn. Look for the Marin Municipal Water District sign by the fire station. Park at the state park parking lot west of Mountain Home Inn and walk east along this fire road, called Gravity Car Road (though it's unmarked), through mixed pines, redwoods, fir, madrone, and scrub. Keep your eyes open for fast-moving mountain bikes. 415/945-1400.

37 Old Mill Park

😺😺😺 (See Marin County map on page 138)

Refresh your dog under cool redwoods right in the town of Mill Valley. The old mill, built in 1834, has been beautifully restored. A wooden bridge over Old Mill Creek leads to well-maintained paths that run along the creek. The creek is dog-accessible, though pooches are supposed to be leashed.

One picnic table here sits within the hugest "fairy ring" we've ever seen—40 feet across. Boy dogs like to imagine the size of the mother tree whose stump engendered this ring of saplings. The park is on Throckmorton Avenue at Olive Street, near the public library. 415/383-1370.

38 Camino Alto Open Space Preserve

😺😺😺🐕 (See Marin County map on page 138)

In this accessible Open Space, your dog may run free on a wide fire trail along a ridge connecting with Mt. Tamalpais. You'll walk through bay laurels, madrones, and chaparral, looking down on soaring vultures and the bay, Highway 1, the hills, and the Headlands. A small imperfection is that you can hear the whoosh of traffic. Just pretend it's the wind. Dogs must be leashed on the regular hiking trails here. Park at the end of Escalon Drive, just west of Camino Alto. 415/499-6387.

39 Bayfront Park

😺😺😺😺🐕 (See Marin County map on page 138)

This good-looking park is well designed for every kind of family activity and for dogs. It has an exercise course, lawns are green and silky, and picnic areas are clean and attractive. The multiuse trails for bicycles, strollers, and whatnot may be used only by leashed dogs (there are bikes galore). But here's the canine payoff: It has a special dog run next to an estuary, where dogs are free to dip their paws. (Tioga, the dog of my freelance editor and researcher Caroline Grannan, learned to swim here. Or rather, she discovered swimming, because, as Caroline says, with labs like Tioga, there's really no learning curve for the dog paddle. It's instantaneous. In the other camp was my old Airedale, Joe, who lived for 13 years and never got the hang of staying afloat, poor beast.)

The dog-use area starts where you see the signs and all the other dogs. Beware, owners of escape artists: The area is a big three acres, but it's not fenced. No scoops or water are furnished, but the Richardson Bay Estuary is right there to jump into.

At the end of the run there's even a marsh that dogs can explore, if you're willing to put a very mucky friend back into the car with you. Luckily, this marsh is all relatively clean muck (oxymoron alert!), free from the dangerous trash that fills many unprotected bay marshes.

For a dog park, this one offers an unparalleled view of Mt. Tam. Horses and bikes pass by harmlessly on their own separate trail in the foreground, and mockingbirds sing in the bushes.

The parking lot is on Sycamore Avenue, just after you cross Camino Alto, next to the wastewater treatment plant. Keep your dog leashed near the steep-sided sewage ponds; dogs have drowned in them. Also, be sure to keep your dog leashed until you've reached the grassy dog-run area; there's a fine if you're caught unleashed. 415/383-1370.

PLACES TO EAT

Balboa Cafe: As with so many PlumpJack properties, this classic American bistro is very welcoming to dogs who want to take their good people out for a meal. Thirsty dogs get water, hungry people get things like blackened Scottish salmon and the Balboa's killer "classic" burger with housemade pickles. Your dog can bring you to the alfresco dining for these treats. 38 Miller Avenue; 415/381-7321.

Champagne French Bakery: Ooh la la! How great that dogs get to tiptoe through the restaurant to the sunny back brick patio and sit with you while you enjoy the perfect croissant and fresh OJ, or any of the other goodies they have here. Jake is becoming smitten with the French and their dog-friendly ways. We discovered this gem when my daughter was volunteering as an usher at the Mill Valley Film Festival, a couple of doors up. *Tres* convenient! 41 Throckmorton; 415/380-0410.

The Depot: This combo bookstore and café has a wonderful brick patio with tables galore, nice white umbrellas for shade, and a decent selection of coffees, sandwiches, and desserts. As I type this, I'm sipping on a watermelon Italian soda, and a dog–not mine, his name is Ozzie–has decided to curl up at my feet. He likes me! Oh wait, it's the crumbs from my lemon cake he's after. Fine. 87 Throckmorton Avenue; 415/383-2665.

Mama's Royal Cafe: It's kitschy, it's divey, it's fun, and it's super dog friendly. Oh, and the food is fabulous too. The breakfasts are out of this world, and the crepes are to drool for. As for dogs, "We LOVE dogs here!" exclaimed a server. How much do they love dogs? "Sometimes we'll give them a little piece of bacon. And we always give them water." Dine with your dog at the umbrella-topped patio tables. The patio is next to the parking lot, but you'll hardly notice. Weekend brunch time can be very busy, but there's often live piano music to help pass the wait. 393 Miller Avenue; 415/388-3261.

PLACES TO STAY

Acqua Hotel: It's water, water everywhere here, including the view from all 49 guest rooms. Some more limited than others in their view, but there's water out there somewhere. If you like H2O, soak in your tub, gaze at Richardson Bay, let your dog drink from the hotel-provided dog bowl (or the toilet, as Jake is prone to doing). If mountains are more your thing, Mount Tamalpais towers in the background in the other direction from the bay. Go take a leashed hike and discover some of the best views in the Bay Area.

All rooms at this Joie de Vivre property have little fridges, LCD TVs, down comforters, and plush robes. Dogs don't fit in the robes very well, but what do they care? Canine guests get use of very comfy dog beds, as well as food and water bowls. Treats and toys also come with their stay. Lucky dogs! Dogs must stay on the first floor, which makes it easy to unwater them. Rates are $129–299. 555 Redwood Highway 94941; 415/380-0400 or 888/662-9555; www.jdvhotels.com.

Larkspur Hotel: Set on the edge of nature, this former Holiday Inn is a good place to go with a pooch who likes to go for hikes. The rooms are attractive and comfortable. Rates are $119–215. Dogs pay a $75 fee for the length of their stay, so you might want to stay a few days to get your money's worth. 160 Shoreline Highway 94941; 415/332-5700; www.larkspurhotels.com.

Corte Madera

Dogs are still banned from all parks here. Will it ever change? "Not that I can see," a city employee tells us. "When people picnic in the park, they don't want to be where dogs have been doing their… you know." Yes, I know. Dogs do doo these things. And people clean them up. But it's not my battle.

PLACES TO EAT

Book Passage Cafe: Whether your dog is illiterate or erudite, he's welcome to join you at the many shaded tables outside this bookstore/café. You can dine on sandwiches, muffins, and a few assorted hot entrées, as well as tasty coffees and healthful smoothies. Dogs aren't allowed inside the bookstore, so if you want to peruse (and who wouldn't—the bookstore is one of the best we've seen), bring a friend and take turns dog-sitting. 51 Tamal Vista Boulevard; 415/927-1503.

Twin Cities Market: Pick up a fresh deli sandwich (with your dog's favorite cold cuts, of course) and eat it with your pooch at the three tables outside. It's casual, but that's how most dogs like it. 118 Corte Madera Avenue; 415/924-7372.

PLACES TO STAY

Marin Suites Hotel: The guest accommodations here are mostly of the spacious suite variety, which works out great when traveling with a dog. You'll get a fully equipped kitchen and separate living room and bedroom. Traditional hotel rooms, with kitchenettes, are also available. Rates are $79–209. Dogs are

$30 extra. 45 Tamal Vista Boulevard 94925; 415/924-3608 or 800/362-3372; www.marinsuites.com.

Tiburon

The "downtown" area of this beautiful sailing village feels like something out of the Florida Keys. It's upscale, but down to earth. Tourists, the well-heeled, the very casual, and an occasional pirate-lookalike mingle here beautifully. There's something for everyone, including dogs who love boats. (See Diversion.)

PARKS, BEACHES, AND RECREATION AREAS

40 Richardson Bay Lineal Park

🐾🐾🐾 (See Marin County map on page 138)

Generally known as the Tiburon Bike Path (and certainly rarely referred to with the odd "Lineal" in its name), this is a terrific multiuse park, unusual because it can be safely enjoyed by both bicyclists and dogs. It stretches two-thirds the length of Tiburon's peninsula and has parking at both ends. The larger lot is at the northern end. A dirt road, Brunini Way (no vehicles), leads into the park at the north end. You'll find a quiet, natural bay shoreline with a bit of marsh. There's some flotsam and jetsam, but only the highest quality, of course.

Keep walking and you'll enter McKegney Green, the wide bike path that runs for two miles along Tiburon Boulevard toward downtown. (It doesn't go all the way, though.) Your dog must be leashed. The path, marked for running trainers, swings past benches overlooking the bay and a kids' jungle gym.

Soon the path splits and goes past both sides of a stretch of soccer fields,

DIVERSION

Make Your Dog Ferry Happy: Dogs aren't allowed to set paw on Angel Island, but they can do something many would consider just as much fun. Dogs are extremely welcome to join their people on the short ferry ride to the island and back, aboard the **Angel Island-Tiburon Ferry.** Dogs just have to promise to stay on the boat while the ferry drops off passengers on the island. The ride embarks from beautiful downtown Tiburon, and takes about 10 minutes each way, plus some time at the island. Dogs thrill to the scents of the salty bay, and people swoon at the sights. You'll get a great view of the Golden Gate Bridge, sweeping vistas of San Francisco, and, of course, of Angel Island.

Captain Maggie McDonogh, fourth generation captain of this gem of a ferry service, loves dogs. Her ferries are the only ones on the bay that welcome dogs on a regular basis. "Dogs are family too! They love coming with us, and we love having them!" she says. The round-trip costs only $5 for humans. Dogs go for free. This is an unbelievable deal. These days, $5 can't even get you half a movie ticket! Take advantage, and take the ride. You will love it, your dog will thank you for it, and you'll get some great photos to boot. When you get to the ferry dock, tell the ticket seller you want a "stay-aboard" fare. You don't have to bring a dog to take advantage of the $5 deal, but you, being the proud owner of this book, will certainly not leave yours behind.

If a half-hour on a ferry just isn't enough, or if you want to be on San Francisco Bay at a very special time of day, you'll be happy to know that dogs are also invited to join their people for a Sunset Cruise. Pack some wine and a picnic, and watch the sun set over the Golden Gate Bridge or into the fog. Even if you never see the sun at all, it's 1.5 hours you're not likely to forget, nor will your dog. Jake has been a few times, and his nose always quivers with excitement, and he always gets loads of love from fellow passengers.

The sunset cruises run Friday and Saturday evenings, May through October. Adults are $20, children 6–12 are $10, ages 3–4 are $5, and dogs are free. Good dogs! Check the website for the Angel Island schedule. Reservations are recommended for the Sunset Cruise. Phone 415/235-4121, or go to the website: www.angelislandferry. com. The ferry dock and office is at 21 Main Street. (Full disclosure: My husband, Craig Hanson, occasionally works as a fill-in captain for the ferry. But I'd rave about its dog-friendliness even if he'd never heard of Capt. Maggie. The thing is that I would probably not know of this deal if it weren't for him. This was insider stuff, but not any more!)

fenced wildlife ponds (no dogs), and a parcourse fitness trail. You can take your dog on either side, but be aware that bicyclists use both. You'll also share this path, on a fair weekend day, with roller skaters and parents pushing strollers. On the green are sunbathers and kite fliers.

The view: Mt. Tamalpais and Belvedere, with the Bay Bridge, San Francisco, and the Golden Gate Bridge peeking out from behind. Bring a jacket—it can be breezy here—and carry water for your dog if you're walking far. The only fountains are for people. Going toward town on Tiburon Boulevard, turn right at the sign that says Blackie's Pasture Road. It leads to the parking lot. 415/435-7373.

PLACES TO EAT

New Morning Cafe: Breakfast is definitely a favorite at this fun eatery, where outdoor tables provide great people watching, and dogs inevitably get pats from those people they're watching. It's a dog-friendly place, and there's always water for the asking. If you're hungry and want to be a bit decadent, I'd recommend the eggs Benedict. Wow, they are good. Jake recommends dropping just a bit on the ground "by accident" if you're with your dog. He's always thinking of others, that dog. 1696 Tiburon Boulevard; 415/435-4315.

Paradise Hamburgers and Ice Cream: This place furnishes bike racks and lots of outdoor tables. There's always a Fido bowl of water outside the door. The owners adore dogs and occasionally give a pooch a special treat. 1694 Tiburon Boulevard; 415/435-8823.

Tiburon Grill: This lovely restaurant is all about grilled foods. Dogs like to be all about grilled foods. It's a match made in heaven. Dine with your dog at the attractive patio dining areas. The Grill is part of the dog-friendly Lodge at Tiburon (see below). 1651 Tiburon Boulevars; 415/435-5996.

PLACES TO STAY

The Lodge at Tiburon: I've passed by here many times on my way to accompany my captain husband on one of the ferry runs he does occasionally for the Angel Island Ferry. (See Diversion.) And I've always sighed and thought how lovely it would be if 1) I could spend a night or two here and 2) the hotel allowed dogs. Well, Part 1 hasn't happened yet, but Part 2 is a reality! I stopped by one day and asked if they allow dogs, and a most enthusiastic clerk told me, "Of course! We love dogs!" Then he looked down at Jake, and dropped the "S" bomb. "But his size may be too big." Well! Fine! Dog size-ism needs to stop. The best dog guests, in my opinion, tend to be bigger dogs. But I didn't get on my soapbox. The size limit here is 65 pounds. Ninety-something-pound Jake would not pass, even if he sucked in his gut all the way, no matter how big my soapbox.

For dogs who do pass the size test, this upscale, California-Craftsman-style lodge is an exquisite place to stay. The rooms are super attractive, peaceful, and comfortable, there's free Wi-Fi, and the pool is an unusual but welcome feature in this neck of the woods. Dogs are invited to join you at the outdoor areas of the lodge, including the poolside fire pit (no dogs in the pool, not even a paw, please) and the sky deck with its radiant fireplace. Rates are $149–279. Dogs pay a $75 cleaning fee per visit, and must stay in ground-floor rooms. 1651 Tiburon Boulevard 94920; 415/435-3133 or 877/411-3436; www.larkspur hotels.com/collection/tiburon.

Muir Beach

PARKS, BEACHES, AND RECREATION AREAS

41 Muir Beach
😸😸😸😸 🐕 (See Marin County map on page 138)

This beach is small, but a real gem, with rugged sand dunes spotted with plants, a parking lot and large picnic area, a small lagoon with tules, and its share of wind. Redwood Creek empties into the ocean here. Dogs are once again allowed off-leash here, which is as it should be.

You can reach Muir Beach via Highway 1. From Highway 1, watch for the turnoff for the beach. 415/388-2596.

Sausalito

Even if you live here, you should play tourist and stroll around Sausalito's harbor in the brilliant sea light (or luminous sea fog). On weekends, it's especially pleasant early in the day, before the ferries disgorge their passengers. The city's attitude toward dogs is relaxed. It's the perfect place to stop and sniff around for awhile.

PARKS, BEACHES, AND RECREATION AREAS

42 Remington Dog Park
😸😸😸😸 🐕 (See Marin County map on page 138)

Your leash-free dog can exercise his paws while you both exercise your social skills at this delightful park. Remington Park is named after the dog whose owner, Dianne Chute, helped raise the money to put the park together a few years back. It's more than an acre, all fenced, on a grassy slope with trees. Dogs have the time of their lives tearing around chasing each other, and humans have a great time chatting. The park comes complete with an informative bulletin board, a leash rack, benches, poop bags, and water. It even has a tent you can hide under in foul weather! Everything is cozy here.

Best of all, on Friday evening, about 100 human patrons and their dogs gather for cocktail hour, with wine, cheese, bread, and of course, doggy treats.

It sounds very Marin, but it's really just very civilized. On a recent summer evening, the park was host to a Mexican happy hour. Margaritas, chips, and salsa made the atmosphere even more festive than the usual Friday night gathering.

From the day it was finished, Remington and his dog friends have made terrific use of this place. "It's the social hub of Sausalito," said the late cartoonist Phil Frank, "where the elite with four feet meet." What a boon to freedom-loving Sausalito dogs, who otherwise must be leashed almost everywhere in town.

From U.S. 101, take the Sausalito/Marin City exit, driving west to Bridgeway. Turn right on Bridgeway and drive south the equivalent of a long city block. Turn right at Ebbtide Avenue and park in the large lot at the end of Ebbtide.

43 Rodeo Beach and Lagoon

😊😊😊😊🐕 (See Marin County map on page 138)

Yahoo and arroooo! Dogs are once again allowed to be leash-free here, as long as they're under voice control! Jake wags himself into a jiggling mass of happiness whenever we visit and take off his leash. Leashes were the law here for a few years—and may be again in the future—but dogs around the Bay Area are praying against this possibility. Meanwhile, enjoy, and be sure to check out the status of the leash law at www.nps.gov/goga.

Rodeo Beach is small but majestic, made of the dark sand common in Marin. Large rocks on shore are covered with "whitewash," birders' polite name for guano, which is the polite name for bird poo, which is the polite name for something we can't print here. Water dogs enjoy this beach, but letting your dog swim in Marin County surf is always risky—currents are strong, and trying to rescue a dog who is being swept away is to risk your own life. Don't turn your back on the surf here. Especially in winter, a "sneaker" wave can sweep you and your dog away.

If your dog promises not to bark and disturb wildlife, he can join you on an interesting walk around Rodeo Lagoon. The lagoon is lined with tules and pickleweed. Ocean water splashes into the lagoon in winter and rainfall swells it until it overflows, continually mixing saltwater and freshwater. Birds love this fecund lagoon. It can be almost too much for a bird dog to take. An attractive wooden walkway leads across the lagoon to the beach.

Heading north on U.S. 101, take the Alexander Avenue exit (the second exit after crossing the Golden Gate Bridge). Stay to the right on the exit ramp to get onto Alexander Avenue. Turn left on Bunker Road, where you'll see a brown sign for the Marin Headlands Visitor Center. Go through the one-way tunnel and drive about two miles. Turn left onto Field Road to reach the Marin Headlands Visitors Center—follow the signs for Rodeo Beach west from there. You can pick up a good trail map at the Visitors Center, or at the website above. 415/331-1540.

44 Marin Headlands Trails

🐾🐾🐾🐾🐕 (See Marin County map on page 138)

From Rodeo Beach, you can circle the lagoon or head up into the hills, and your well-behaved dog can run naked (leash-free) beside you! You're in for a gorgeous walk—or a gorgeous and challenging walk, depending on the weather. Look at a map of the Bay Area, and it will be obvious why the headlands' trees all grow at an eastward slant. In summer especially, cold ocean air funnels through the Golden Gate, sucked in by the Central Valley's heat—chilling the headlands and the inhabitants of western San Francisco with fog and wind. The Bay Area may be "air-conditioned by God," but the headlands sit right at the air inflow, and it's set on "high." Never come here without at least one jacket.

Your dog will love the wind. The combination of fishy breeze and aromatic brush from the hillsides sends many into olfactory ecstasy. What looks from a distance like green fuzz on these headlands is a profusion of wildflowers and low brush. Indian paintbrush, hemlock, sticky monkeyflower, ferns, dock, morning glory, blackberry, sage, and thousands more species grow here—even some stunted but effective poison oak on the windward sides. (On the lee of the hills, it's not stunted.) Groves of eucalyptus grow on the crests. You hear a lovely low rustle and roar of wind, surf, birds, and insects—and the squeak and groan of eucalyptuses rubbing against each other. Pinch some sage between your fingers and sniff; if you can ever leave California again after that, you're a strong person.

The Golden Gate National Recreation Area (GGNRA), which oversees this 12,000-acre piece of heaven known as the Marin Headlands, permits dogs only on the Coastal Trail and the Miwok Trail these days, and if they're under voice control they can run leash-free. The trails are exquisite for humans and their sidekicks. Sights include the mighty Pacific Ocean, World War II gun emplacements, the Golden Gate Bridge, and San Francisco. As the trail rises and falls, you will discover a blessing: You'll be intermittently sheltered from the wind, and in these pockets, if the sun warms your back, it's pure paradise. (Except for the ticks. This is tick country, so search carefully when you get home.)

The most direct starting point for the dog-friendly trail access, should you not happen to already be at Rodeo Beach, is around the Marin Headlands Visitor Center. Heading north on U.S. 101, take the Alexander Avenue exit (the second exit after crossing the Golden Gate Bridge). Stay to the right on the exit ramp to get onto Alexander Avenue. Turn left on Bunker Road, where you'll see a brown sign for the Marin Headlands Visitor Center. Go through the one-way tunnel and drive about two miles. Turn left onto Field Road. The visitor center will be on the right side of the road, and you'll have access to trail maps, toilets, picnic tables, and other simple pleasures of the hiking life. 415/331-1540.

PLACES TO EAT

Just a few of Sausalito's pooch-friendly restaurants:

Farley Bar: There's nothing like having a wonderful restaurant and bar named after one of the most gracious, kind, talented people you've ever run across. Or actually, after his most famous comic character and comic strip. Phil Frank, the illustrator of this book and all the Dog Lover's Companion books, and syndicated cartoonist extraordinaire, died far too young, of brain caner, in 2007. But he lives on in so many ways, in so many places. His illustrations in my books touch many thousands of dog lovers with each new edition. His spirit lives on through the pages you are holding in your hand.

And Farley Bar, named after his popular reporter character in the eponymous comic strip, pays special homage to Sausalito's most beloved cartoonist. Inside, it looks like a place old-style reporter Farley would love. The seating is rich leather and the ambiance is one of fun sophistication, with a leaning toward the casually quirky. Best of all, it's decorated with photos of Phil, and many of his framed Farley comic strips. Outside, dogs and their people delight in sitting on the restaurant's big porch and dining on some of the Bay Area's best burgers and other really tasty food. Oh, you can get any kind of drink here, too. It's a bar, after all. Farley wouldn't have it any other way.

While you're here with your dog, be sure to raise a toast to Phil. And give your dog an extra scratch behind the ears for him. The restaurant is in the Fort Baker/Cavallo Point part of Sausalito, at 601 Murray Circle; 415/339-4750.

Fish: This fabulous eatery on the Sausalito waterfront is one of the most fun restaurants around. The fish is fresh, the harborside tables are to drool for, and the servers love dogs. Dogs get big bowls of water and samples of dog treats made with salmon! If your dog likes the treats (and she will), you can buy them here. The website is worth checking out: It's www.331fish.com. You can get the latest fish news and local bay and ocean-related activity schedules there, too. You can even click on the "fish.cam" to see what's happening at the restaurant at any given minute. What we especially love about the restaurant's location is that it's next to a dog-friendly point of land at Clipper Yacht Harbor. You'll see the Mutt Mitt dispenser. Dogs enjoy the bay views and the scents and sounds of the nearby harbor seals. The restaurant is at 350 Harbor Drive; 415/331-3474.

Poggio: Care for a side of white-tablecloth romance while your dog sits next to you and pretends not to notice? This casual, fun, top-rated Italian restaurant is just the place for you. The food is great, the people-watching better. During a late-summer visit, I had the sweet-corn, cherry tomato, and fresh mozzarella frittata. It was the second-best frittata I'd ever had, and with my Italian background, I've sampled my fair share. (For the record, the best was my mom's.) 777 Bridgeway; 415/332-7771.

Scoma's: Want fresh salmon and a magnificent view of the bay? Come to this waterfront eatery and dine with your well-behaved dog on the deck. 588 Bridgeway; 415/332-9551.

Tommy's Wok: This fun Chinese restaurant is just a bone's throw from Remington Park, so it's a great place to dine after your dog burns up all his energy. The food is delicious, leaning more toward Szechuan dishes but accommodating Cantonese-loving palates as well. Dine with your good doggy at the four outdoor tables. 3001 Bridgeway; 415/332-5818.

PLACES TO STAY

Cavallo Point–The Lodge at the Golden Gate: This is one of the most amazing spots to spend the night with or without a dog in California. The gorgeously restored historic buildings of Fort Baker, a former U.S. Army post, now house exquisite rooms and suites—many of which welcome canine guests. Most rooms come with to-drool-for views of San Francisco Bay, or even the Golden Gate Bridge. Relax by your fireplace in the hotel-provided organic cotton robe. Stroll the expansive, lush, green grounds (after you've changed back into your clothes, preferably). Enjoy a meal at Farley Bar, named after the popular comic strip of the man who filled this book with its wonderful illustrations.

If you err on the side of modern, you'll wag to know that about half of the rooms here are in non-historic buildings that embody a contemporary style. Whatever your style, dogs are very happy here, and feel most welcome. The dog-friendly rooms include use of a plush bed and pet food bowls. Rates are $265–550. Dogs are $75 per stay. 601 Murray Circle 94965; 415/339-4750 or 888/651-2003; www.cavallopoint.com/lodging.html.

178

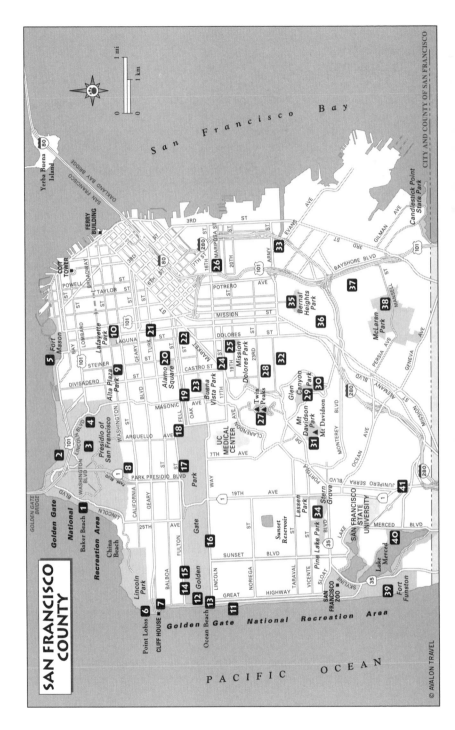

CHAPTER 7

San Francisco County

San Francisco is as beloved by dogs as it is by humans. From the Golden Gate Bridge to Fisherman's Wharf, from the Bay to the Breakers, this is one of the most dog-friendly cities on earth.

Dogs feel right at home here. Look at Jake. He feels incredibly at home here. OK, so San Francisco *is* his home. But even so, this is a city that makes its canine residents and visitors feel very welcome. The finest hotels here permit dogs, as do some of the most popular tourist spots, including Fisherman's Wharf, Pier 39, and the Golden Gate Bridge. Dog-friendly restaurants abound. No public transportation anywhere compares with San Francisco's, where canines can ride cable cars, streetcars, and buses. Dogs can go to a Giants ballgame, attend a Lutheran church every Sunday, and shop at swank stores in posh neighborhoods. They even get their own special evening at a popular brasserie.

PICK OF THE LITTER—
SAN FRANCISCO COUNTY

MOST SPECTACULAR LEASH-FREE PARK
Land's End (page 187)

BEST LEASH-FREE BEACHES
Baker Beach (page 183)
Crissy Field (page 184)
Ocean Beach (page 189)

DOG HEAVEN
Fort Funston (page 205)

MOST DOG-FRIENDLY PLACES TO EAT
Calzone's Pizza Cucina (page 209)
Judy's Cafe (page 210)
Rose's Cafe (page 212)
Zazie (page 214)

MOST BUCOLIC OUTDOOR DINING
Park Chalet Garden Restaurant (page 211)

BEST NIGHT FOR DINING WITH DOG
Mondays at Zazie's "Bring Your Dog to Dinner" Night
(page 214)

BEST B&B SUITE FOR YOUR INNER YOGI
**Broderick Victorian Bed & Breakfast's Penthouse Suite,
with its own circular yoga room** (page 215)

BEST DIGS FOR LITERARY DOGS AND THEIR PEOPLE/
MOST APPROPRIATE DOG-FRIENDLY HOTEL NAME
Hotel Rex (page 219)

HOTEL THAT MAKES DOGS FEEL LIKE SALTY SEA CAPTAINS
Argonaut Hotel (page 214)

BOUTIQUE HOTEL CHAINS THAT GO
THE EXTRA MILE FOR DOGS
Kimpton Hotels
Joie de Vivre Hotels

BEST PLACES TO BUY FINE ATTIRE
Saks Fifth Avenue (page 195)
Wilkes Bashford Company (page 195)

BEST WALK WITH/AS A TOURIST
Golden Gate Bridge walk (page 183)

MOST DOG-FRIENDLY CHURCH
St. Mary & St. Martha Lutheran Church (page 196)

BEST RIDE
San Francisco cable cars (page 207)

BEST DAY TO HAVE A BALL
San Francisco Giants' Dog Days of Summer (page 200)

BEST PLACE TO CATCH GREAT CONCERTS
Stern Grove Festival (page 203)

As for parks where dogs can run leash-free, the City by the Bay is replete with these gems. Some are diamonds, some are cubic zirconia, and a couple aren't worthy of a Cracker Jack box. The city runs about two dozen leash-free areas, known here as Dog Play Areas (DPAs). Golden Gate National Recreation Area (GGNRA) is in charge of such beauties as Fort Funston (Dog Heaven), Crissy Field, and Ocean Beach.

It's been a roller-coaster ride for dog lovers contending with the GGNRA's leashes-on, leashes-off decrees for the last few years, and it isn't necessarily over. At press time, the GGNRA was considering restrictions on dog access to its beaches and parklands, ranging from banning dogs completely to greatly curtailing off-leash areas. Please call ahead or look for signage before throwing your leash to the wind. For updates or to find out what you can do to help retain the leash-free lifestyle, go to the SFDOG website, www.sfdog.org. For official updates, check out the GGNRA's "dog management" page at www.nps.gov/goga/parkmgmt/dog-management.htm. You can also phone the GGNRA dog-policy liaisons at 415/561-4732.

And be sure to check out a terrific, highly informative website of Eco-Dog, a coalition of local dog groups whose goal is to promote the co-existence of responsible off-leash dog recreation with other forms of outdoor recreation. Eco-Dog supports the protection of natural resources, but not to the exclusion of our four-legged friends. Visit www.eco-dog.org to get updates on the GGNRA situation, and to find out ways you can help protect these and other lands for future generations of humans *and* dogs.

San Francisco

San Francisco is the only city in San Francisco County. When you have a city like this, who could ask for anything more?

PARKS, BEACHES, AND RECREATION AREAS

Dogs are allowed on-leash in any San Francisco park, and off-leash in portions of a whopping 24 city-run parks. The off-leash segments of these parks are known as Dog Play Areas and are often marked by brown signs. Many are being upgraded with poop-bag dispensers and triple-decker water fountains. This is a huge improvement from a few years ago, when many of the dog areas were in danger of closing or being severely restricted. At press time, well-behaved dogs are also allowed to be leash-free on many GGNRA properties, but this could change any time, so be sure to check signs or the GGNRA website, www.nps.gov/goga, before letting your dog run around in the nude. SFDOG's helpful website should also have plenty of updates: www.sfdog.org. So should Eco Dog's: www.eco-dog.org.

You may notice fewer trees and familiar plants in some of San Francisco's most beautiful parks lately. It's not because of blight or urban development. In fact, quite the opposite. It's part of a master plan by the San Francisco Recreation & Parks Natural Areas Program (NAP), which seeks to restore certain park areas to their more "native" habitats to increase biodiversity. I've talked to one volunteer who says they're turning the clock back about 150 years. Hey, why not go all the way and take it back 28 million years? Just add water (the Pacific Ocean, to be precise) and voila! A truly natural, native habitat, and lots of happy ancient aquatic life. I'm just sayin'! (OK, I admit NAP's desire for biodiversity is commendable, but it slays me to see trees being cut down for this. Jake, who has a vested interest in all things arboreal, agrees. For an official look at the program, go here: www.sfnap.org.)

❶ Baker Beach

🐾🐾🐾🐾 ⚞ (See San Francisco County map on page 178)

This beach brings your dog almost within a bone's throw of the Golden Gate Bridge. And what a sight it is. Though in summer you shouldn't hold out much hope for a sunny day here, this sandy shoreline is ideal for a romp in the misty air. And dogs really appreciate Baker Beach in the summer. It's almost always cool and breezy.

If you like to sunbathe without a bathing suit and want to take your dog

DIVERSION

Saunter Across the Golden Gate: Like their people, dogs are thrilled to walk San Francisco's most famous landmark, spanning 1.9 miles from the city to Marin County. It's open 5 A.M.–6 P.M. daily to human and canine pedestrians, no fee.

The **Golden Gate Bridge** folks ask only that 1) if your dog can't contain his excitement over the views, you *please* pick up his poop (even if he's not so keen on the scenery and does his number, you'll need to scoop); and 2) your dog wear a leash. You both probably will want to wear sweaters, too—it can be a little nippy when making your way across.

Joe never had a problem walking on the bridge, but Jake won't set paw on it. As soon as he gets near the free span, he starts trembling, turning around to almost tiptoe his way back to the part of the walkway that's on terra firma. I think the slight vibration from the cars makes his 95-pound body very shaky. We've only tried it twice, but that's enough torture for one dog. Driving is the only way he's doing the bridge from now on.

You'll find vista points with parking lots on the northeast (Marin County) and southeast (San Francisco) sides of the bridge. These are the best embarkation points for your walk. For more info, call 415/921-5858.

along, the very north end of the beach (closest to the bridge) is perfect. It's the only official nude beach in Northern California where dogs are welcome. (It's also the part of the beach that allows dogs to be leash-free. Go figure.) Just make sure your dog doesn't get too up close and personal with exposed cobathers. Jake had cause to sniff out an interesting stick during a walk not long ago, and ended up sniffing out a man's bare tush too. Fortunately the owner of the tush took it in stride and told me that dogs seem to be drawn to him. I leashed Jake and walked away, red-faced, not sure how to respond beyond another apology while looking at an invisible object far in the distance. (The usual reply I give people who are flattered by Jake's attention, "Dogs know good people when they see them," seemed just plain wrong in this situation.)

The south end (of the beach) is also intriguing, with trails meandering through wooded areas and lots of picnic tables for leisurely lunches. Battery Chamberlain, with its 95,000-pound cannon aimed toward the sea, looms nearby.

From either direction, take Lincoln Boulevard to Bowley Street, and then make the first turn into the two parking lots. 415/561-4700.

🐾 Crissy Field

🐾🐾🐾🐾🐕 (See San Francisco County map on page 178)

There's nothing quite like Crissy Field at sunset. As the orange sun disappears behind the Golden Gate Bridge, you'll be viewing one of the most stunning blends of natural and man-made wonders in the world.

Crissy Field, part of the Golden Gate National Recreation Area, is a jewel of a park any time of day. Leash-free dogs can chase and cavort up and down the beach and jump into the bay any time of year in the eastern portion of Crissy Field. That's the majority of this area, from about 500 feet east of the Coast Guard station all the way east (away from the Golden Gate Bridge, in case you're from the other coast) to where most people park, and beyond. The far western portion requires leashes most of the year, thanks to our feathered friends, the snowy plovers, who have protected status. Leashes are the law in this Wildlife Protection Area from about July to May. Yes, that's a long time, and it can vary, depending on when the plovers return. Look for signage, or check the official status at www.nps.gov/goga.

Your dog will find the views here are to drool for. As you walk westward, you'll see the Golden Gate Bridge before you, Alcatraz and bits of the city skyline behind you. Sailboats sometimes glide so close you can hear the sails flapping in the wind. A 20-acre marsh lends a satisfying air of swampiness. (For its $25 million price tag, it should lend something.) Keep your dog out of it, by the way.

Enter on Mason Street in the Marina district and drive past the warehouses. Go right on Mitchell Street and through the parking lot. If you go too far east, you may run into a sea of sailboarders. On those days, try starting your walk close to the western edge of the parking lot. 415/561-4700.

🔳 Presidio National Park

🐾 🐾 🐾 🐾 (See San Francisco County map on page 178)

Dogs and their people like to pretend that the Presidio is their very own country estate, complete with acre after rolling acre (1,480 in all!) of secret pathways, open meadows, and dense groves of eucalyptus and pine. It's truly a magnificent spread, and dogs, who must be leashed here these days, love it despite their tethers.

These days, the park is drawing more visitors than ever, but there are still some out-of-the-way areas that even the most adventurous tourists and their dogs will have a difficult time finding. A hike that takes you away from it all starts when you park at the golf course parking lot just inside the Arguello Boulevard gate. Cross the street (carefully—it can get busy on this road) and follow the path down the hill. It will quickly widen and loop past wildflowers and seasonal sweet peas. Bear left at the first major fork and hike through a thick forest area, then bear right when that path gives you a choice. You'll hike up and down a gentle sequence of hills. Pull over and enjoy the larger hills to the west. Dogs thrill at dragging their people up and down them for no apparent reason. You'll run into a few more side trails along the way.

A slightly more tame walk starts to the west of Julius Kahn Playground on West Pacific Avenue. Again enter on Arguello, but immediately bear right. Parking will be on your right on the bottom of the hill. Cross the street and you'll see a plastic-bag dispenser for scooping the poop. Begin here and follow any number of paths.

The area near the park's Lombard Street entrance makes for a fun stroll in a more manicured setting. This is where you'll find Lucas's beautiful Letterman Digital Arts Center and the grassy 23-acre public park he created on the grounds. You and your leashed dog will be wowed by this creation, which includes a man-made stream and large pond, natural California boulders, comfy seating areas, and unbeatable views of the Golden Gate Bridge, the Palace of Fine Arts, and the bay. I have a scavenger hunt mission for you: Find the Yoda fountain. A clue: It's close to one of the buildings. Advice: You might have to ask a guard permission to see it, but it's worth it. Bring a camera. (Thank you to Carol Copsey and her notorious socialite dog, Bella Pearl, for introducing us to this heavenly part of the Presidio.) While in the area, sniff out the center's Perk Presidio Café for a convenient and attractive place to get some coffee and basic eats. 415/561-4947.

🔳 Palace of Fine Arts

🐾 🐾 🐾 (See San Francisco County map on page 178)

The glory of ancient Rome embraces you even as you approach this relic of the 1915 Panama-Pacific Exposition. From the huge colonnaded rotunda to the serene reflecting pool, the place drips with Romanesque splendor.

The Palace is especially grand under its night lighting. It's also an ideal place to take your dog while the kids go to the Exploratorium inside. Walk around the paved path that winds through the grand columns and around the pond.

But keep your eyes peeled for people feeding the multitudes of pigeons, ducks, and geese. Dogs like to break up the feeding frenzy with an abrupt tug on the mandatory leash. Feathers fly and dried bread scatters everywhere.

The best place to enter for the full Roman effect is on Baker Street, between North Point and Jefferson Streets. Dogs are not allowed inside the buildings, although Joe did sneak into the Exploratorium one fine afternoon. (It's a long story.) He got as far as the tornado demonstration machine when he was nabbed and whisked away. 415/831-2700.

🄳 Fort Mason
🐾🐾🐾 (See San Francisco County map on page 178)

This park, perched high above the bay, is full of surprises. Depending on the disposition of your dog, some of the surprises are great fun. One can be downright frightening.

DIVERSION

Give Your Dog the Gift of Horse Heinie: Ahh, there's nothing like a horse-and-carriage ride to make your whole crew happy. People love the steady clip-clop of the trusty equine and the oddly familiar jiggling of the carriage as it parades down beloved tourist areas. And dogs? As I've discussed elsewhere, they're smitten with the scent of horse petard. One of Jake's happiest moments came behind a **Waterfront Carriage Service** horse one cold summer evening. We were with a couple of tourist friends when we saw the horse and carriage in the Fisherman's Wharf area. We decided to hop on for a ride. (Note: "Hop" is a gracious word for what Jake had to do to get up in the carriage.) We were all enjoying a good chat and learning about the history of the area from our friendly driver when the horse slowed down, and ever so discreetly, thanks to a giant poop bag that was attached to him (note to self: must get one for Jake), did his business.

Well you'd have thought Jake had won the doggy lottery. His tail started wagging his body. His nose quivered with joy. His body actually seemed to shake, although for his sake I'll assume it was the carriage's jiggling resuming as the horse picked up the pace again. Even after the ride was over, no matter where we strolled in the area that night, he always seemed to be checking around for his new equine friend.

You can hitch the ride of your dog's life on Embarcadero (street) at Powell Street, around Pier 41, just a couple of blocks to the west of Pier 39, the famous tourist destination. No need for reservations. Just show up after 1 P.M. and look for a horse and buggy in the vicinity. The phone number they provide hasn't led to a real person or recording any time I've tried it, but for the record: 415/771-8687.

The best stands right in the middle of the wide-open field that constitutes the main part of the park. It's a fire hydrant, and it sticks out like a sore yellow thumb from its flat green surroundings. Joyous male dogs bound up and pay it homage time and time again.

The object that seems to take dogs aback, although people find it riveting, is a gigantic bronze statue of Phillip Burton, who helped secure the national park system, including the GGNRA. Several feet taller and broader than life (although even when alive, Burton was larger than life), with outstretched hand, it can send a dog fleeing as far as his mandatory leash will allow.

Lower Fort Mason is also interesting to investigate. You can walk alongside the piers and sniff the bay, or peer at the liberty ship *Jeremiah O'Brien.*

Enter the lower Fort Mason parking lot at Buchanan Street and take the stairs all the way up to upper Fort Mason. (Huff, puff.) Or park along Bay Street or Laguna Street and walk in. 415/556-0560.

6 Land's End

🐾🐾🐾🐾🦮 (See San Francisco County map on page 178)

This is probably the most spectacular park in San Francisco. You won't believe your eyes and your leashed dog won't believe his nose. And neither of you will believe your ears—it's so far removed from traffic that all you hear are foghorns, the calls of birds, and the wind whistling through the pines and eucalyptus. One sound you won't hear if your dog is under voice control is the wind whistling past your leash. As of this writing, dogs can once again be leash-free in this piece of pooch paradise!

The towering cliffs, high above the crashing tide below, overlook virtually no civilization. At times, all you can see are ocean, cliffs, trees, wildflowers, and boats. It looks more like Mendocino did 100 years ago—at least until you round one final bend and the Golden Gate Bridge jars your senses back to semi-urban reality.

There are many entrance points, but we like to start from the parking lot at the end of Camino del Mar. Go down the wooden steps to the wide trail and turn right. As you hike, you'll come to occasional wood benches overlooking wildly beautiful seascapes. Take a moment to sit down. Your dog will appreciate the chance to contemplate the wondrous odors here.

The park service has made many improvements to Land's End in recent years, but despite some serious manicuring, most of it still retains its original wild feel. Some of its features are fun for dogs and people. A very long wooden stairway leads from the main path all the way down to a beautiful rock-strewn beach with great views of the Golden Gate. The trip down is worth the rather rigorous hike back up. Other side trails will take you up hills, down hills, down to the beach, and up to clifftops. Try them all, but keep your eyes peeled for poison oak on the more narrow trails.

A very convenient entry point is at the parking lot on Point Lobos Avenue (which is what Geary Street turns into toward the ocean) just above the Cliff House and Louie's restaurant. But we like to park in the lot at the end of Camino del Mar, a little street just above that lot. You can take the wooden stairs down to a popular path, as described above, or amble along a wide trail that starts on the east end of the parking lot. 415/561-4700.

7 Sutro Heights Park
🐾🐾🐾 (See San Francisco County map on page 178)

This gem of a park set high on a cliff overlooking the Pacific Ocean is bypassed by most tourists. They just whiz by from one San Francisco coastal destination to the next, blissfully unaware that this lush green park houses the ruins of the stately home of former mayor Adolf Sutro, the renaissance man behind the Sutro Baths and other wonders of 1800s San Francisco.

The views of the ocean are spectacular, the Victorian-style gardens sweet, the statue of Diana still revered (with an ever-present scattering of flowers), and the path around the park is a must-visit for dogs who don't mind a little leash time. If you want to burn off steam first, visit Land's End for a leash-free hike. You can park at the lot on the south side of Point Lobos Avenue (what Geary Boulevard turns into when it gets out to the ocean), just up the road from the Cliff House. If that lot is full, the one across the street is a good alternative. For a little more exercise, try entering at the other end, at Balboa and La Playa streets, where you'll hike up a fairly long wooden staircase to the more manicured part of the park. 415/561-4700.

8 Mountain Lake Park
🐾🐾🐾🐕 (See San Francisco County map on page 178)

In this sociable park, your dog can cavort with other dogs while you shoot the breeze with other dog people. The off-leash area is between two signs on the east side of the park. You'll find a bench for humans and a pretty good safety net of trees and grass between dogs and the outside world.

The favorite game among dogs here involves a big green bush. One dog usually starts running around it for no apparent reason. Circle after circle, he'll attract more and more dogs into chasing him until almost every dog is swirling around in a dizzying loop. Watch too closely and you can get seasick.

Dogs find the rest of the park mildly entertaining, although they have to be leashed. The park's namesake lake is little more than a pond. Ducks and a couple of swans live here, and the temptation may be too much for your dog. We've seen dogs drag their owners ankle-deep into the muddy pond in pursuit of a duck dinner. The park is also home to an attractive playground and a decent heart parcourse fitness trail.

To reach the dog-run area, enter on 8th Avenue at Lake Street. 415/831-2700.

9 Alta Plaza Park

(See San Francisco County map on page 178)

Smack in the middle of Pacific Heights, this park is where all the best breeds and most magnificent mutts gather daily. They flock to the hill on the north side of the park and conduct their dog business in the most discriminating fashion. It's not uncommon to see 25 dogs trotting around the park. Owners often address each other by their dogs' names—"Maggie's mom! How are you?"

For a real treat, visit here on the first Sunday of each month, when loads of pugs hold their monthly social gathering. It's a sight you must see at least once in your life. The gathering of pug mugs starts around 2:30 P.M. See www.geocities.com/pugsunday for more details.

The park's off-leash run is actually on the other side of the playground and tennis courts, on the second level up from Clay Street. Bushes line the paved walkway, and it's far enough from traffic that you don't have to worry too much about cars.

The park is bordered by Jackson, Clay, Steiner, and Scott Streets. 415/831-2700.

10 Lafayette Park

(See San Francisco County map on page 178)

This four-square-block park gets lots of dog traffic. The park is hilly and green and studded with palm trees, pines, and well-trimmed bushes. The official dog-run area is near Sacramento Street, between Octavia and Gough streets. As you enter the park from the main Sacramento Street entrance, it's on your right. But most dogs gather atop the hill to the left, around two huge, smelly garbage cans.

The park is bounded by Laguna, Gough, Sacramento, and Washington Streets. 415/831-2700.

11 Ocean Beach

(See San Francisco County map on page 178)

This broad, four-mile-long beach with a crashing surf isn't exactly Palm Beach. It's usually cold and windy and dotted with seaweed, jellyfish, jagged bits of shells, and less savory deposits from the Pacific. In other words, dogs think it's grand.

Ocean Beach is one of those places that's not usually on the radar of tourists. By the time they make it all the way out to this end of the world, they tend to spend their valuable time at the Cliff House or Beach Chalet restaurants. Only on the hottest days will you find a significant number of people here, and by significant I mean a smattering compared with beaches in the southern climes of the state. There's always plenty of room for running around without stepping over a sea of sun worshippers.

This is once again a pretty dog-friendly stretch of sand: Dogs can be off-leash year-round in the more populous section of the beach, from Stairwell 21 (just south of the Beach Chalet) all the way to the northern end of the beach, just below the Cliff House. (Basically Stairwell 1). The other year-round off-leash section goes from Sloat Boulevard south. In between these two areas is what's known as a Snowy Plover Protection Area, and unfortunately dogs are permitted off-leash only between May and July. To me, that sounds like June is the only month of leash-free bliss on this long segment of dune-lined beach, but GGNRA park officials say it varies and can be open to leash-free dogs as early as May. Oh boy, two months! It all depends on where the plover, a threatened bird, is hanging out at that time of year. So look for signs or go to the GGNRA website, www.nps.gov/goga, to get the official word.

You can park along the ocean, between the Cliff House and Balboa Street. Walk south on the sidewalk until you hit the beach. Or park in the spaces between Fulton Street and Lincoln Way. A parking lot is also at Sloat Boulevard, but beach access can be limited because of erosion. 415/561-4700.

12 Golden Gate Park
🐾🐾🐾🐕 (See San Francisco County map on page 178)

This famed city park provides much dog bliss, but only in the places where dogs are supposed to be leashed. Four areas are set aside for leashless dogs, but dogs in the know like to avoid those places, for good reason. The following listings are for both leash and off-leash areas, from west to east, and north to south. For information about any area in the park, call 415/831-2700.

13 Golden Gate Park (Beach Chalet)
🐾🐾 (See San Francisco County map on page 178)

The paths in back of the Beach Chalet (near the soccer fields between the windmills near the ocean) run along the edge of the fields and can be a little unsavory at times, although they're looking better these days. To leashed dogs, they're full of good smells and interesting characters. The dog-friendly Park Chalet restaurant is right here, a perfect place to stop for some tasty chow after a little romp around the park (or vice versa).

This area also includes the hilly, piney area up behind the archery field. We haven't heard of any impalements up there, but be careful.

14 Golden Gate Park Dog Run
🐾🐾🐕 (See San Francisco County map on page 178)

This fenced-in dog exercise area has the dubious distinction of being right next to a field full of buffalo. Some dogs adore the location, especially when the wind is blowing in just the right direction. It's the only fenced-in dog run in the city, so it's really the only game in town for escape artists. But the park's fans aren't just dogs who walk on the wild side. All sizes and shapes of dogs come here for playtime. So many dogs use it that much of it is grassless and dusty.

The place can sometimes get a little rough around the edges when the usual dog crowd isn't around. People who like their dogs tough will occasionally drop in and hang out with something to swig while their dogs strut around. It's not usually a problem, though, especially during the normal dog rush hours (before work and after work for 9-to-5ers, and all day on weekends).

We've found more amorous dogs here than in any other park, so if your dog isn't in the mood (or you don't want her to be), this isn't the place to take her. For some reason, Jake, like dear Joe before him, gets accosted at almost every visit, so it's not one of his favorite places. He's flattered, but he's not that kind of dog.

The Dog Run is at 38th Avenue and Fulton Street. Park on Fulton Street and walk in, or take 36th Avenue into the park and go right at the first paved road. Drive all the way to the end, and there it is.

15 Golden Gate Park (by the Polo Grounds)

😀😀😀 (See San Francisco County map on page 178)

Dogs who enjoy playing Frisbee go to the meadow just east of the polo field. It's known for wide-open dells, good bushes, and plenty of gopher holes for old sports. Leashes are mandatory, if you follow the law. Your best bet here is to come early in the morning. A walk around the dirt track above the grassy Polo Grounds is a favorite of many dogs and their leashed people, and the parcourse around the dirt track (on the other side of the trees and bushes) makes for a fun leashed walk with your furry friend. Jake likes to do the 6-inch-tall log hops but isn't a big fan of jumping jacks.

16 Golden Gate Park (South Side)

😀😀🐕 (See San Francisco County map on page 178)

Two areas set aside for leash-free dogs are slivers along the south end of the park. One is between 2nd and 7th Avenues and bounded on the north and south by Lincoln Way and Martin Luther King Jr. Drive. It's a good length, but it's not terribly wide. The other is on the south side of the polo field, between 34th and 38th avenues and Middle and Martin Luther King Jr. drives. Bring your dog to these sections if he's very good off leash. They're too close to busy traffic for less disciplined dogs.

17 Golden Gate Park (Stow Lake/Strawberry Hill)

😀😀😀 (See San Francisco County map on page 178)

The summit of the man-made mountain at Stow Lake is truly a sniffer's paradise. Dogs who like to look at ducks will also enjoy the lake area. The path winds up Strawberry Hill to a breathtaking 360-degree view of the city.

Unfortunately, dogs are not supposed to be off leash. It's best to avoid this walk on weekends, when bikers and hikers and wee ones are everywhere.

Stow Lake is between 15th and 19th Avenues. From John F. Kennedy or Martin Luther King Jr. Drives, follow the Stow Lake signs.

18 Golden Gate Park (Northeast Corner)
🐾 🐕 (See San Francisco County map on page 178)

Dogs are allowed off-leash on one of the narrow fields at the northeast corner of the park, up by the horseshoe courts. It's a strange little area with hills and dales and dirt paths. Homeless people live here, and some don't keep good house. You'll see the campfire remains, old sleeping bags, and trash of every type. It's best to avoid this place, except in the middle of the day. Enter at Stanyan and Grove Streets.

19 Golden Gate Park (The Panhandle)
🐾 🐾 🐾 (See San Francisco County map on page 178)

That long, thin strip of park that extends eight blocks from the east end of the park to Baker Street is a great hangout for cool dogs. It's got a real Haight-Ashbury influence in parts, and although dogs must be leashed, they love to saunter around visiting other dogs wearing bandannas.

20 Alamo Square Park
🐾 🐾 🐾 🐕 (See San Francisco County map on page 178)

A postcard comes to life in this park for you and your leashed dog. This is where the famed Painted Ladies hold court over the city. These six brightly colored Victorian homes are even better in person than on a postcard.

Walk up the east side of the park, near Steiner Street, to enjoy the view of the old houses with the modern city skyline in the background. (Dogs need to be leashed in this half of the park.) Even if your dog doesn't care about architecture, she'll love the grassy hills that make up this park.

Dogs who like to run around all nudie (sans leash) are joyful these days because the city has given the OK to an official leash-free area on the park's west half. Hooray! (This had been a de facto leash-free area forever. Now it has the city's seal of approval.)

The park is bordered by Fulton, Hayes, Scott, and Steiner Streets. 415/831-2700.

21 Jefferson Square Park
🐾 🐕 (See San Francisco County map on page 178)

It was a toss-up whether to give the tiny off-leash section of this park one paw or two paws, but in the end, Jake's pained look told me that a single paw was our rating. He was badly in need of a leash-free run, and I brought him here thinking he'd get to dash about. But the off-leash section here is so tiny and so close to busy streets that I'd have made even obedient Lassie stay on a leash. The park is attractive enough, with green grass, some trees, and even poop bags, but it doesn't make up for its kibble-sized leash-free area that's dangerously close to traffic. The doggy area is in the northwest corner of this rectangular park, at Eddy and Laguna Streets. 415/831-2700.

22 Duboce Park

🐾🐾🦮 (See San Francisco County map on page 178)

Even before Duboce Park got the official OK to be off-leash a few years ago, it was a leash-free park in practice for ages and is extremely popular with dog people. I still won't take Jake off-leash here, not because I'm some kind of goody-two-shoes but because it's not a big area, and dogs are never more than a few fast steps from the nearest street. Jake isn't quite ready for being off leash here, but the dogs who come here seem to have no problem running free and staying off the streets. The park is at Duboce Avenue between Steiner and Scott Streets. 415/831-2700.

23 Buena Vista Park

🐾🐾🐾🐾🦮 (See San Francisco County map on page 178)

The presence of vagrants who sometimes congregate at the front of the park has scared off lots of would-be park users, but it shouldn't. They're generally a friendly lot, posing no threat to folks exploring the park's upper limits with a dog.

This park is a real find for anyone living near the Haight-Ashbury district. Hike along the myriad dirt and paved trails winding through the hills, enveloped by eucalyptus and redwood trees. Sadly, the San Francisco Natural Areas Program, which seeks to restores parkland to the landscape of 150 years ago, is causing a frightful deforestation on some parts of the hill. But hey, at least the rain gutters beside the paths can stay: Some of them are lined with pieces of tombstone from a nearby cemetery. The cemetery's occupants, who died in the 1800s, were moved to the oh-so-quiet town of Colma. The gutters give the park a historical, haunted feeling.

From the top of the park, you can see the ocean, the bay, the Marin headlands, and both the Golden Gate and Bay bridges. Birds sing everywhere, and there are lots of benches to rest on. Dogs are allowed off leash at the woodsy west side of the park, near Central Street.

A note: Sometimes people meet for assignations at the top of the park. Concealing shrubs and bushes have gotten haircuts of late, but this area is still a "hot spot," so to speak. If this bothers you or your dog, avoid this lovers' lane.

Enter at Buena Vista Avenue West and Central Street, or from Haight Street. 415/831-2700.

🔢 Corona Heights Park/Red Rock Park

🐾🐾🐾🦴 (See San Francisco County map on page 178)

The rust-colored boulders atop this park cast long, surreal shadows at dawn. If you and your dog are early risers, it's worth the hike to the summit to witness this. And there's a fine view any time of day of downtown and the Castro district.

Unfortunately, dogs aren't allowed off leash on hikes up the hill. Until a few years ago, the off-leash area was a roomy square of grass at the foot of the park. The leash-free section has now been made smaller (about 0.75 acre) and is completely fenced. It was a compromise between the dog people and the

DIVERSION

Take Me Out to the Ballgame: Can't make it to the San Francisco Giants' Dog Days of Summer? Try a stroll around the outside of AT&T Park. A wide promenade flanks right field along **McCovey Cove.** At game time, you and the pooch can get a dog's-eye view of the game alongside other nonticketed folks.

Or make a day of it and walk the entire waterfront of San Francisco with your dog from here. Head west along the promenade, which turns into a sidewalk. You'll come to a grassy marina, complete with a poop-bag station. Continuing west, you'll pass the Embarcadero, Fisherman's Wharf, the Marina District, and, finally, beautiful Crissy Field. Keep walking west and you'll be under the Golden Gate Bridge. AT&T Park is at 24 Willie Mays Plaza. Call 415/972-2000 or visit the SF Giants' website: www.sfgiants.com.

DIVERSIONS

These Stores Are for the Dogs! Dogs who enjoy shopping with their people love San Francisco. Following are a few of the more pooch-friendly retail spots for the leashed and well behaved.

Beach Street: This isn't a store but a kind of outdoor tourist market where you can shop for baubles, bangles, and T-shirts with your leashed dog at any of dozens of little stands up and down this Fisherman's Wharf area street. The bulk of the stands on Beach Street are between Hyde and Polk Streets.

Neiman Marcus: Even jaded dogs can be agog when they visit this upscale store's beautiful atrium lobby. 150 Stockton Street; 415/362-3900.

Saks Fifth Avenue: Keep your dog under tight rein and she's welcome here. 384 Post Street; 415/986-4300.

Sports Basement: This doesn't really fit in with the high-end stores on this list, but outdoor-oriented dogs feel very comfortable visiting this fun, hip outdoor gear shop. The location south of Market Street is very dog friendly. (The store near Crissy Field has a no-dogs policy, alas.) The prices are lower than most outdoor outfitters, and you can even get yoga gear, stylin' shoes, and dog accoutrements (including canine backpacks). 1590 Bryant Street; 415/437-0100.

Wilkes Bashford Company: Pooches of any size are welcome to peruse this upscale Union Square store (it's to drool for), as long as they're clean and don't conduct any dog business. "I'm a nut about dogs," says Wilkes Bashford, the store's owner. "Dogs are a vital part of life." And he says all the dogs who've visited his store have been very well behaved. Bashford has been bringing his dogs to the store since 1968. Little Callie goes to work with Bashford just about every day. And even when Bashford is out of town on business, Callie makes her rounds at the store. Bashford's driver takes her there in the morning and drives her home in the afternoon. 375 Sutter Street; 415/986-4380.

folks who like to sunbathe there without getting stomped upon and sniffed at. Because of heavy use, the fenced dog park is no longer grassy, but the surrounding area—leashes mandatory—is lush. (The grass truly is greener on the other side of this fence.)

After a bit of leashless playing, you can don a leash and take your pooch up the hill. Fences keep dogs and people from falling down the steep cliffs and from treading on native habitat. Keep in mind that there's virtually no shade, so if you have a black rug of a dog, think twice about climbing the hill on hot, sunny days.

The park is at Museum Way and Roosevelt Avenue. 415/831-2700.

25 Dolores Park

🐾🐾🐕 (See San Francisco County map on page 178)

You can get a little history lesson while walking your dog here. A statue of Miguel Hidalgo overlooks the park, and Mexico's liberty bell hangs at the Dolores Street entrance.

History may not impress your dog, but a wide-open space for running off leash will. It's behind the tennis courts.

There are two problems with this area, though: 1) It's easy for your dog to

DIVERSION

Go to Church With Your Pooch! (Oh My Dog...): When Jake and I walked into **St. Mary & St. Martha Lutheran Church** in the Mission District one bright Sunday morning, the pastor smiled. None of the parishioners looked askance. The only churchgoers who stared were the other canines. We entered, appropriately enough, to the hymn "All Creatures of our God and King" and sat down in a row of this small, cheerfully colorful church, next to Bruce Engle and his shockingly calm Jack Russell terriers, Einstein and Emma Sue.

This wasn't a special service for pets. Dogs are welcome to go to Sunday services every week. Normally at least four or five dogs attend, but this was Labor Day weekend, and the only canines were Bruce's dogs and Jake. Bruce told me that a man named Alvin usually sits at the back of the church and plies the dogs with bits of turkey when they get restless, but it being a holiday, Alvin was gone, too.

About 10 minutes into the service, Jake started groaning and trying to leave. (No fault of Pastor Ron, who is an animated, kindly man.) To entice Jake to be quiet, I gave him one of the large treats I had brought for backup. It was too hard to break, so I gave it to him whole, and he started crunching away contentedly. It was at that very second—horror of horrors!—that Pastor Ron asked parishioners to pause for a moment of silence. The church went quiet, except for the CRUNCH, slurp, gruffle, CRUNCH that echoed off the tile floors and around the walls. There was nothing to do but pray that the moment of silence or the treat would be finished quickly. Mercifully the "silence" ended just as Jake started Hoovering the crumbs off the floor.

The service continued, and Jake eventually fell asleep on the cool tile floor (praise the Lord). But within a breath of this restful blessed event, Pastor Ron asked us all to rise, and up sprang energetic Jake. After a reading by a parishioner, Jake yawned one of those ridiculously loud, squeaky dog yawns. This drew an amused titter or two, including one from the reader.

The service lasted about an hour, and I'm relieved to report that Jake did very well overall. During communion, jazz pianist Richard run into the road—even if she's the voice control type, she could find herself in Church Street traffic just by running a little too far to catch a ball; and 2) you have to be on the lookout that your dog doesn't run over people who live in the park. Joe once slid into a sleeping homeless woman and scared her so bad she screamed and ran away.

Enter anywhere on Dolores or Church Streets, between 18th and 20th Streets. The off-leash area is south of the tennis courts and north of the soccer field. 415/831-2700.

Daquioag played an uplifting Bill Evans–like tune that would have been equally fitting at a hip café, and Jake thumped his tail almost in time with the beat. Jake did eventually repose on the cool tile floor, he shook paws with a couple of churchgoers when Pastor Ron asked us all to offer each other a handshake of peace, he did no leg-lifts or barks, and he didn't even sneak a scone off the table at the coffee social that happens after each service. (Yes, dogs can join you for an after-service cuppa Joe!)

This is an embracing, friendly place. You don't have to be Lutheran to attend. The church offers shelter to the homeless, and daycare and food programs for the poor. Pastor Ron and Pastor Ed (who was gone that day because of the holiday; he came from another dog-friendly Lutheran church that had to close because of earthquake retrofit financial issues) love dogs and will make you and your well-enough-behaved one feel very welcome here.

You can choose from an English-language service at 10 A.M. or Spanish at 11. The first Sunday of October is the church's blessing of the animals for St. Francis Day. This is a most appropriate place to celebrate it. 1050 South Van Ness Avenue. 415/647-2717.

26 McKinley Square

🐾🐾🐕 (See San Francisco County map on page 178)

The view from this little patch of land is, shall we say, interesting. You can see for miles and miles, and the view includes several other leash-free parks, such as Buena Vista, Corona Heights, Mission Dolores, and Bernal Heights Parks. But you can also see such lovely sights as U.S. 101, with its cars rushing madcap-fashion just a couple of hundred feet down the hill from you. And if you ever craved a view of San Francisco General Hospital's most austere, Dickensian brick buildings, this is the place to come. If you had really long arms, you could almost reach out and touch them. Actually, depending on the direction of the wind, on some days they reach out and touch you—the steam from the hospital's huge chimneys has been known to slip right up to this hilltop park.

Dogs are permitted off leash in the back section of the park, between the playground and the community gardens. Signs will point you in the right direction. It's nothing beautiful, just a wide path with a little running room on a hillside dotted with brush and occasional trees.

The off-leash section is on 20th Street and San Bruno Avenue, just a few blocks from the heart of the Potrero Hill business district. 415/831-2700.

27 Twin Peaks

🐾🐾 (See San Francisco County map on page 178)

So dogs aren't allowed at the Top of the Mark. So what! The view from up here will put all those "No Dogs Allowed" establishments to shame, and it's cheaper to entertain guests up here—it's free, in fact.

The summits of the Twin Peaks are higher than 900 feet. It's usually cold up here, so bundle up. You can drive to the northern peak and park in the lot. It's very touristy, and on this peak, signs tell you what you're looking at—Tiburon, Nob Hill, Mt. Diablo, Japantown, and Mt. Tamalpais. Your dog won't get much exercise, though, since all he can do is walk around the paved viewing area on leash. And frankly, many dogs are bored by the marvelous vistas.

For your dog's sake, try exploring the other peak. It's a bare hill with wooden stairs up one side. While dogs must be on leash, it's not bad exercise. And the view—at almost 20 feet higher than the first peak—is *magnificent.* From here you can see other potential walks for you and your dog on the lower hills, where the views are almost as dynamic and the air is a little warmer. Be sure to keep him on leash, because the road is never far away.

The Twin Peaks are on Twin Peaks Boulevard, just north of Portola Drive. 415/831-2700.

28 Douglass Park

🐾🐾🐾🐾🐕 (See San Francisco County map on page 178)

The leash-free section at Douglass Park used to be a steep hillside with fences that were falling apart. It was so bad and difficult to get to (and to stay on!)

that I decided not to waste space on it in previous editions. But now the city has changed the locale, and it's a completely different animal: a big, attractive, grassy field flanked by tall trees. It's actually a barely used softball field, so your dog can make like Barry Bonds and run the bases and then go out for a fly ball (of the lobbed tennis variety) to right field. There's plenty of room for dogs to run and play, and boy, do they.

Escape artist dogs are pretty safe here, although the park is not totally enclosed. The area near the entrance has no barrier. But the park is so big that you can keep your activities to a far-flung section of the field if escape is a concern.

The park has good views of downtown from the back fence area (it has some very tall fences in back from its softball days). If you want to sit and sip your coffee while your dog gallops around, you'll have to be a bump on a log: The only place to repose is a big log bordering the outfield. The leash-free part of the park is all the way at the top, on Douglass at 27th Street. 415/831-2700.

29 Glen Canyon Park

🐾🐾🐾 (See San Francisco County map on page 178)

From the cypress forests to the streams and grassy hills, this 122-acre park was made for you and your dog. The nature trail in the middle of the park follows a muddy creek and is so overgrown with brush and bramble that at times you nearly have to crawl. It's as though the trail were blazed for dogs. There are so many dragonflies of all colors and sizes near the creek, and so much lush vegetation, that you may wonder if you've stepped back to the age of the dinosaurs. But it's not carnivorous giant reptiles you have to watch out for here—it's poison oak. There's a lot, so watch out, and tell your dog to do so, too.

Park at Bosworth Street and O'Shaughnessy Boulevard and walk down a dirt trail past a recreation center, through the redwoods and loud birds. Stay away from the paved road—it can look deserted for hours on end, and then a car suddenly whizzes by. Your dog is supposed to be leashed, but you should still be aware of the road. The area down the path a bit is swarming with kids year-round, since it houses a preschool during the school year and a day camp during the summer. (Additionally, kids also inundate the park's ball fields on weekends and on weekday afternoons after school, so you'd be best to make a sojourn here during earlier hours on weekdays, and again, make sure that leash is attached.) At this point, you can go left and up a hill for some secluded picnic spots or keep going and take the nature trail. When you finally emerge from the dragonflies and dense greenery, take any of several trails up the open, rolling hills and enjoy a panorama of the park. There are lots of options for side trails, too.

The part of the park that's easiest to access is at Bosworth Street and O'Shaughnessy Boulevard. There's only street parking, and it can get tight at times. If you'd like to avoid the paved road and all those kiddies for a bit longer,

DOG-EAR YOUR CALENDAR

You won't strike out with your dog if you bring her to the **Dog Days of Summer** at AT&T Park. In fact, you'll score a home run. If you thought hot dogs and baseball go together, you should see just plain dog dogs and baseball. It's a match made in dog heaven!

At Dog Days of Summer, your pooch gets to join you for a baseball game on a set day in August. You'll sit together in "The Dog Zone" (a.k.a. the bleachers) and watch the San Francisco Giants pound the heck out of the visiting team (we hope). But that's not all. Before the game, you and your dog can take part in a poochy parade around the field! Not many dogs (or humans) can say they've cruised around a pro ballpark. There's also usually some kind of contest, be it a costume or "stupid pet trick" soiree. Cost for the day is $66 for one human and you can bring one dog. Additional humans in your party (sans dogs) are about $28. Dogs have to wear ID and rabies tags. 415/972-2000; www.sfgiants.com.

the best entrance is at the west end of Christopher Playground, just behind the Diamond Heights shopping center on Diamond Heights Boulevard, north of Goldmine Street. (Gotta love those rich street names.) A trail goes around Christopher Playground's ball field and leads down to Glen Canyon Park. 415/831-2700.

30 Walter Haas Playground

🐾 🦮 (See San Francisco County map on page 178)

No, even leashed dogs aren't allowed on the swings and slides at this charming playground, but just up the hill is a teensy-weensy fenced dog park where dogs can run leash-free. It's the most barren dog park I've seen, but it's on purpose: The clay ground with nary a sprig of grass is meant to be that way because it's easy to maintain. If your dog poops here, there's no way to ignore it. It sticks up off the flat earth in such an obvious manner that it's almost like it's waving a flag saying in a squeaky little voice, "Pick me up!"

If your boy dog needs a mark for a leg lift, his choices are the water fountain (bad idea, since a dog bowl is on the bottom level), the attractive low benches (bad idea, since people sit on them), or the few large-ish rocks that have been placed on the ground most likely with this purpose in mind (your best bet). Jake, however, chose none of the above the first time we visited. We threw the ball across the 0.3-acre enclosure a few times before he started looking desperate to get out. We leashed up and went on our way, and as soon as he was out he found the first tuft of grass and watered it for about 20 seconds.

My human child, Laura, asked me to mention that this seems like an excellent place to train a dog, and she's right. (Smarty pants kid!) With minimal distractions, especially when other dogs aren't around, you can really work on those stay and recall commands. The park is at the top of a windy hill that provides great views of the bay and the East Bay, including Mt. Diablo. You can also look down at the grass that surrounds the playground below. At this dog play area, the grass really is greener on the other side of the fence. It's at the intersection of Diamond Heights Boulevard and Addison Street. There are entrances on both streets. 415/831-2700.

31 Mount Davidson

🐾🐾🐾 (See San Francisco County map on page 178)

Hiking to the peak of this park can be a religious experience—literally. As you emerge from the tall pine and eucalyptus trees leading to the 927-foot summit, a concrete structure looms in the distance. As you get closer you'll see that it's a gigantic cross, 103 feet tall. It's so huge, and in such a prominent spot—at the end of a long, wide path surrounded by trees—that it can be a startling sight. On his first encounter, Joe backed out of his collar and collided with a tree. Since leashes are the law here, we had to quickly put him back together.

In 1934, President Franklin Delano Roosevelt became the first person to flick the switch and light the cross. These days it's only lighted the night before Easter and a couple of other holidays. There's been controversy about keeping the cross (a religious symbol) in the park (a city-run property). That church and state–mixing thing just wasn't making some folks happy. Thank God (so to speak), an Armenian group bought the property surrounding the cross. The cross, an intriguing landmark for generations—much more than a religious icon—will remain.

Since you enter the trails at such a high altitude, it's only about a 10-minute pilgrimage to the peak. But you can make it a much longer walk by experimenting with different trails. Note that 1) the trails can get very muddy, and 2) they're almost always nearly deserted. My wonderful research editor, Caroline Grannan, walks her trusty dog Tioga here and notes that this lack of hikers "is probably because it's practically impossible to find, even with GPS and a good map. The streets are like a plate of spaghetti."

You can bring your well-behaved dog to the legendary Easter Sunrise Service, an interdenominational affair that starts at around 5:30 A.M. One mappable entry point for a good hike is at Dalewood Way and Lansdale Avenue. 415/831-2700.

32 Upper Noe Park

🐾🐕 (See San Francisco County map on page 178)

At last sniff, the leash-free section of this park was a tiny little area of compacted dirt. It was fenced and had water and two benches but no shade and no real appeal other than being an off-leash area. (To be fair, regular users say it's better than it used to be when the ground was a sandy, dusty mess.) The off-leash section is on Day and Sanchez Streets, east of the ballfield. (You can enter only on Day Street at this point.) 415/831-2700.

33 Potrero Hill Mini Park

🐾 (See San Francisco County map on page 178)

If you value your safety, don't go to the designated off-leash part of this park, even if your dog is crossing her legs in need of an off-leash romp. A friend was mugged twice at gunpoint when she used to play tennis at the courts adjacent to the dog run. (For some reason she no longer plays tennis there.) The leash-free section of this tiny park is a postage-stamp-sized lawn next to a tiny, ancient playground. A steep, uncleared patch of land that stretches from the nearby housing projects to the lawn is also supposed to be part of the dog run. The city needs to rethink this whole setup. The park is at 22nd and Arkansas Streets. 415/831-2700.

34 Pine Lake Park/Stern Grove

🐾🐾🐾🐾🐾 (See San Francisco County map on page 178)

These are two parks, but they're attached, have no line of demarcation, and share a common parking lot used by most park-goers, so we're putting them in one listing. But for reference's sake, this gorgeous 64-acre contiguous open space is made up of Pine Lake Park to the west and Stern Grove to the east. Now that your dog has his compass, let's talk a little about these beauties.

Dogs love it here, because it's a treasure of trees, hills, meadows, birds, fresh air, and leash-free areas. The best place for dogs to run off leash is just to the west of the parking lot (to the left, as you enter via the directions below—officially Pine Lake Park), where there's a wide-open meadow in a valley between two hills. It's not fenced (yay!) but thanks to its location it's safe from traffic, and a real treat with all the surrounding trees on the slopes. Many people come here to shoot the breeze with each other while their dogs run around, but the walk west on the meadow is a pleasant one. Note that during summer there's a city-run children's camp at the very west end of this meadow and beyond. Dogs need to stay away, even on leash. If you visit during other seasons, leash up here and you'll have a relaxing stroll around the lake that gives Pine Lake Park its name. (Actually, the lake is called Laguna Puerca, so if the park were named for it, it would be called Pig Lake Park. Nice moniker.)

The slopes on the north side have a couple of dirt trails dogs enjoy, but dogs are supposed to be leashed here. One of our favorite on-leash walks is to the east (right, as you enter) of the parking lot, where you start on a paved trail, cross over a grassy area to the dirt trails on the north slopes, and enjoy a super vista of the stage at the famed Stern Grove concert area. (See the Diversion *Groove at the Grove* for more on these summer Sunday concerts.)

DIVERSION

Groove at the Grove: If you and your dog like music and don't mind crowds, a Sunday afternoon at a **Stern Grove Festival** concert can be big fun. You can hear and see (if you get close enough) a variety of top performers at this beautiful outdoor concert area in dog-friendly Stern Grove.

The festival runs through the summer, and there's no fee for admission. Dogs can't take in the performances from the main meadow, but they're allowed on the peripheral hills, on leash. (But if you want to bring vino, apparently you can't drink it on the hill. Maybe festival organizers are worried you'll get tipsy and roll down to the stage.) Another option is to go to the west meadow, which permits dogs and wine. Bring a picnic, a stuffed Kong, and, of course, a poop bag. You won't be able to see the performance from here, but you'll get an earful. Concerts start at 2 P.M. but get there significantly earlier for best seating. Keep in mind that your dog can run off steam before or after the concert in Pine Lake Park/Stern Grove's leash-free area to the west of the parking lot (the one west of the performance area). Stern Grove's main entrance is at 19th Avenue and Sloat Boulevard. 415/252-6252; www.sterngrove.org.

We like visiting on nonconcert days. We keep heading east on our choice of trails, and then descend and walk past the beautiful Trocadero Clubhouse to a thick grove of redwoods surrounding a small pond. It's a peaceful, meditative place, and you can enjoy the tranquility from a memorial bench under the trees. It's not necessarily as peaceful if you have a water dog obsessed with getting at a floating pinecone (I'll name no names, Jake), but it's still a great end to a loop hike here.

The official off-leash area for the Stern Grove end of the park is on Stern Grove's north side, on Wawona Street between 21st and 23rd Avenues. It's a bit close to traffic, and the other meadow is a much better option. The two off-leash areas are now connected by a 0.2-mile trail where dogs can be off leash! The parking lot on which I've based all directions is just north of Sloat Boulevard, at Crestlake and Vale Streets. 415/831-2700.

35 Bernal Heights Park

😊😊😊🐕 (See San Francisco County map on page 178)

On one visit to this park, a dozen wolf-shepherds were the only dogs atop the amber hill. They ran and played in such pure wolf fashion that it was hard to believe they weren't the genuine item. The icy wind hit the power lines overhead and made a low, arctic whistle. The scene left an indelible impression that even in the middle of a city such as San Francisco, the wild is just beneath the surface. (To attest to this, a coyote has taken up residence here. Hardly anyone sees it, and it bothers no one, so fear not.)

The rugged hills here are fairly rigorous for bipeds, but dogs have a magnificent time bolting up and down. Humans can enjoy the view of the Golden Gate and Bay bridges. The vista makes up for the austere look of the treeless park. Dogs are allowed off leash on the hills bordered by Bernal Heights Boulevard. It can be very windy and cold, so bundle up.

Enter at Carver Street and Bernal Heights Boulevard, or keep going on Bernal Heights Boulevard until just past Anderson Street. 415/831-2700.

36 St. Mary's Park
🐾 🐾 🐕 (See San Francisco County map on page 178)

If it weren't for its teeny size, St. Mary's dog park would score three paws. It's an attractive place with friendly people and well-manicured grass that somehow withstands the pounding of paws day after day. It's totally enclosed and has three picnic tables and occasional shade from trees on a steep adjacent hillside. The leash-free section of St. Mary's is very close to I-280 (and the constant drone of traffic). From the park's main entrance on Murray Street at Justin Drive, walk immediately to the right and follow a paved path downhill past a playground and to the dog park, which will be on your left. A closer entrance is a block south, on Benton Avenue at Justin Drive. 415/831-2700.

37 Crocker Amazon Playground
🧍 🐕 (See San Francisco County map on page 178)

You'd only want to bring your dog here for an off-leash romp if 1) you live near here; 2) a friend or loved one is playing a game at the adjacent ball fields; or 3) you enjoy run-down areas with power lines overhead. At this fence-free, leash-free area of the larger Crocker Amazon Playground (a misnomer, since most of this large park is not a playground), you'll walk on dirt and crunchy twigs under power lines and too close to a tiny playground and the ballpark for comfort unless your dog is über-good. In its favor, it sports many eucalyptus trees, which are appreciated by dogs of the male persuasion.

The leash-free area is on the northeast side of the park, between LaGrande and Dublin streets. Your best bet is to park on LaGrande and follow the paved path past the mini playground. You'll soon come to a rather ramshackle flat area with a poop bag dispenser, which is where you can unleash. You can also enter this section from the more findable Geneva Avenue. Drive into the parking lot on the 1600 block of Geneva, leash up, walk on the paved trail past the skateboard park (if devoid of boarders you could mistake it for an abandoned swimming pool) and up wooden stairs that bear the sign Dog Play Area. It'll be at the top of the stairs. 415/831-2700.

38 McLaren Park

🐾🐾🐾🐕 (See San Francisco County map on page 178)

In almost any other neighborhood, the 59-acre section of leash-free land on a hilltop with super views of the city would be a huge favorite with the canine set. It has everything dogs and their people love, including leash-free paved and dirt trails, tons of trees, grassy slopes, and killer vistas. But you won't usually find many dogs here, and it's most likely because of location, location, location: Part of the off-leash area is very close to the Sunnydale Housing Project, the largest housing project in San Francisco and one of the worst in the area in terms of living conditions and shootings. People who haven't been to this park say they'd never go. People who live nearby say maybe it's not a great idea.

That said, I've never had any problems when hiking here with Jake, and the few people we've passed have mostly been families, joggers, or dog walkers. Maybe we've just been lucky, maybe it's because Jake is 95 pounds of muscle (OK, there's a little fat and a lot of dewlap too), but I've talked with other park users and they say this underused park area is a safe (usually preceded by "as far as I can tell") and pleasant undiscovered gem.

The leash-free area is the hilltop bounded by Shelley Drive. Most of McLaren's trails run through remote wooded areas and windswept hills with sweeping views. This area is rife with trails, so you can park just about anywhere along Shelley Drive and begin your hike. One decent starting point is where Shelley meets Cambridge Street. There's even a stand with poop bags there. Bring water; we haven't found any. Dogs aren't allowed at the Greek-style Jerry Garcia Amphitheater or the picnic areas. 415/831-2700.

39 Fort Funston

🐾🐾🐾🐾🐕 (See San Francisco County map on page 178)

Fort Funston is paws down Jake's favorite place to run around in San Francisco. He's not alone. This magnificent park, set on seaside cliffs that tower up to 200 feet above the Pacific, has everything it takes to make it dog heaven on earth. Trails wind through bluffs where you'll have stunning views of the ocean, some trails take you down to the beach itself, and happy leash-free dogs and their contented human counterparts abound.

As I write this, it's once again officially OK to be leash-free in all of Fort Funston except for a 12-acre section that's closed because it's a bank-swallow nesting habitat. Some decisions are in the works about the fate of the rest of Fort Funston's wonderful off-leash designation, but our paws are crossed that the decision-makers do the right thing and continue the decades-old off-leash tradition here (and in other parts of the Golden Gate National Recreation Area).

This generously sized leash-free beauty is truly a mecca for dogs. What's so magical about Fort Funston is that humans enjoy it at least as much as dogs do. If you have a dog in the Bay Area and haven't visited Fort Funston, you haven't had one of the ultimate doggy experiences. So get your tail over here and see what real dog bliss is all about.

Fort Funston is located along Highway 35, south of the San Francisco Zoo. It's about 0.5 mile south of the turnoff to John Muir Drive. You'll see the signs. (If you get to the Daly City limits, you've gone too far south.) There's also some roadside parking near the John Muir Drive intersection. Use caution when parking here, though, because a few people I know have had their cars broken into in this area. 415/561-4700.

40 Lake Merced
🐾🐾🐕 (See San Francisco County map on page 178)

As the city's largest body of water, Lake Merced is favored by Labrador retrievers, Portuguese water dogs, springer spaniels, and the like. An ideal spot to explore is the footbridge area near the south end of the lake. A couple of sandy beaches there are safe from traffic, but dogs are supposed to be leashed anyway. Once you cross the bridge, you'll find an inviting area with lots of little trees. This is where you'll find one of two double-decker drinking fountains for humans and their best friends. Lap up if you're going to hike around the entire lake: It's about a five-mile walk on paved trails and can be heavily used on weekends.

The off-leash section of Lake Merced is at the north lake area, at Lake Merced Boulevard and Middlefield Drive. Park on Middlefield and cross Lake Merced Boulevard at the light. You'll enter a small grassy/weedy section and come to a narrow dirt trail overlooking the lake's northeast bowl. We don't recommend letting dogs off leash until you're a bit into the park, because menacing traffic is so close by. There are birds galore and purple wildflowers in spring. The park is a tease, though, because there's no decent way to get to the lake from here— it's down a very formidable slope covered with impenetrable brush. Jake did once lead me on a journey down there to smell some duck guano coming from quackers nesting in trees above, and I lived to tell about it, but it's not high on my list of must-try-agains. 415/831-2700.

41 Brotherhood Mini Park
🐾🐾🐕 (See San Francisco County map on page 178)

This is a park built by a city that knows how to use its limited space. Weighing in at less than an acre, this fenced park along busy Brotherhood Way is squeezed onto a narrow tree-dotted slope at the southeast end of Brotherhood. It's a good place to let your dog run around if you're near the southwest part of the city and don't have time for Fort Funston. It's also conveniently located if you're on your way to Highway 101 or 280 from this neighborhood. It's very close to on-ramps for both.

Inside the fenced area you'll find poop bags, benches, really cool gnarled trees that like to grow horizontally, and some upright ones for shade. Dogs

DIVERSIONS

Hop on a Bus: It's good to be a dog in San Francisco. Dogs are allowed on **Muni buses** and streetcars as long as it's not commute time (dog hours are 9 A.M.–3 P.M. and 7 P.M.–5 A.M.). Only one dog is permitted per vehicle. Dogs must be on a short leash and muzzled, no matter how little or how sweet. (There are many muzzles dogs barely notice. Shop around 'til you find one your dog doesn't despise.) Bus driver Tom Brown told us about the creative, but ineffective, ways some people muzzle their dogs. "This one man had a part–pit bull dog, and he put a little rubber band around its mouth," said Brown. "No way that dog was getting on my bus."

Dogs pay the same fare as owners. If you're an adult, you pay $2, and your dog does, too. Dogs of seniors pay the senior rate. Lap-sized dogs can stay on your lap, but all others are consigned to the floor. Keep your dog from getting underfoot and be sure he's well walked before he gets on. Call 415/673-6864 for more information.

Ride Halfway to the Stars: Not many world-famous tourist attractions permit pooches. Can dogs ascend the Eiffel Tower? No. Can they visit the Vatican? No. Can they ride in a beautiful old **San Francisco cable car?** They sure can! (They can also go on the Golden Gate Bridge. See the Diversion *Saunter Across the Golden Gate* for details.)

Jake the Dog has mixed feelings about the cable car privilege. He doesn't mind the clanging of the bells, as his predecessor Joe did. But he's not too keen on wearing a muzzle (a requirement, along with a leash; the muzzle can be a gentle nylon one that most dogs, not including Jake, barely notice), and he really doesn't care for the hills. On a recent descent to Fisherman's Wharf, he tried to scramble from the floor to my lap, and we both slid down the bench and smack into the open newspaper of a surprised commuter. "Welcome to the sports section," he said with a bemused grin.

Opinions vary about whether dogs should ride inside or outside. Some drivers think the outside is better because the cable noise isn't so amplified, and dogs don't get so nervous. Others say the outside is too dangerous—that a dog could panic and jump off. I opt for inside, but if you have a small dog and can hold her securely on your lap, riding outside is the best way to get the full San Francisco experience.

Only one dog is permitted per cable car. Dogs aren't allowed during peak commute times (5–9 A.M. and 3–7 P.M.), and you should never take your dog on a crowded cable car. Off-season and away from touristy areas are your best bets. Dogs pay the same fare as their person. If you pay the full $5 adult rate, your dog does too. For more information, call 415/673-MUNI (415/673-6864).

enjoy running up and down the slope and the wooden stairs near the Alemany Boulevard entrance. Got a thirsty dog? Head to the water fountain just outside the Alemany gate. It's got a doggy level bowl and levels for short and tall humans, too (sans bowls, of course).

There's an entrance along Brotherhood Way, the street known for its diversity of churches and religious schools; no houses or other businesses reside here. But since there's no parking on this section of Brotherhood, your best bet is the entrance on Alemany Boulevard, which parallels Brotherhood one narrow block to the south. Park along the street and go in through the double-gated entrance, making sure to shut the gates behind you so no other dogs escape into traffic. Be sure the double gates along Brotherhood are closed, too, because that traffic really gets busy. The Alemany entrance is just west of where Alemany Boulevard intersects with the east end of Brotherhood (just east of Arch Street). 415/831-2700.

PLACES TO EAT

For a city known for its cool, foggy weather, San Francisco sure has a lot of sidewalk cafés. Here's a sampling:

Absinthe Brasserie: This elegant, forward-thinking restaurant with a Gallic bent is a power-lunch place for City Hall types. The lunch menu offers several varieties of oysters, caviar at $38 for a half-ounce, an interesting assortment of cheeses, and an upscale sandwich and main dish menu. Dogs dine at the outside tables. 398 Hayes Street; 415/551-1590.

Angelina's Caffe: Conveniently situated one-half block from Cal's Discount Pet Supply, Angelina's is a good place for you and your dog to take a break from shopping. It's got everything from soup to pine nuts, plus a large variety of coffees. Enjoy them at one of six sidewalk tables. You can also stock on up on Italian souvenirs here, but watch out for the red, white, and green hats. 6000 California Street; 415/221-7801.

Belden Taverna: Want to go to Paris, but just don't have the funds? Visit this delightful eatery in San Francisco's "French Quarter." (Belden Place—which makes up the "French Quarter"—is a little alley in the Financial District. It's filled not with cars, but with café tables. From my unscientific survey, dogs are welcome at all of them.) It's not a French restaurant per se, but the food is exquisite, and you'll feel positively Parisian dining with your pooch at the outdoor tables. 52 Belden Place; 415/986-8887.

Café Bastille: And speaking of the "French Quarter" (see previous entry, Belden Taverna), this popular Belden Place French eatery is a hit with people with dogs. Enjoy dining in a very French-feeling setting with lots of other happy diners who wouldn't think twice of giving you the "look" about having your dog with you here. A word of advice: Order the *coq au vin.* 22 Belden Place; 415/986-5673.

Cafe Zoetrope: Dogs are welcome to join their people at any of 12 white-cloth–covered tables outside this upscale North Beach/Financial District restaurant owned by Francis Ford Coppola. Apparently if you come here enough, you're bound to run into the famous bearded director himself. If it's cool outside, the alfresco dining area will be plenty comfy, thanks to well-placed heat lamps. 916 Kearney Street; 415/291-1700.

Calzone's Pizza Cucina: You and your dog can dine on wonderful pastas, pizzas, calzones, seafood, and steak at this North Beach restaurant. It has about a trillion outdoor tables to choose from. They're lovely, tiled works of art set under a canopy. On chilly evenings (or days) you'll be warmed by myriad heat lamps. This is a great place to watch the North Beach scene pass by.

Your dog will be happy to know that the waitstaff offers dogs treats and water! Jake would have preferred some of my fresh fettuccine with chicken, asparagus, roasted tomatoes, garlic, and other delicious ingredients, but the food was so good that I wasn't in the sharing mood despite his hungry brown eyes. 430 Columbus Avenue; 415/397-3600.

Cioppino's: Dogs love coming to this well-known Fisherman's Wharf seafood restaurant because they know they're more than welcome. The folks here always provide water to thirsty pooches. You can dine at any of oodles of plastic sidewalk tables here. 400 Jefferson Street; 415/775-9311.

Dolores Park Cafe: Eat here and you're directly across the street from the off-leash area of Dolores Park. The food's OK and the servers have been overworked when we've visited on the weekend, but it's a decent place for a quick hot drink or smoothie (try the Chai Crush). Sit at the handful of sidewalk tables with your dog. 501 Dolores Street; 415/621-2936.

Duboce Park Cafe: This corner café with the logo of a dog running with a leash with no person attached is right across the street from the leash-free Duboce Park, so if you want a place to enjoy some tasty food or just a cup of coffee after a social excursion to the park, this is mighty convenient. Dogs dine at the sidewalk tables and are offered water. Treats are served "irregularly," says a server. This café is a first cousin of the Dolores Park Cafe. 2 Sanchez Street; 415/621-1108.

Fisherman's Pizzeria: If you and your salty mutt are sniffing around Fisherman's Wharf for pizza, you'll get a decent meal here. A sign above the entrance features a fisherman and his dog in a little boat, so you'll know you and your canine crew are welcome. Dine at the seven sidewalk tables. 2800 Leavenworth; 415/928-2998.

Ghirardelli Chocolate Ice Cream and Chocolate Shop: Here's where you can get some of that famous rich Ghirardelli ice cream with all the fixings. Just remember: The more your dog gets, the fewer sit-ups you have to do. Don't share your chocolate, though. It can be very bad for dogs, as you surely know by now. Dine at the outdoor tables. The restaurant is in the lower floor of Ghirardelli Square, one of the classiest tourist shopping centers we've seen. It used to be a chocolate factory, and if someone in your party holds your dog's leash, you can go inside the ice-creamery and still see some delectable milk chocolate being swirled about in a giant copper contraption that makes me want to dive into it every time I see it. 900 North Point Street. 415/474-3938.

Grove Cafe: This coffeehouse is so popular you might need a shoehorn to find room at the plentiful outdoor tables here. But if you and your dog like the Chestnut Street coffee scene, you'll enjoy sipping your Joe among the Marina District masses. You can wash down your coffee with some fine sandwiches, salads, and pastries. 2250 Chestnut Street, 415/474-4843.

Java Beach: After a morning of combing Ocean Beach, you can catch some rays and eat some lunch on one of the benches outside this über-popular yet mellow soup, sandwich, beer, and coffee café. 1396 La Playa at the Great Highway; 415/665-5282.

Judy's Cafe: Judy's is a beloved little weekend brunch hangout that offers great traditional brunch fare in huge portions. The omelettes are top contenders with the sourdough French toast (mmm). Dogs love Judy's because they're offered treats and water by the friendly waitstaff. Jake usually prefers fallen bits of human food, since he's a fan of syrup, of all things (and yes, I know he's not supposed to have any). Dine at the few outdoor tables with your happy dog. It's best to visit on a weekday. We send a thank-you to Elway, a West Highland terrier, and his mom, Tori, who told us about Judy's dog-friendliness after a trip here from their home in San Diego. 2268 Chestnut Street; 415/922-4588.

La Mediterranée: Dog owners are lucky—there are two of these top Mediterranean/Greek restaurants in the city; each puts tables outside in decent weather and has a dog-loving staff. Try the vegetarian Middle-East plate. Even meat-eaters enjoy it. The restaurant at 2210 Fillmore Street, 415/921-2956, has only a couple of tiny outdoor tables. (The area inside is fairly tiny, too.) The restaurant at 288 Noe Street, 415/431-7210, has several roomy sidewalk tables, some of which are covered by an awning.

La Terrasse: The food at this French restaurant is FAB-u-LOUS, as a friend describes it, and where better to eat it with your dog than at the restaurant's heated patio that seats 50? The Sunday brunch is a favorite; instead of waffles and their kin you're offered more substantial midday items like smoked salmon pizza made with crème fraîche. Lunch items include sautéed skate with brown butter and wood-roasted squab forestiere. La Terrasse is in the Presidio, close to the off-leash beach at Crissy Field. 215 Lincoln Boulevard; 415/922-3463.

Liverpool Lil's: You can see two wonderful sights from this fun English pub: 1) the Golden Gate Bridge; and 2) the western end of the Presidio. Enjoy a drink and fish and chips with your dog at your side at the six pleasant outdoor tables. 2942 Lyon Street; 415/921-6664.

Mocca on Maiden Lane: Now your dog can dine in one of the most posh streets of the Union Square area. Just a bone's throw from the finest stores in San Francisco, Mocca is a European-style café famed for its many types of salads. Dine at the zillions of umbrella-topped tables right on the street, which is closed to traffic. 174 Maiden Lane; 415/956-1188.

Mona Lisa Restaurant: This family-owned and -operated North Beach restaurant is our little secret, OK? We discovered it one day while roaming around without Joe Dog and had a most sumptuous feast inside. Everything we ordered, from salad to pasta to main dish to dessert, was wonderful. Plenty of insiders know about the Mona Lisa, but it's off the radar screen for most. We like that. But of course, after this appears, it will be on many a dog's radar. The pizza here has been called the best in North Beach by many a patron. Pooches get to join their people at four outdoor tables. 353 Columbus Avenue; 415/989-4917.

Palomino: I'll always remember this Embarcadero-area restaurant as the place my literary attorney, Karl Olson, former publisher, Vicki Morgan, and I had a happy champagne toast after we emerged as victors in a copyright infringement case against a copycat dog book. That was in 1996. This restaurant is going just as strong as ever, but until recently, I hadn't thought to put it in this book. That's because I hadn't seen the patio dining. Dogs are welcome to join you at the comfy heated outdoor patio. Reader Ellen Rose and her dog Boo wrote to clue me in after they enjoyed dinner and a drink with friends there one evening. We sniffed it out and Jake gave it a big thumbs up. I think it had something to do with the bleu-cheese potato wedge he managed to wrangle from someone at our table. Thrice. 345 Spear Street; 415/512-7400.

Paragon: This popular brasserie-style restaurant is literally a bone's throw (via the arm of a major-league pitcher) from AT&T Park. As you may have seen elsewhere in this chapter, the park and area around it can be a really fun place to visit with a dog. Dine at the lively outdoor seating with your best pal at your side, and then take her out to the ballgame—or at least near it. 701 Second Street; 415/537-9020.

Park Chalet Garden Restaurant: If you could choose one restaurant in the Bay Area to visit with your dog, the Park Chalet should be high on your list, if not right at the top: This fabulous, dog-friendly restaurant resides in one of the most special locations of any restaurant Jake and I have visited: It's where beautiful Golden Gate Park meets the magnificent Pacific Ocean. In fact, it's right across the street from part of Ocean Beach that's leash-free year round, and it's officially within Golden Gate Park, next to some great on-leash walking areas.

The garden seating area is huge and grassy, graced by trees and gardens, and sided with lawns that kids tumble around in. It's truly a bucolic culinary experience. The flatbread pizzas are a real treat, and the rest of the menu is an eclectic mix of healthy international cuisine and standard American fare. Thirsty dogs get a bowl of water. The Park Chalet is behind and under its famed sister, the Beach Chalet restaurant (which has no outdoor seating), at 1000 Great Highway at the very west end of Golden Gate Park. 415/386-8439.

Pier 39: If your dog doesn't mind flocks of tourists, you'll find a wide selection of decent eateries with outdoor tables for the two of you here. Your dog gets to smell the bay and sniff at the sea lions below. Pier 39 is off the Embarcadero, near Jefferson Street. Here are a couple of the restaurants where you and your dog are allowed (and they're not allowed at all restaurants' outdoor tables, so ask before settling in with your dog). **Chowder's** has fried seafood and several types of chowder, making Pier 39 really feel like a pier, 415/391-4737; **Sal's Pizzeria** offers several special pizzas that will give you and your dog a real taste of San Francisco, 415/398-1198.

Sometimes it's fun to just grab a snack at one of a few walk-up windows on the pier as you stroll around. Jake highly recommends ordering a little bagful of hot and crispy-yet-gooey doughnuts from Trish's Mini Donuts, and then accidentally dropping one right in front of your dog.

Primo Patio Cafe: If you and the pooch need sustenance before or after a good sniff around AT&T Park, this casual Caribbean restaurant is a primo place to visit. It's just a block or so away from the San Francisco Giants' home, and the food is mouthwatering. Dine with your dugout dog at the two sidewalk tables here. (Sorry, no dogs in the garden section of the restaurant, since they would have to walk through the indoor section and past the kitchen.) 214 Townsend Street; 415/957-1129.

Rose's Cafe: As soon as you sit down to dine with your dog at this elegant Italian-Californian restaurant's lovely side patio, you'll know you've come to one of the most dog-friendly restaurants around. Your dog will almost immediately be greeted by someone from the staff (often the dog-loving manager, Matthew) and given a big bowl of water. Then comes the gourmet house-made dog biscuit, available for a fairly good price. Throughout the meal comes plenty of attention, often from other diners, sometimes from the folks who run Rose's.

My introduction to Rose's came several years back, when I got a letter from reader Carol Copsey, and her dog, Bella, a flirty American Eskimo. She was a frequent patron and wanted to let Joe and me know about Bella's favorite restaurant. I phoned her, and we got together one cool summer evening for dinner at Rose's. Joe was immediately smitten by Bella's fluffy good looks, but he fell asleep somewhere between the second and third gourmet dog biscuit. Bella didn't know what to make of Joe's snoozing on their date, but she pulled through after another nibble of dog treat. We had a wonderful time dining under the cream-colored awning, heat lamps getting us warm enough to take off our wraps. More recently, Jake came here with Bella to celebrate her birthday, and she watched in muffled awe (or more likely shocked disgust) as he wolfed down three-quarters of the mashed-potato-frosting-topped ground turkey birthday cake in one breath. (We made this cake; it's not a menu item.)

The food here is superb. The menu changes frequently, but here are a few dishes to be sure to order if you see them listed: bruschetta with fresh tomatoes, garlic, and basil; peaches, kadota figs, and prosciutto; crescenza-stuffed focaccia; soft polenta with gorgonzola; sautéed sweet white corn; local albacore with tomato, fennel, romano beans, and tapenade. The desserts are every bit as delicious.

It can get pretty busy here at times, so try to come when it's less hectic, for your dog's sake as well as that of other patrons. A good bet is to phone for reservations and mention that you'll be bringing your well-behaved furry friend along. There are also a few tables along the front of the restaurant, but if you have a choice, the side area is the best. 2298 Union Street; 415/775-2200.

Sea Breeze Café: Come here for delicious comfort food with a European twist. If you're here for weekend brunch, try the brown sugar and vanilla cream oatmeal; the weather in the Outer Sunset district is usually just right for this kind of cozy dish. But what dogs like best is that the café owners love dogs and welcome them at the sidewalk tables with a bowl of fresh water. (You can get tasty, natural dog treats at the natural food store next door.) 3940 Judah Street; 415/242-6022.

Squat & Gobble: Dogs love visiting the Castro's Squat and Gobble café and crepery. Not only are the servers really friendly, but the sidewalk alfresco dining area is spacious and there's always a bowl of water for thirsty dogs. Try the Zorba the Greek crepe. It's to drool for. (Jake urges any dogs reading this to convince their people to order the Gobble Burger instead.) 3600 16th Street (at Market and Noe); 415/552-2125. Other Squat & Gobble locations with dog-friendly outdoor seating include: Lower Haight, 237 Fillmore Street, 415/487-0551; Marina, 2263 Chestnut Street, 415/441-2200; and West Portal (with only a couple of sidewalk tables), at 1 West Portal Avenue, 415/665-9900.

Steps of Rome: "Of course we allow dogs!" exclaimed a manager on a recent visit. "We love dogs!" This big and bustling North Beach restaurant is a really fun place for a meal or just coffee and people-watching. The staff is friendly, and the atmosphere is very Italian, in a modern kind of way. And the food—*delicioso!* I love it here because I'm a big risotto fan, and Steps features a different risotto daily. The sidewalk tables for you and your dog are plentiful and popular. 348 Columbus Avenue; 415/397-0435.

Universal Cafe: This charming little Potrero Hill restaurant is very popular with the pooch set. The very friendly staffers here love dogs and provide them water and kind words. The restaurant features a variety of magnificent dishes with a California twist. If it's on the menu, be sure to try the caramelized onion pizza with prosciutto, fontina, and ricotta. Dine with your happy dog at the five outdoor tables. 2814 19th Street; 415/821-4608.

Zazie: This French bistro in the Cole Valley neighborhood may come last in the restaurant listings, but it's at the top of many a dog's list. Sure, dogs are welcome at the sidewalk tables to join you for really yummy meal. (Keep in mind it gets crowded, especially on weekends, especially at brunch. It must be the Tahiti French toast.) But on Monday evenings, it's *Bring Your Dog to Dinner* night at this popular brasserie. Dogs and their people get to dine in the lovely little heated back patio, where pooches aren't permitted on other days. Dogs get free treats, and human adults get $10 off a bottle of wine! Gotta love it! Everyone dining back there is a dog-lover, so no worries about getting the evil eye. This fantastic weekly ritual is brilliant. I hope other restaurants follow suit. 941 Cole Street; 415/564-5332.

PLACES TO STAY

The City by the Bay has some of the most wonderful dog-friendly hotels anywhere.

Argonaut Hotel: The terms "boutique hotel" and "Fisherman's Wharf" are strange bedfellows. But yes, Virginia, there can be sophisticated, whimsical luxury in the midst of junky trinket and t-shirt shops. The brick building was built in 1907, right after the big quake of 1906. The near-waterfront beauty sports a decidedly nautical feel. I think of it as Navy Chic. Rooms feature a quirky blend of blue carpeting dotted with yellow stars, bedding with anchor and compass themes, and striped yellow walls. If the St. Francis Yacht Club were a hotel, this is what the rooms would look like.

The views from here are terrific. You're just up the street from the historic Hyde Street Pier and all its old sailing ships. Depending on your room, you may also see the Golden Gate Bridge, Alcatraz, and Ghirardelli Square. If you head out to any of these places, be sure to be back at the hotel at 5 P.M. for the daily free wine tasting. We hear it's not to be missed.

As if all this isn't wonderful enough, your dog gets treated like the captain of an important ship here. They really go all out to make dogs feel welcome at this Kimpton hotel. When your dog arrives, his or her name gets written on a chalkboard that's the shape of a dog silhouette. The chalkboard is often full of names, since dogs love to drag their people here. The lobby also is home to a canine cookie jar. If you'd like use of a dog bed or food and water bowls, all you have to do is ask. And how's this for unique? The hotel features a doggy mini bar, from which your dog can choose—for a price—from a variety of stuffed toys. The bellman toy seems to be a popular choice around here. In addition, the hotel will provide you with a list of pet sitters, should you tire of watching your dog tear an effigy of an innocent hotel worker from limb to limb. Rates are $149–389. 495 Jefferson Street at Hyde Street 94109; 415/563-0800 or 866/415-0704; www.argonauthotel.com.

Best Western Tuscan Inn: The Kimpton hotel chain runs this Best Western. You can tell by the nice touches, including a big fireplace in the lobby, and really fun, peppy rooms, colorful rooms. All rooms come with little fridges, which is always handy when traveling with dogs. If you book certain rates, your dog can have access to special leashes and pooch treats. But all dog guests get free snacks in the lobby. Human guests get a daily wine reception in the lobby, and complimentary organic coffee and tea. Rates are $119–289. Northpoint Street 94133; 415/561-1100 or 800/648-4626; www.tuscaninn.com.

Broderick Victorian Bed & Breakfast: Wow, what a treat to be able to stay in a genuine Victorian bed & breakfast with your dog! Each of five private, peaceful guest suites has its own bathroom, but our favorite—the penthouse suite—has a gorgeous, circular yoga room, topped by a lofty, cone-shaped ceiling. (It's the "witch's hat" portion of the Victorian.) The suite is a spacious 800 square feet, with fantastic views of the city. Dogs are welcome in any of the suites with prior approval. Midas, the inn's golden retriever/host, will make you feel right at home. A light and tasty continental breakfast comes with your stay. Rates are $120–250. Dogs are $25 extra. The business address is 1751 Pacific Avenue, #6, 94115; 415/867-8708; www.broderickvictorian.com.

Galleria Park Hotel: This gorgeous boutique hotel has gone from being managed by one super-dog-friendly hotel group (Kimpton) to another (Joie de Vivre), and it's better than ever. You'll find an urban oasis at this 1911 Art Nouveau–style hotel. If you like the architecture here, be sure to take the hotel's San Francisco architecture walking tour, which is free to guests. (Dogs are welcome, but can't go inside some buildings.) You'll also get a complimentary evening wine service when you stay here.

The Galleria Park is a very calming, peaceful place to stay, especially if you stay in a courtyard room. Street rooms are fun, and brighter, but not quite as hushed. Here's a fun and unique feature: Dogs are welcome to join you at the third-floor garden area. It's a half-acre with nice city views and decent space for dog-walking. There's also a jogging track up there, should you feel like picking up the pace a bit. Canine guests also get treats and comfy dog beds.

Rates are among the best in the Union Square area: $99–299. 191 Sutter Street 94104; 415/781-3060 or 800/792-9639; www.galleriapark.com.

Harbor Court Hotel: The Harbor Court is homey and restful at the same time it's a happening place. Dogs who stay here can get the Pet Retreat package, which features a pet bed and pad, a rawhide bone, water and food bowls, bottled water, and poop bags. Rates are $189–239. 165 Steuart Street 94105; 415/882-1300 or 866/792-6283; www.harborcourthotel.com.

Hotel Abri: The only thing missing in this grand colonial-style hotel is Thomas Jefferson a couple of blocks off Union Square. This Larkspur-Collection hotel is housed in a landmark 1906 building. But inside it's chic and modern all the way, with a bit of midcentury style, but not so much that it's kitschy. The rooms are done up in relaxing earth tones that lend an air of tranquility to this vibrant spot off Union Square. The beds are super comfy, the WiFi is free, and the 42-inch flat screen TV with smart panel will keep you and your dog watching the best of Animal Planet until it fades to infomercials in the wee hours. Dogs are welcome warmly, with a little bag of treats. Rates are $145–285. 127 Ellis Street 94102; 415/392-8800 or 866/778-6169; www .hotel-abri.com.

Hotel Beresford: This Union Square–area hotel bills itself as "the friendliest hotel in San Francisco." Is it true? We don't know, as we haven't done a personality survey of the city's hotel employees. But we can say that the staff members we've encountered here have been very friendly and helpful. When asked if there's a size limit on pet guests, a chipper front desk manager replied, "No, as long as you don't bring an elephant." We like the attitude.

The family-owned hotel features attractive rooms—nothing fancy, but comfortable and clean. You'll get a decent continental breakfast with your stay. Humans get to eat at the hotel's adjacent restaurant, the White Horse Tavern. It has a real English pub feel, but the food is actually delicious—and even healthful, if you order right.

Rates are $89–169. Dogs are $25 per visit. 635 Sutter Street 94102; 415/673-9900 or 800/533-6533; www.beresford.com.

Hotel Beresford Arms: The sister hotel of the Hotel Beresford, this one is bigger and more elegant, with a few extra amenities. The lobby, complete with pillars and a chandelier, is a bit grander. You and the pooch can stay in a standard room or a suite with a kitchen. A continental breakfast and a fun afternoon tea and wine social come with your stay. As an added attraction, the hotel advertises that its rooms feature whirlpool baths and bidets. (We aren't sure of the lure of the latter and assume that these bidets are not of the whirlpool bath variety.)

While this hotel is the prettier of the two, it's a little tougher on dogs. Pooches need to be in the smallish range (the front desk clerk or phone reservationist will help you decide if your dog is smallish), must stay on the third (smoking) floor, and are not allowed in the elevator. With this no-elevator rule, you might want to employ the porter to take up your bags, should they put the "lug" in luggage.

On the outside, the hotel looks like any of the many decent old brick-facade apartment buildings in the slightly-off-Union-Square neighborhood. It's not the Ritz, but it is a comfy place to stay with your wee dog. Rates are $109–299. Dogs are $25 per visit. 701 Post Street 94109; 415/673-2600 or 800/533-6533; www.beresford.com.

Hotel Carlton: If you like eco-friendly, you'll feel good about staying at this city-hall-area hotel. Not only does it have its own solar panels–a rarity for hotels here–but it's received all kinds of green certifications. It's a soothing place, with quiet colors jazzed up with splashes of brightness to keep things interesting. (Speaking of quiet, if you prefer a quieter room, ask for one that doesn't face the street. Market Street is not known for its serenity.) The rooms have a modern, clean feel, and come with free WiFi, and marble-topped writing desks. Dogs don't get as many great amenities as they do at most other Joie de Vivre properties, but if they ask ever so nicely, they can get use of an organic dog bed. (Hmm. It's not like a dog's going to eat the thing. Well, Jake might...) A small bed-cleaning charge may apply. Rates are $79–229. The lower range is a really good price for this city. 1075 Market Street 94109; 415/673-0242 or 800/922-7586; www.jdvhotels.com.

Hotel Del Sol: This midcentury motorlodge has blossomed into a cheery, airy, casual boutique hotel. It's embodies a kind of colorful Cal-Mex feel without the souvenir-shop look. The heated outdoor pool is a rarity in this foggy city, but on warm days it's great to float on your back while looking up at the tall palms and at the yellow hotel exterior. It's almost Caribbean–and it's not often you get to say that in San Francisco! This Joie de Vivre property is the perfect antidote to a foggy day.

This Marina District hotel is big on families and dogs. Kids get free beach balls, sunglasses, and visors. (Who are they trying to fool? This is chilly San Francisco. But it's a fun idea.) They also have access to a pretty extensive children's video ending library. Guests get complementary cookies in the afternoon and a light continental breakfast in the morning. Dogs enjoy use of comfy dog beds and handy pet bowls. Even adult humans have extras here, like free Wi-Fi, and free Town Car service downtown during certain times of day. Rates are $149–299. 3100 Webster Street 94123; 415/921-5520 or 877/433-5765; www.jdvhotels.com.

Hotel Kabuki: From the Japanese garden to the lovely and very comfortable Japanese-inspired rooms, this Japantown hotel is a delectably different from many other dog-friendly hotels. Don't worry that it looks like a standalone "eh" apartment building from the outside. It's what's inside that counts.

Dogs get use of pet beds and bowls here, and humans get free Wi-Fi. Book directly through Joie de Vivre to get a free pass to the nearby Kabuki Hot Springs communal bath area. It's heaven. Don't miss your chance to soak your troubles away. Just make sure someone else is with your dog, since dogs are verboten in the spa. Hotel rates are $89–249. 1625 Post Street 94115; 415/922-3200 or 800/533-4567; www.jdvhotels.com.

Hotel Monaco: You and your dog will have *so* much fun at this upscale, sophisticated, whimsical hotel near Union Square. Upon entering the main lobby, you'll be wowed by the gorgeous two-story-tall French-style fireplace. (It's like the famed fireplace in *Citizen Kane,* only without the austere emotional surroundings.) Louis Armstrong hits and other sumptuous music floats around the high ceilings, which sport wonderful, light-hearted murals of the sky and hot-air balloons.

The rooms here are sumptuous, with opulent decor. You'll find a variety of furnishings, including canopied beds (with thick, rich material for the canopy), Chinese-style armoires, and cushy ottomans. If you need more room, you can stay in a gorgeous suite that comes with a big whirlpool tub and entertainment center with DVD.

The hotel's mission is to seduce and pamper, and dogs are not excluded from this noble cause. The Monaco offers something called the Bone A Petit Pet Package. It includes bottled water, poop bags, dog towels, quality chew toys, and gourmet dog cookies. You can also ask the front desk for Lassie, Babe, or Dr. Doolittle videos. The price for all this: $0! Yes, free! But you have to mention the Pet Package when you make your reservation. In addition, so that your furry friend won't be lonely if you need to step out, dog-walking or sitting services are available for a fee.

Rates are $119–650. Don't forget to ask for the Pet Package when making your reservation. The Monaco, a Kimpton hotel, is directly across from the Curran Theater. 501 Geary Street 94102; 415/292-0100 or 800/214-4220; www.monaco-sf.com.

Hotel Nikko: Dogs of all shapes and sizes are welcome to spend the night with you at this luxurious member of the exclusive JAL Hotels chain, near Union Square. It used to be that only small dogs were allowed here, so we applaud this gracious acceptance of larger dogs. Stay here and you get to sleep on a Subarashee Yume sumptuous pillow-top bed designed just for the Hotel Nikko. It's topped by Frette linens and a down comforter. It's best to bring your dog's own bed so the feathers won't fly.

Rates are $199–655. 222 Mason Street 94102; 415/394-1111; www.hotel nikkosf.com.

Hotel Palomar: It's sophisticated, it's luxurious, it's South of Market, and it's got an amazing dog package called the Woof for Wellness, which includes all-natural botanical spa sprays and treats, a cool leopard-print bed and "plateware," a toy, gourmet treats, and for those whiffy canine orifices, doggy breath drops and Sweet Smell Ear Care. Dogs love it here, and are often greeted by the Maverick, a chocolate Lab who serves as the hotel's canine goodwill ambassador.

The rooms here are bright and chic, yet super comfy. Oranges and reds add pop to the circumstances. And speaking of orange, if you don't come with your dog (perish the thought!), you may receive a surprise visitor: A goldfish to call your own for the night. Guests find them relaxing, and fish probably find a change of scene a bubbly new experience. Rates are $179–369. 12 4th Street 94103; 415/348-1111 or 877/294-9711; www.hotelpalomar-sf.com.

Hotel Rex: With a name like Hotel Rex, how could this shining gem not allow dogs? Literary dogs love this exquisite Union Square hotel. So do dogs who can't read. The lobby and rooms are modeled after downtown San Francisco literary and art salons of the 1920s and 1930s. How's that for a niche style? Joie de Vivre, which manages the Rex, describes the lobby as "clubby," and with its furnishings, artwork, books, and unique *object d'art,* you do feel rather as if you've stumbled into a literary salon from decades past. The guest rooms are a slight nod to that era, with unique pieces from local artisans. The beds are comfy, the TVs flat, and the dogs are happy. Not only do pooches get to stay with their favorite people, but they get to sleep on a great loaner dog bed, and eat and drink from swank hotel pet bowls. Treats are available for the asking, but you usually don't have to ask, because the folks here love dogs.

If you're here in the late afternoon, you'll get a free glass of wine. Nice touch in such literary circles! The hotel is quiet and peaceful, despite its location. This is a great place to get a good night's sleep. If I didn't live in San Francisco, I'd probably be a regular. Rates are $119–319. 562 Sutter Street 94102; 415/433-4434; 800/433-4434; www.jdvhotels.com.

Hotel Triton: If you're hankering for a wonderfully unique, creative, fun, intimate, whimsical, sophisticated place to stay, hanker no more, and book yourself any of the 140 rooms at the Hotel Triton. It's as if Betty Boop, Salvador Dali, Pee-wee Herman, and Ub Iwerks somehow came together to create their dream lodging.

I normally consider it a sign of laziness when guidebook authors lift material straight out of a brochure, but I shall do this here with the noble purpose of letting the creative Triton folks speak for themselves: "Totally hip without the attitude, the Hotel Triton is not for your average Joe, but for guests with imagination and style. A tarot reading during nightly wine hour, whimsical sculptured furniture, and a twinkly eyed staff" (I pause to attest to the fact that their eyes do, indeed, seem to sparkle a little more than those of most other hotel staffers) "await you at this fun and funky gem."

Room rates are $149–379. The Triton, a Kimpton hotel, is right across the street from the Dragon Gate entrance to Chinatown, just east of Union Square. 342 Grant Avenue 94108; 415/394-0500 or 800/433-6611; www.hotel triton.com.

Hotel Vitale: This stunning luxury hotel is probably the most soothing and spa-like of the dog-friendly hotels in San Francisco. You'll find the ambiance here inspirational for treating yourself well in this retreat on the city's

Embarcadero Waterfront. Sure, the place has big flat-screen TVs, free WiFi, and other gizmos to keep you plugged into the rest of the world. But unplug for a while during your stay. Soak in your room's big tub, and relax in the hotel-provided bathrobe and slippers. Dive deep into your super-comfortable bed's down bedding. Choose a pillow from the hotel's "pillow library" for the perfect night's sleep. Visit Spa Vitale and enjoy a soak in a private rooftop tub. Go across the street to the gourmet paradise of the Ferry Building Marketplace. The possibilities for a healthful, relaxing getaway on the city's edge are endless.

Your dog may not get to enjoy some of the more relaxing features of this Joie de Vivre hotel, but seeing you in such a relaxed and happy state will surely put a smile on her snout. If that doesn't do it, the doggy bed and bowls the Vitale makes available to all pooch guests should inspire some wagging. Rates are $219–456. 8 Mission Street 94105; 415/278-3700; www.hotelvitale.com.

Laurel Inn: This hip, midcentury-style Joie de Vivre hotel is great fun to visit. Each room is actually set up like a stylish city studio apartment, with a little sitting/dining area. It's convenient for dogs who like to have a little room in their room. And dogs feel especially welcome here: Their room comes with a dog bed, food and water bowls, and treats–all free! Humans get a very nice complimentary continental breakfast. Afternoon comes with cookies and lemonade. Or if you want something a bit stronger, head to the inn's chic, plush, retro Swank Cocktail Club. You'll feel like you're on the set of *Mad Men*.

The hotel is conveniently situated in a lovely neighborhood just far enough from downtown to be able to get great views of it from some of the rooms. It's also just a bone's throw from the magnificent Presidio National Park. Rates are $169–239. 444 Presidio Avenue 94115; 415/567-8467; www.thelaurelinn.com.

The Marina Motel: This charming 1930s motel is a few blocks from two great places to walk your dog—Crissy Field and the Presidio. It has a bougainvillea- and fuchsia-festooned courtyard and little wrought iron balconies,

which makes it feel less motelly and more Mediterranean. Some rooms have kitchens, and every room comes with free parking for one car. This alone is worth the room price in this neighborhood! Rates are $95–219. Dogs are $10 extra. 2576 Lombard Street 94123; 800/346-6118; www.marinamotel.com.

Ocean Park Motel: This art deco gem is San Francisco's very first motel. It was completed in 1937, one month before the Golden Gate Bridge. "When we took the place over (in 1977), deco was pretty much a lost art," says owner Marc Duffett. "But my wife and I put everything into this place to preserve the deco flair and at the same time make it homey."

Conveniently situated just a long block from Ocean Beach and the San Francisco Zoo, this pleasant motel provides a quiet, safe atmosphere away from the hectic pace (and price) of downtown. You can hear the foghorns from the motel's relaxing hot tub. You can also hear the streetcars, but it's not bad. And there's a special little play area for human kids. Accommodations range from rooms to suites, some with kitchens. Rates are $100–195. Dogs are $10–20 extra, depending on size. 2690 46th Avenue; 415/566-7020; www .oceanparkmotel.com.

The Palace Hotel: Dogs at the Palace? I know what you're thinking: These must be those itsy-bitsy dogs you can't see until you step on them and they shriek, right? Wrong! This four-diamond luxury hotel welcomes any size dog to stay here, and it's thrilling to me that they're able to hunker down at this gorgeous old downtown hotel. Today the Palace, tomorrow the White House! Dogs can't have tea with you in the gorgeous tearoom, the Garden Court, but if you want a version of the famous Tea at the Palace, you can simply order room service. Jazz Brunch at the Garden Court is as famous as high tea, but the jazz musicians probably don't do room service. Rates are $349–699. Dogs are $100 extra. 2 New Montgomery Street 94105; 415/512-1111; www.sfpalace.com.

The Prescott Hotel: Enjoy quiet luxury at this beautiful hotel. This Kimpton hotel harkens back to another era, with timeless elegance in a relaxing, traditional setting. The rich color scheme, custom-made cherrywood furniture, and extremely comfortable beds will take you miles away from the buzzing just outside the hotel's doors. But being a Kimpton, the style is anything but staid. It's alive and modern, despite the elegant old-style feel.

"Enough!" your dog may be saying. "Who cares about colors and hoity-toity stuff? What about me?" Good question! Dogs are beloved here, and are given use of a plush pet bed and pet bowls upon arrival. They also get high-end treats. And it's all free. That ought to put the wag back in your dog. Rates are $139–310. 545 Post Street 94102; 415/563-0303 or 866/271-3632; www .prescotthotel.com.

San Francisco Marriott Fisherman's Wharf: Stay here and you and your pooch are just two blocks from all the T-shirt and souvenir shops that have taken over Fisherman's Wharf. Actually, some fishing boats still live at the Wharf, and some local crabs still frequent the restaurants, so it's not as commercialized as it looks at first (and second) glance. The rooms are decent, and your stay includes use of the hotel's health club and sauna. Dogs need to be under 50 pounds to stay here. Rates are $159–299. Dogs are $100 extra. 1250 Columbus Avenue 94133; 415/775-7555 or 800/228-9290.

The Serrano Hotel: This opulent Spanish-revival luxury boutique hotel mixes timeless elegance in the lobby with an utterly fun, rich décor in the rooms. Striped red-and-white curtains and red-and-blue bed skirts give guest rooms a lively, mod-yet-comfy Mediterranean ambiance. If you like quirky, this is a great hotel for you!

But dogs don't care much about the red and white stripes, since they'll probably look grey and orange to them. What they love is how welcome they feel here. Staffers are always happy to see nice dogs, and they provide pooches with a "Pet Palace Package" that includes designer mineral water, gourmet dog treats, and poop cleanup bags. Your dog may not jump for joy about the latter, but they do come in handy. Rates are $119–349. 405 Taylor Street 94102; 415/885-2500 or 866/289-6561; www.serranohotel.com.

The Sir Francis Drake Hotel: This luxurious old Union Square hotel is famous for its Beefeater doorman who helps tourists and hotel guests alike. Jake likes the Beefeater almost as much as he likes beef. So do other doggy visitors, who tend to get excited about this man in plush red and a cool hat.

This hotel has been a stylin' place since 1928, and since it's become a Kimpton hotel, it's also become a little more mod and super-dog-friendly. If you opt for the Pet Package during your stay, you can get a dog bowl with "in-room water service daily," a Sir Francis Drake Hotel chew toy, and a few other goodies. It's not always available but rates for the package start at $189. You can choose a plain old stay at the hotel and it'll run you $120–419. Should you care to dance, the concierge will help you find a dog-sitter so you can cut a rug or two at the marvelous Harry Denton's Starlight Lounge, at the top of the hotel. 450 Powell Street 94102; 415/392-7755 or 800/795-7129; www .sirfrancisdrake.com.

Taj Campton Place: The European ambience and superb service make this a luxury hotel your dog will never forget. The rooms are magnificently comfortable, peaceful, elegant, and filled with extra touches that really make your stay here stand out. Some of the king rooms even feature sweet window seats with roman shades—the perfect place for relaxing with your furry friend, as long as she is under the 50-pound weight limit.

The hotel is just a half block away from Union Square. Rates are $305–1,940. Dogs are $100 extra per visit. 340 Stockton Street 94108; 415/781-5555; www .camptonplace.com.

TraveLodge by the Bay: Some rooms here have private patios. A few even have extra-length beds, should you find that you're tall. This motel is just three blocks from the part of Lombard Street that's known as "the crookedest street in the world." Rates are $69–169. Dogs are $20 extra. 1450 Lombard Street 94123; 415/673-0691; www.travelodgebythebay.com.

Villa Florence Hotel: Are you at Union Square, or in a comfortable, calming Tuscan villa? If you don't peek out your window of this Larkspur Collection hotel, you and your dog might feel like you're in *bella Italia*. The mural of Florence that graces the lobby of this 100-year-old building is so realistic that you'd swear you saw the leaves of the trees rustle. Fortunately the trees are in the background, so your boy dog won't get any big ideas.

The guest rooms are done up in rich yellows and subdued greens, with stylish Italian accents. The ridiculously comfortable beds make it a little too easy to settle in and take advantage of the free Wi-Fi and flat-screen smart-panel TVs in each room. If you want a quiet night sleep, we hear it's best to ask for an inside room, where the noise from Union Square is pretty much inaudible.

Dogs who stay here are supposed to be under 60 pounds. Exceptions are made, but the friendly front-desk clerk was relieved when he found out 90-pound Jake and I just wanted to tour the premises, not stay there. Rates are $139–289. 225 Powell Street 94102; 415/397-7700; www.villaflorence.com.

Westin St. Francis: The cable car stops in front of this historic landmark, so there's no excuse for not taking your dog on it. (See the Diversion *Ride Halfway to the Stars* for more about dogs on cable cars.) After a day of sniffing around San Francisco, your relatively small dog (30 pounds is the max allowed here) can crash on the Heavenly Pet Bed supplied by the St. Francis. It's a miniature version of the delectably comfortable Heavenly Bed that humans get to sleep on here. Dogs love this, but they're also grateful that humans get one Heavenly item dogs don't: the Heavenly Bath. Rates are $269–749. 335 Powell Street 94102; 415/397-7000; www.westinstfrancis.com.

W Hotel: Need a dose of opulent optimism? Stay here, where the room types have names like Wonderful Room, Spectacular Room, Fabulous Room, and Extreme Wow Suite. All the rooms are the lap of luxury, with goose-down comforters and luxury spa goodies. And speaking of laps, it's not just lap dogs who can stay here. Any size dog is welcome!

Dogs have another reason for thinking this place is wonderful, spectacular, and fabulous: Pooches who stay here get use of a dog bed and bowls and are given swanky treats and signature waste bags (and there's nothing like a signature waste bag for picking up the poo). Walks can be arranged if you can't do it yourself. Rates are $329–689. Suite fees start at $480. Dogs pay $100 for the length of their stay, "be it one night, or 101 nights," as the friendly concierge told me. I like a hotelier who thinks in dog movie terms. 181 3rd Street 94103; 415/777-5300; www.whotel.com.

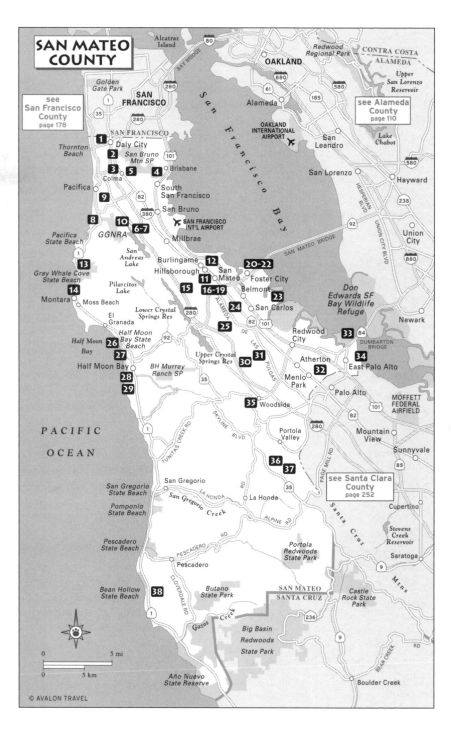

SAN MATEO COUNTY

see San Francisco County page 178

see Alameda County page 110

see Santa Clara County page 252

PACIFIC OCEAN

© AVALON TRAVEL

CHAPTER 8

San Mateo County

From the cool and foggy beaches of the coast to the warm and sunny inland communities, there's something for every dog's taste in San Mateo County. Sadly, the 15,000 acres of county parklands still ban dogs. Nothing has worked to change the county's ironclad law. (If it's any comfort to your dog, the county parks department is considering a ban on another human companion: cigarettes. Jake and his friends think when this ban takes effect, the county should eliminate the ban on dogs so there aren't too many rules. Good idea, dogs.)

Many beaches allow leashed dogs, but there's no sandy off-leash haven here. You'll have to head to San Francisco for a leash-free romp on a beach. The Midpeninsula Regional Open Space District is a dog's best friend (second best, counting you), with four preserves in San Mateo County that allow dogs. One, Pulgas Ridge Open Space Preserve in San Carlos, even has a 17.5-acre off-leash area. Be sure to follow extremely good doggy etiquette at all the district's preserves, because there are a lot of antidoggers out there who would love to get the district to take away our privileges.

PICK OF THE LITTER—SAN MATEO COUNTY

MOST PRIM AND TRIM DOG PARK
Foster City Dog Playground, Foster City (page 239)

BEST PUBLIC ART IN A DOG PARK
10-foot-tall "American Dog" statue that greets visitors to Centennial Way Dog Park, South San Francisco (page 229)

BEST DOG PARK CRAMMED BETWEEN INDUSTRIAL BUILDINGS
Brisbane Dog Park, Brisbane (page 228)

BEST CHUNK OF LEASH-FREE LAND
17.5 acres within Pulgas Ridge Open Space Preserve, San Carlos (page 245)

BEST LEASH-FREE PARKS BUILT ON A DUMP
Seal Point Park Dog Park, San Mateo (page 237)
Bayfront Park, Menlo Park (page 247)

SMALLEST DOG PARK EVER
Mission Hills Park Dog Area, Daly City (page 227)

MOST DOG-FRIENDLY PLACES TO EAT
City Pub, Redwood City (page 241)
Cameron's Inn, Half Moon Bay (page 244)

MOST BEAUTIFUL *AND* DOG-FRIENDLY PLACE TO STAY
Seal Cove Inn, Moss Beach (page 235)

BEST SOCIAL HIKE
Midpeninsula Regional Open Space District canine hikes (page 228)

BEST PLACE TO BOOK BROWSE WITH BOWZER
Kepler's Books, Menlo Park (page 246)

The district has unique rules about poop-scooping. Scooping the poop is required in places, but because of limited trash disposal sites, if you kick the poop off the trail, that's usually considered OK. (Helpful hint: Don't wear open-toed sandals.) Retractable leashes up to 25 feet long are OK, but be sure to reel your dog to the standard six-foot length when you're within 100 feet of parking lots, roads, trailheads, picnic areas, and restrooms, and when you're within 50 feet of other people or any body of water, including creeks.

The district provides excellent park info, dog rules, and maps on its website, www.openspace.org. Or phone 650/691-1200 for doggy details.

Daly City

PARKS, BEACHES, AND RECREATION AREAS

◨ Palisades Dog Park

◉✖ (See San Mateo County map on page 224)

This is the second-smallest dog park I've ever seen. (For the smallest, see *Mission Hills,* the next listing.) It's not much bigger than many backyards in the area. It's fenced and has double gates for dog safety, but it's not signed, and there's nothing in it at all except for some petrified poops scattered around the thick grass.

The park is conveniently situated if you're on Highway 35/Skyline Boulevard and your dog starts crossing his legs. Turn west on Westridge Avenue and you'll see Palisades Park at the end of the road. Look to the right of the playground and you'll see the teeny dog park. 650/991-8006.

◨ Mission Hills Park Dog Area

♟✖ (See San Mateo County map on page 224)

Welcome to what is very likely the smallest dog park in California. I appreciate the fact that Daly City has tried to make a little something for dogs to run off leash, but this one's so small that a dog can barely trot before crashing into a fence. Jake just poked around for about 30 seconds, then stood at the gate looking plaintively to get out.

The park is about the size of a dining room and living room in a not-so-big house. The ground is dirt and weeds, and there's no water, and no place to sit. But there are two medium trees within, plus a double-gated entry, should you chance to encounter another dog here. (You probably won't.) The dog area is in Mission Hills Park, a small urban affair that has a little playground and a basketball court. It's at Frankfort and Gutenburg Streets. Enter on Gutenburg on leash, walk past the playground, and you'll see a chain-link fence surrounding the postage stamp, er, dog park. 650/991-8006.

Colma

PARKS, BEACHES, AND RECREATION AREAS

🖈 Bark Park

🐾 🐕 (See San Mateo County map on page 224)

If this park were only bigger, it would get more paws. Colma, where the Bay Area buries its people and dogs, is no stranger to lush, green lawns. And this tiny park–about 30 by 90 feet, does have a fabulously green lawn. Around it is a little walking path. I think that's more for looks than exercise, unless you are a turtle or snail, in which case this is not a good place to be. Around the walking path you'll find dense green hedges. There's water, should your dog get thirsty after rolling in the grass. The park is at the west end of D Street, off Clark Avenue. 650/985-5678.

Brisbane

PARKS, BEACHES, AND RECREATION AREAS

🖈 Brisbane Dog Park

🐾 🐾 🐕 (See San Mateo County map on page 224)

The setting isn't pretty—it's a long, narrow park nestled between industrial buildings and a parking lot—and at a quarter acre, it's very small for a dog park. But the park gets two paws up because the people here have done a lot with this tiny space. It's all grass, and has all the usual park amenities, includ-

DIVERSION

Hike with Like-Minded Hounds: Want to take your dog for a hike but don't like the way the conversation kind of peters out after the first "How ya doin,' buddy? Are you a good boy?!" Sounds like it's time for a **docent-led dog hike.** These hikes, run by **The Midpeninsula Regional Open Space District,** provide a fun way to meet other dog people and to learn about your stomping grounds.

The hikes take place in some of the district's dog-friendly preserves a few times a year. They have themes like "fall hiking" or "day's end hikes." The day's end hikes are actually at night and loop by a pet cemetery. Dogs are not a requirement for any of the hikes, but you might want one at your side for that one.

The docent-led hikes are generally free, but reservations are necessary. Check out www.openspace.org/activities/ideas_for_dogs.asp for upcoming dog hikes, or phone 650/691-1200.

ing a picnic table and water. But it's the extras that set this little park apart: It has a fun wood play structure for dogs (some climb on it, Jake manages to squeeze through it), wading pools, a leash rack, and potted plants along the sides. They are watered regularly, and it gives you the feeling that people really care for this park. The park is at 50 Park Place, just west of Bayshore Boulevard. 415/508-2142.

South San Francisco

PARKS, BEACHES, AND RECREATION AREAS

🖪 Centennial Way Dog Park

😺😺😺😺 🐕 (See San Mateo County map on page 224)

This two-acre park is a huge hit with dogs and their people. It's a long park, so there's a chance to move around if you and your dog don't just come to "go for a talk" with the other friendly folks who visit. In fact, it has a looped path to inspire you to take yourself for a walk. The groundcover has something for everyone, except perhaps horses. There's decomposed granite, artificial turf, and wood chips. No real grass, but the miniature horse who visited here a couple of times didn't seem to mind. (I'm told the dogs were a little shocked to such an odd-looking "dog," with long hair streaming from his neck and forehead. I'm sure some rejoiced when he made horse manure.)

The park has separate sections for large and small dogs, water, some shade from trees (depending on where the sun is), poop bags, and a feature that's very unique, indeed: A whimsical 10-foot-tall steel statue of a dog, with a giant bone-shape cut from in his center. The statue, American Dog, by Massachusetts artist Dale Rogers, is hard to describe. You'll just have to come see it in person. The dog park is in back of Orange Memorial Park. The park is at 35 West Orange Avenue, near Memorial Drive. Look for the giant metal dog. 650/829-3837.

PLACES TO STAY

Embassy Suites: The striking nine-story atrium here is home to palm trees, a delightful breakfast area, and a large koi pond filled with some real bruisers—one that must weigh in at 25 pounds. The rooms are all suites, with dark wood cabinetry that adds a luxurious touch.

Dogs are supposed to weigh less than 100 pounds to stay here, so Jake will be monitoring his waistline if he needs to visit, and praying they don't make him do a weigh-in. A grassy area off the parking lot is available for a late-night amble if your dog needs a toilet break. Rates are $129–199. Dogs pay a $50 flat fee for the length of their stay. 250 Gateway Boulevard 94080; 650/589-3400.

La Quinta Inn San Francisco Airport: Rates are $69–129. 20 Airport Boulevard 94080; 650/583-2223; www.laquinta.com.

San Bruno

PARKS, BEACHES, AND RECREATION AREAS

One of the state's original dog parks, the San Bruno Dog Exercise Area, has closed, but in its place—at another location—is a fresh addition, Commodore Dog Park.

6 Commodore Dog Park

😺😺😺🐕 (See San Mateo County map on page 224)

The location is ideal for visitors passing by on the highway, as well as for dogs who have any business to conduct at San Francisco International Airport. The park is at the intersection of Highways 280 and 380, so close to the airport that you can almost feel the breeze of planes as they take off. (The noise level can be a little startling for noise-sensitive pooches and people. Old Airedale Joe would have had a heart attack. Jake, however, doesn't appear to even notice.)

It's a small but attractive park, set within the larger Commodore Park. The dog park has sufficient shade from mature trees, water (for people and dogs), separate areas for large and small dogs, benches, and enough grass to make it worth a roll.

The park is at Commodore and Cherry Avenues, at the east end of Commodore Park. Traveling south on Highway 280, take the San Bruno Avenue exit. In about a half mile you'll come to San Bruno Avenue West. Turn left and drive 0.2 mile to Cherry Avenue. Go left on Cherry and drive 0.3 mile to the park. You'll pass under Highway 380, and the park will be on your right. 650/616-7195.

7 Sweeney Ridge

😺😺😺😺 (See San Mateo County map on page 224)

If your dog appreciates breathtaking vistas of the Bay Area, with a rainbow assortment of wildflowers in the foreground, this 1,000-acre park is a rare treat. But if your canine is like most, he can take or leave such a magnificent panorama.

Still, if you like stunning views and a vigorous uphill climb, take the Sneath Lane entrance. It may be toasty when you start, but bring a couple of thick wool sweaters if you plan to hike along the ridge—it's cold and often foggy up there. The furrier your dog, the more she'll take to the invigorating conditions.

The Skyline College entrance is ideal if you want a more moderate grade, but both trailheads will take you to the same place. The leash law here can come in handy if your dog is of the pulling mentality. Just say "mush" on those steep slopes.

From different parts of the ridge, you'll be able to see the ocean (and the Farallon Islands, on a good day), as well as Mt. Tamalpais in Marin, Mt. Diablo to the east, and Montara Mountain to the south. Judging by all the canines with flaring nostrils, the scents from all four directions must be as enticing as the views.

For the Sneath Lane entrance, take San Bruno's Sneath Lane all the way to the end. There's usually plenty of parking. The Skyline College entrance, off College Drive, is in the southeast corner of campus, near Lot 2. 415/239-2366 or 415/556-8371.

Pacifica

PARKS, BEACHES, AND RECREATION AREAS

The stairs to a small off-leash Pacifica beach washed out since this book's last edition, so now leashes are the law in all Pacifica beaches.

🖫 Linda Mar Beach/Pacifica State Beach

😾 😾 😾 (See San Mateo County map on page 224)

Even though this is a state beach, leashed dogs are welcome here. It's run by the city of Pacifica, so it doesn't have to follow the more stringent "no dogs" rules being enforced by most other state beaches in coastal San Mateo County. The setting alone warrants a visit. With green rolling hills in the distance behind you and the pounding sea before you, you and your dog won't regret stopping here. This is Surfer Heaven, so if your dog likes to see surfers doing their thing, this is the place to come.

The beach also provides an easy access point to a coastal multiuse trail that will take you north over bluffs with great views of the coastline, and all the way to Pacifica's jagged Rockaway Beach area. It's a decidedly more wild affair than Linda Mar, and dogs enjoy poking around. The trek from beach to beach about three miles. A word of warning: Keep your dog on leash at the beach, even if you think there's no enforcement around. Rangers are using dune buggies to speed up to off-leashers and issue pricey tickets. A friend of a friend recently ended up with citations for $200 for two dogs.

Linda Mar Beach is also known as Taco Bell Beach in some circles, for its proximity to this long-surviving wood-clad member of the fast-food chain (the most attractive Taco Bell exterior we've seen, for what it's worth). You'll find the beach, and Taco Bell, on Highway 1. Park between Crespi Drive and Linda Mar Boulevard. 415/738-7381.

🖲 Milagra Ridge

😾 😾 😾 😾 (See San Mateo County map on page 224)

Follow the trail up to the top of the tallest hill and you'll end up with both an incredible view of the Pacific and a perfect plateau for a picnic. You'll see hillsides covered with ice plant and even a few Monterey pines along the way. Visit in the spring if you want to be wowed by wildflowers.

Despite the leash law, dogs really seem to enjoy this park. Make sure to keep them on the trail, as the environment here is fragile. And keep your eyes peeled for the Mission Blue butterfly. This park is one of its last habitats. Milagra Ridge is especially magical at night. You've never seen the full moon until you've seen it from here.

Enter on Sharp Park Road in Pacifica, between Highway 1 and Skyline Boulevard. 415/239-2366 or 415/556-8371.

🔟 Sweeney Ridge
🐾🐾🐾🐾 (See San Mateo County map on page 224)
See the *San Bruno* section for this listing.

PLACES TO STAY

Pacifica Motor Inn: A very cute smiling dog on the inn's website has a cartoon bubble coming out of his mouth saying, "Dogs love the Pacifica Motor Inn… And a good bone!" So have no fear: Dogs are welcome here. And it's a bone's throw to Rockaway Beach and the dog-friendly coastal trail at Linda Mar Beach. The inn is pretty decent for a motel and has two floors, and some rooms have ocean views. It's set in a fun little seaside neighborhood.

Rates are $89–159. Dogs are $15 extra. 200 Rockaway Beach Avenue 94044; 650/359-7700 or 800/522-3772; www.pacificamotorinn.com.

Millbrae

Dogs are no longer allowed on trails surrounding Crystal Springs Reservoir, and they are howling. But they can still spend the night.

PLACES TO STAY

Clarion Hotel: Rates are $89–249. 401 East Millbrae Avenue 94030; 650/692-6363; www.clarionhotels.com.

Westin San Francisco Airport: If you're traveling by air and need to stay somewhere with your dog, this is about the most convenient and luxurious place you can stay. It's only two minutes from the airport. Each of the 390 rooms is well appointed and has a very comfortable bed, known as the Heavenly Bed. So that dogs don't feel left out, dogs who stay here get their own Heavenly Pet Bed. Pooches we've talked with say the beds are dreamy. For humans, there are Mutt Mitts (not exciting, but very handy) and better yet, there's a fitness center and a yummy Mediterranean-style bistro. Rates are $129–379. Dogs are $50 per stay. 1 Old Bayshore Highway 94030; 650/692-3500 or 800/228-3000; www.starwood.com.

Burlingame
PARKS, BEACHES, AND RECREATION AREAS

🔟 Burlingame Dog Exercise Park
🐾🐾🐾🐕 (See San Mateo County map on page 224)

The half-grass, half–fine gravel park is a popular place, with a very different shape than most dog parks. It's very long, almost as long as two football fields end to end, and not extremely wide (anywhere from 30 feet to 70 feet). This lends itself very well to the park's name: It's a dog *exercise* park. With a shape like this, forward movement beckons. You and your dog can stand around and chat and sniff (as most do here), or you can really walk in this fenced park. In more typical squarish dog parks, you'd look kind of foolish taking a hike.

The trees are growing from their original sapling stage, and starting to provide a little shade, and targets for boy dogs. Speaking of bathroom habits, one drawback to this park is that it's right next to a sewage treatment plant. This can make the park a little whiffy at times, depending on which way the wind is blowing, but it's usually not a problem. In fact, as far as dogs are concerned, the stinkier the better.

A nice bonus if you use this park: There's a great path you can follow. You can pick up the path behind the dog park. You have to leash up to use it, but it's a good walk. It's within Bayside Park, on the Old Bayshore Freeway between Anza Boulevard and Broadway. 650/558-7300.

🔢 Washington Park
🐾🐾🐕 (See San Mateo County map on page 224)

Good news: Early rising dogs can now go off-leash in the area behind the recreation center, on the east side of the park, from 6 A.M. to 7:30 A.M. The rest of the time they must be leashed. This relatively small park has the look of an old college campus. Its trees are big and old and mostly deciduous, making autumn a particularly brilliant time. Bring a lunch and eat it on the thick, knotty old redwood picnic tables. They're something out of the Enchanted Forest. The park is at 850 Burlingame Avenue below Carolan Avenue. 650/558-7300.

PLACES TO EAT

It's fun to stroll down Burlingame Avenue, between El Camino Real and California Drive. The stores are upscale, the people generally like good dogs, and there are plenty of restaurants where you can enjoy a tasty meal with your dog at an outdoor table. Here are three to get you started:

Cafe La Scala: The outdoor area at this exquisite Italian restaurant has dozens of tables, but it's still very romantic, with beautiful flowers, soft music, and pastoral murals. It's all very Florentine. Dogs need to sit at the edge of the patio area. In cooler months, the area is warmed by heat lamps. 1219 Burlingame Avenue; 650/347-3035.

Copenhagen Bakery & Cafe: We've enjoyed some magnificently rich, flavorful, top-notch baked treats here. But if you're hankering for a real meal, the café has a full menu of scrumptious dishes, from appetizers (try the soft polenta with wild mushrooms and gorgonzola) to salads to steaks (yes, steaks at a café, doggy). Enjoy them at a couple of lovely sidewalk tables. 1216 Burlingame Avenue; 650/342-1357.

Trapeze European Cafe: OK, this one's around the corner and down a half block from popular Burlingame Avenue, but your dog will thank you for the extra jaunt. The servers we've had here adore dogs, and Jake got a bowl of water and lots of pats when we dined at one of the few sidewalk tables. The fruits and veggies are pesticide-free, the meat is free-range, and the chefs know how to make the ingredients shine. 266 Lorton Avene; 650/344-4242.

PLACES TO STAY

San Francisco Airport Marriott: If you need to stay near the airport, and your dog appreciates good views of San Francisco Bay, you couldn't ask for a better hotel. Rates are $99–219, and dogs pay $75 for the length of their stay. 1800 Old Bayshore Highway 94010; 650/692-9100.

Vagabond Inn: With these prices, it's a wonder they still call it Vagabond Inn. Rates are $79–99. Dogs are $10 extra. 1640 Bayshore Highway 94010; 650/692-4040.

Montara

PARKS, BEACHES, AND RECREATION AREAS

🔢 McNee Ranch State Park

🐾🐾🐾🐾 (See San Mateo County map on page 224)

State parks usually ban dogs completely, or at least from all but paved roadways. But McNee is a refreshing exception to the rule. At McNee, you can hike at the same level as the soaring gulls and watch the gem-blue ocean below. The higher you go up Montara Mountain, the more magnificent the view. Hardly a soul knows about this park, so if it's peace you want, it's peace you'll get.

And if it's a workout you want, you'll get that, too. Just strap on a day pack and bring lots of water for you and your dog. If you do the full hike, you'll ascend from sea level to 1,898 feet in a couple of hours. As you hike up and away from the ocean and the road, you lose all sounds of civilization, and Highway 1 fades into a thin ribbon and disappears below.

As soon as you go through the gate at the bottom of the park, follow the narrow trails to the left up the hills. You may be tempted to take the wide and winding paved road from the start, but to avoid any bikers, take the little trails. Besides, they lead to much better vistas.

Eventually, you'll come to a point where you have a choice of going left or right on a wider part of the trail. It's a choice between paradise and heaven. Left will lead you to a stunning view of the Golden Gate Bridge and the Farallon Islands. Right will bring you to the top of the ridge, where you see Mt. Diablo and the rest of San Francisco Bay.

This was one of Joe's favorite parks, despite the leash law. Still, he always managed to slide down several steep grassy hills on his back, wriggling and moaning in ecstasy all the way.

It's easy to miss this park since there aren't any signs and there's no official parking lot. From Highway 1 in Montara, park at the far northern end of the Montara State Beach parking lot and walk across the road. Be careful as you walk along Highway 1, because there's hardly any room on the shoulder. You'll see a gate on a dirt road just north of you and a small state property sign. That's where you go in. A few cars can also park next to the gate on the sides of the dirt road. But don't block the gate or your car probably won't be there when you get back. 650/726-8820.

🐾 Montara State Beach

🐾🐾🐾🐾 (See San Mateo County map on page 224)

This long, wide beach has more nooks and crannies than your dog will be able to investigate. Around mid-beach, you'll find several little inlets carved into the mini-cliffs. Take your dog back there at low tide and you'll find all sorts of water, grass, mud, and beach flotsam. It's a good place for her to get her paws wet while obeying the leash law. The water at the inlets is as calm as pond water. This is where Joe first dared to walk in water. It was only a centimeter deep, but he licked his paws in triumph all the way home.

With the recent banning of dogs at other state beaches in the area, this one has been taking a pounding of late. I know it's hard, but please keep your dog on leash, or this beach could go the way of so many others.

Off Highway 1, park in the little lot behind the building that used to house the Chart House restaurant. There's also a parking area on the north side of the beach, off Highway 1. 650/726-8820.

Moss Beach

PLACES TO STAY

Seal Cove Inn: What a spectacular place to vacation with a dog! This 10-room inn looks like an old English manor. The sprawling inn is set on gorgeous land with wildflowers, big trees, and views of parkland and the ocean. The inn is a combination of boutique hotel and bed and breakfast. It's intimate like a bed and breakfast, and with a scrumptious breakfast served in the dining room next to the fireplace. The inn serves afternoon tea and hors d'ouevres, and there's even a turndown service with gourmet chocolates. On the boutique hotel side, the dog-friendly rooms are large, airy, and have log-burning fireplaces. A beautiful pane-glass door opens right to the garden, which is perfect for dogs, who feel no great urge to walk through the rest of the inn just to water the trees.

Dogs feel extra welcome here. When the arrive in their room, they'll find a dog bed, bowls for food and water, treats, and poop bags. There's free Wi-Fi, should your dog want to write to his friends and brag about what a great time he's having. Rates are $225–250. Dogs are $65 per stay. 221 Cypress Avenue 94038; 800/995-9987; www.sealcoveinn.com.

Hillsborough

PARKS, BEACHES, AND RECREATION AREAS

15 Vista Park

🐕 (See San Mateo County map on page 224)

You can visit this park only if you live here, unless you choose to walk miles to get to it—there's no street parking for blocks, and no parking lot. And chances are that if you live in this town, your backyard is bigger anyway. A little section in the back has several tall eucalyptus trees that leashed neighborhood dogs call their own. It's good for sniffs when you can't get to a better park. Poop bags are provided.

The park is at Vista and Culebra Roads. 650/579-3800.

San Mateo

PARKS, BEACHES, AND RECREATION AREAS

At press time, the city was undergoing a Rover Renaissance, of sorts. A pilot program was underway at four city parks to test out an off-leash program that would spread the off-leash bliss around the city. If all goes well, the parks will have permanent off-leash areas we'll include in the book's next edition. But for the record, here are the off-leash areas, and their hours. Call 650/522-7420 or check online to see if the parks are official before heading there.

- Central Park (which we describe here): 50 East 5th Street, at Fitzgerald Field only, 6–8 A.M.
- Beresford Park: 2720 Alameda de las Pulgas, Chanteloup Field only, 6–8 A.M.
- Los Prados Park: 1837 Bahia Street, fenced area in the southwestern part of the park near the south diamond, 6 A.M.–8 P.M.
- Bayside-Joinville Park: 2111 Kehoe Avenue, fenced area near the wastewater treatment plant off Detroit Drive, 6 A.M.–10 P.M.

16 Central Park

🐾🐾🐾 (See San Mateo County map on page 224)

This is a lush, green, miniature version of Golden Gate Park. There's even a Japanese garden, and although no dogs are allowed inside, the Japanese ambience spills outside. The days we've visited, there was always something going on at the outdoor stage in back of the recreation center. A couple of large meadows are bordered by big shady redwoods. There's even a pint-sized railroad that takes up part of a small field. (Something not found in Golden Gate Park.) Someone told us that dogs have been known to chase the cars as they chug along the track. Leashes are a must, although at press time, an experimental off-leash program was going on at the park's Fitzgerald Field between 6 A.M. and 8 A.M. daily. Call the number below before throwing your dog's leash to the wind, or a canine cop may be throwing a ticket in your face.

The park is on East 5th Avenue at El Camino Real. 650/522-7420.

17 Seal Point Park Dog Park

🐾🐾🐾🐕 (See San Mateo County map on page 224)

I never thought I'd give three paws to a dog park that's 1) Under enormous utility towers 2) built on an old city dump 3) devoid of trees or grass and 4) occasionally gets rather whiffy (thanks either to old dump smells wafting up or bacterial action in a nearby lagoon; we've heard both theories).

Sounds appealing, huh?

But three paws it is, thanks to its size, layout, and features. The dog park is a big three acres. That's a large chunk of land for a dog park these days. A small portion of that is carved out for a separate small-dog park, but the bulk of the acreage is in one large, long piece of land. The configuration forces people (and thus dogs) to walk, and prevents the usual grouping activity I like to call "taking your dog for a talk." You have to take a short hike to even get to the area that has four benches where you can plop down under a shade structure. People and dogs do socialize here, but this setup tends to keep dog imbroglios to a minimum, and by my vastly unscientific observation, seems to lead to a generally fitter group of park users than I've seen at other dog parks.

Many park-goers also leash up and continue their walk in the surrounding parklands, so fitness-wise it's a double-winner. The larger Seal Point Park has become a recreational hot spot, with a few popular multi-use trails that lead to great views of San Francisco Bay.

Both the small and large dog sections sport a line of fire hydrants near the entryway, which makes for a fun and functional aesthetic. Since the only targets for boy dog leg lifts are benches, some large rocks, and the concrete base of the utility towers, the hydrants come in handy. A path of decomposed granite winds through a park surface of what appears to be more decomposed granite; the native grass it was supposed to wind through didn't do so well. A watering station is outside the double gates of the park, which can be a little inconvenient if your dog needs a snoutful on the opposite end of the park, but if you bring a little bottle for this you'll be all set. Exit U.S. 101 at 3rd Street and drive east about 0.6 mile. Go left at the main park entrance, and once in the park, drive to the parking lots on the right. 650/522-7420.

18 Laurelwood Park

🐾🐾🐾 (See San Mateo County map on page 224)

A small, clear stream winds the length of this rural park in the suburbs. Joe Dog never wanted anything to do with the water and jumped from one side to the other without getting a toenail damp. But Jake, a.k.a. Mr. Water, delights in its fresh scents and enticing sounds. Follow the bike trail—heeding the leash law, as this is a popular spot for bikers—along the stream, and enjoy tree-covered hillsides in a virtually suburb-free environment. Only a few blocks from the Laurelwood Shopping Center, this park is an ideal getaway after a quick shopping trip. The kids can use the playground at the foot of the bike trail.

The park is at Glendora and Cedarwood Drives. 650/522-7420.

19 Beresford Park

🐾🐾 (See San Mateo County map on page 224)

The bulk of this park is made up of sports fields. But venture behind the garden center and you and your pooch can enjoy a pleasant little leashed romp on a large grassy field. Many youthful-but-shady pine trees are growing well despite dozens of daily assaults from male dogs. Several picnic tables and a large children's play area near the field make this an adequate spot for a weekend afternoon with the family. People are friendly here—we were twice offered soda and beer by locals, who wanted Jake to "hang" with them. Note: At press time the park's Chanteloup Field was part of an off-leash pilot program between 6 A.M. to 8 A.M. daily. We hope this sticks. We'll let you know in the next edition.

The park is on Parkside Way at Alameda de las Pulgas. 650/522-7420.

PLACES TO STAY

Residence Inn by Marriott: There's a walking path not far from here, so it's a good place to stay with your pooch. Besides, it's a comfy lodging—not quite home, but it tries to come close. Rates are $99–214. Dogs are $75 fee per visit. 2000 Winward Way 94404; 650/574-4700; www.marriott.com.

Foster City

PARKS, BEACHES, AND RECREATION AREAS

As my Foster City informant, Kirk Amspoker, told me, Foster City isn't a big city, but there are a lot of dog-friendly people here. Since the book's last edition, the city has added dedicated off-leash areas during morning hours at five locations. We'll describe two—Boothbay and Sea Cloud. The other three are:

• Edgewater Park: At Edgewater Boulevard and Regulus Street, 5–8 A.M.

• Catamaran Park: At Shell Boulevard and Catamaran Street, 5–8 A.M.

• Farragut Park: At Beach Park Boulevard and Farragut Street, 5–8 A.M.

20 Foster City Dog Playground

🐾🐾🐾🐕 (See San Mateo County map on page 224)

This tidy, neat, petite fenced park with artificial grass is a little like a Stepford Wife: Lovely to look at, but perfect to the point of being scary. When I visited with Jake, I spent the whole time silently praying that he'd poop on the refined gravel ground cover (formally known as decomposed granite), not on the carpetlike artifical turf. The turf is the modern version of Astroturf, and it's like a green rug that aspires to be golf-course grass. I asked a nice gent there what happens if a dog does go to the bathroom on it, and he pointed to a poop-bag dispenser (no problem), and also to a scrub brush and bucket of water near the water fountain (ah, the Cinderella routine).

Park fan Kirk Amspoker contacted me after reading the above description in a previous edition, and told me that "non-Cinderellas are welcome.… The only time I've ever seen the water and brush used was for a dog with (how should I say) less-than-solid poop." So if your dog has firm poo, a bag will do. (Ah, the subjects we cover in this book.)

In the end, Jake didn't poop anywhere. He was having too much fun playing chase games with his new friends and learning to run through an agility tire and over an agility jump. Big dogs have their own section, which is great, because the small-dog section had really tiny, breakable dogs when we visited. (The small-dog section had the air of a casual country club, with the well-dressed dog people reposing on a variety of lawn chairs.) The entire park is less than a half acre, but dogs greatly enjoy themselves. There's shade from two large green shade structures, and water, scoops, picnic tables, and benches. A couple of very cute rusted-metal dog sculptures grace one end of the park.

Exit eastbound Highway 92 at Foster City Boulevard, go left at the offramp, and then right within a block at Foster City Boulevard. Travel about 0.7 mile and go right on Bounty Drive, and then left almost immediately into the parking lot. 650/286-3382.

21 Boothbay Park

🐾🐾🐾🐕 (See San Mateo County map on page 224)

Dogs are allowed off leash at this pretty, green, relatively small park between 6 A.M. and 8 A.M. Some nice dog folks gather around 7 A.M. to walk the park's trail together. By the time the off-leash hours are over, the early-rising kiddies are starting to hit the very cool playground. The park is at Edgewater Boulevard and Boothbay Avenue; 650/286-3382.

22 Sea Cloud Park

😊😊😊🐕 (See San Mateo County map on page 224)

The park's name is dreamy, and so is the fact that between 5 A.M. and 9 A.M. dogs may be off leash in the signed off-leash area in the southwest section of the park. Just drive down to the last part of the parking lot, and it's on your right. It's a big, grassy area, with a few large trees and a couple of picnic tables off to the side. We've heard that during the doggy hours, people can get a little territorial, trying to shoo away newbies. When we visited, it was after the off-leash hours were over, so we didn't witness whether or not this was true. I hope it's not, but all it takes is one. The park is at Pitcairn Drive and Sea Cloud Drive. 650/286-3382.

PLACES TO EAT

Dogs dig dining at Foster City's lagoon-side restaurants. Here's one that welcomes dogs. Others do, too, but don't jump at the chance to advertise it.

Plaza Gourmet: Good dogs can dine with you on the attractive wood-planked deck. If your dog is thirsty, a fresh bowl of water is hers for the asking. 929C Edgewater Boulevard; 650/638-0214.

Redwood City

PARKS, BEACHES, AND RECREATION AREAS

23 Shore Dogs Park

😊😊😊🐕 (See San Mateo County map on page 224)

This park is only 0.75 acre, but it doesn't matter. Dogs and their people are simply overjoyed just to have some legal off-leash romping room after so many years of being banned from all city parks. It can get mighty windy here, and it's quite a sight to see dogs joyously running around with their ears flapping, and then standing still only to have their ears continue to flap.

As its name may tell you, Shore Dogs Park is near the water. And what dog doesn't dig being able to sniff the odors wafting off of San Francisco Bay? During winter and fall, the park's location gives you and your dog a front-row seat to the shorebird migration. Your dog's jaw will drop as she watches an egret flap its gigantic wings. The birds have nothing to fear, as the park is fenced, and dogs can't fly.

Poop bags are provided, large and small dogs have separate sections, and there's a little "greeting area" where dogs can sniff each other out before entering. The park is off Redwood Shores Parkway, near the end of Radio Road, in Redwood Shores. 650/654-6538.

PLACES TO EAT

Citrine Bistro: If you're picking up a friend at a movie at the giant Cineplex next door, why not bring the dog along and head for a nosh at this fun, lively bistro with a wide selection of tasty foods? It's a kind of a Cal-American-Mediterranean fusion place. You can get a variety of foods, from a big smoked-pork sandwich to a light hummus salad. Dogs suggest the former. Speaking of dogs, we'd like to thank Zelda the Wonderful, and her equally wonderful person, Jacquie Steiner, for the tip about this place. 885 Middlefield Road; 650/261-3591.

City Pub: Like pub food? Dine at the outdoor tables here at this charming hangout. If your dog is thirsty, the staff will happily provide a big bowl of water. And if treats are in stock, they'll supply a couple for your lucky dog. 2620 Broadway; 650/363-2620.

Milagro's: The outdoor tables at this upscale Mexican restaurant are warm and cozy year-round, thanks to some effective heat lamps. 1099 Middlefield Road; 650/369-4730.

Belmont

PARKS, BEACHES, AND RECREATION AREAS

24 Cipriani Park Dog Exercise Area

🐾🐾🐾🐕 (See San Mateo County map on page 224)

This 0.75-acre fenced park is a treat for leash-free pooches and their chauffeurs. That's partly because of all the social events that take place here: There are frequent potlucks, seminars on topics such as canine first aid, and even a couple of fairs a year. In addition, the park has all good dog-park amenities, including poop bags, water, picnic tables, attractive surroundings, and separate sections for large and small dogs.

The park is at 2525 Buena Vista Avenue, behind the Cipriani School. 650/595-7441.

25 Twin Pines Park

🐾🐾🐾 (See San Mateo County map on page 224)

This park is a hidden treasure, nestled among eucalyptus trees just outside the business district of Belmont. You'd never guess the dog wonders that await within. Your dog may hardly notice she's leashed. The main trail is paved and winds through sweet-smelling trees and brush. A clear stream runs below. In dry seasons, it's only about two feet deep, but in good years it swells to several feet. Dogs love to go down to the stream and wet their whistles. Past the picnic area are numerous small, quiet dirt trails that can take you up the woodsy hill or alongside the stream.

It's at 1225 Ralston Avenue, behind the police department. 650/595-7441.

El Granada

PLACES TO STAY

Harbor View Inn: Each of the 17 comfortable rooms at this upscale motel features a wonderful bay window seat, where you can get a very good view of the ocean and the harbor. You'll have to look over Highway 1, since you're on the east side of the road, but it's a nice touch you don't usually find at motels. They'll point you in the direction of a couple of hush-hush dog-walking spots nearby. Rates are $69–189. Dogs are $10 extra per stay. 51 Avenue Alhambra 94018; 650/726-2329; www.harborviewinn.net.

Half Moon Bay

This is a delightful place to come for a day of sniffing around the enchanting old "downtown" and checking out the beautiful ocean views. It's a real treat on days that are scorching elsewhere: This area is air-conditioned by the god of woolly sheepdogs. No matter how steaming hot it is elsewhere, you can almost always count on cool weather here. It's often chilly and foggy in the summer, wet and windy in the winter, and moderate in the fall and spring.

PARKS, BEACHES, AND RECREATION AREAS

Dogs are no longer allowed on the sand at any of the four Half Moon Bay State Beach areas, but they're still welcome to take a stroll on the scenic blufftop paths that stretch almost from one end of Half Moon Bay to the other—Surfer's Beach, Half Moon Bay State Beach, and Bluff Top Park offer easy trail access.

Fortunately for sand-loving hounds, two city beaches permit leashed beasts.

26 Surfer's Beach

🐾🐾 (See San Mateo County map on page 224)

Water dogs dig being able to dip their paws in the water here. On almost any day, no matter how cold and gray it is, you'll find loads of surfers waiting for the perfect wave. The beach isn't big or wide, and it can be crowded at times, but it's a fun place to take a little stroll with your leashed dog. A trail that starts here takes you miles down the shore. It's a terrific, flat, easy, and very scenic hike. Jake highly recommends it.

Surfer's Beach is on Highway 1 and Coronado Street, just south of Pillar Point Harbor. 650/726-8820.

27 Half Moon Bay State Beach Trail

😺 😺 😺 (See San Mateo County map on page 224)

This name is a misnomer. Thanks to the threatened snowy plover bird, and to people who abused the leashed-dog privilege, dogs are no longer allowed on the beach, even if they promise to wear their leashes and behave perfectly. But they are welcome on the paved blufftop trail here. The views are excellent, the sea air uplifting.

You can hook up with the trail here at several points. There's signage along different spots of Highway 1. At the very west end of Kelly Avenue you'll find Francis Beach and the entrance for the campground. At the west end of Venice Boulevard is Venice Beach (not to be confused with its radically different counterpart in Los Angeles County), and at the west end of Young Avenue you'll find both Dunes Beach and Roosevelt Beach.

This isn't the place to come for a 15-minute romp: If you park in the lots, it costs $6–10. You can park a little away on the street, or take your car down to the city-run Bluff Top Park, which has not only a paved trail, but a leashed-dog-friendly sandy beach—for free!

If you can ignore all the RVs and crowds of tents, the area above Francis Beach is a stunning camping spot. Perched on ice plant–covered dunes above the Pacific, it's one of the most accessible beach camping areas in the Bay Area. All of the 52 campsites are available on a first-come, first-served basis. Sites are $35–50 for the first vehicle, and $10 per additional vehicle.

From Highway 1, follow the brown and white signs to the appropriate beach. 650/726-8820.

28 Bluff Top Park

😺 😺 😺 (See San Mateo County map on page 224)

This is a splendid area to visit with a leashed dog. The beach is beautiful, long, and fairly wide, and the bluff top has a couple of fun and scenic trails. If you're hankering for a great walk, you can hoof it through other park and beach areas for several miles—almost all the way to the Half Moon Bay harbor.

From Highway 1, take Poplar Avenue west all the way to the end. A parking lot will be on your left. 650/726-8297.

29 Half Moon Bay Dog Park

😺 😺 🐕 (See San Mateo County map on page 224)

This 15,000-square-foot dog park is just "temporary" (and has been for several years now) until the long-awaited Coastside Dog Park is up and running. That one's been years in the planning and debating stages, so don't let your dog hold his dog breath. In fact, when I asked a former dog park coordinator about when the park might become a reality, he asked me if I was over 30. I said yes. "Not in your lifetime," he replied. Apparently there's been a lot of frustration about how the city has handled some issues.

The park is a disheveled mass of landscaping bark and scattered dog toys surrounded by temporary and not terribly attractive fencing. In other words, dogs love it here. Jake goes kooky when he arrives at this park, running around with every dog toy in his smiling face until we have to leave. And he never wants to leave. It goes to show that a dog park doesn't have to be fancy to be a hit with the canine crowd.

From Highway 1, turn west on Wavecrest Street (you'll find the super-dog-friendly eatery Cameron's at this intersection) and continue down the bumpy old road about 0.3 mile almost to the end. You'll see a brown sign that says all dogs must be on a leash. Immediately after that is a little dirt road to the right. Follow that past the horseshoe pits and you'll be there. For an update on the park situation, check out www.coastdogs.org. 650/726-8297.

PLACES TO EAT

Cameron's Inn: English pub grub and rich and creamy fountain treats are the specialty here, but burgers, pizza, and salads are big sellers, too. Dine with your pooch at the big outdoor patio. Dogs who are lucky enough to come to this funky, charming, British treasure get to sniff out a double-decker bus out front. (It makes for a very cute photo.) The folks here love dogs and provide them treats and water. Cameron's is a bone's throw from Half Moon Bay's temporary dog park. 1410 South Cabrillo Highway/Highway 1; 650/726-5705.

Casey's Cafe: The outdoor seating here is attractive, with several umbrella-topped tables in a pretty plaza. If you like to play games other than fetch, you'll be pleased to know that on warm evenings you can play your favorite board game at the outdoor tables while snacking with your dog at your side. (If he's a border collie you can even use him as your game partner.) Casey's is right next to the Zaballa House lodging, 328 Main Street; 650/560-4880.

Half Moon Bay Brewing Company: Good beer, good food, good dog-friendly ambience, and good sniffs from the waterfront. What else could a dog want? A bowl of water? It's yours for the asking. This fun eatery and drinkery is in nearby Princeton's Pillar Point Harbor, at 390 Capistrano Road; 650/728-2739.

PLACES TO STAY

Holiday Inn Express: Just five blocks from Half Moon Bay State Beach, and a few blocks from downtown, this dog-friendly hotel is conveniently situated for adventure-seeking pooches and their people. Rates are $99–149. Dogs are $15 extra. 230 Cabrillo Highway 94019; 650/726-3400; www.hiexpress.com/halfmoonbay.

Zaballa House: Dogs and their human roommates get to stay in the attractive rooms and suites in back of this Victorian inn's main building—the oldest standing house in Half Moon Bay, built in 1859. Dogs don't mind the more modern digs. The rooms are spacious and very attractive, and all have fireplaces. Suites come with fireplaces, kitchenettes, whirlpool tubs, and private decks.

The owners of the inn really enjoy dog guests. "A lot of pets are nicer than their people," says one of the innkeepers. If you visit at the right time, the front-desk person might take a photo of you and your dog to put in the VIP Dog Guest photo album. The album is tucked away, and sometimes employees don't seem to know of its existence, but it's there.

The inn is right in beautiful downtown Half Moon Bay, next to some mighty dog-friendly eateries. Rates are $129–275. Dogs pay $10 extra. 324 Main Street 94019; 650/726-9123; www.zaballahouse.net.

San Carlos

PARKS, BEACHES, AND RECREATION AREAS

30 Heather Park

🐾🐾🐾 🦴 (See San Mateo County map on page 224)

This is one of the few fenced-in dog parks we've ever seen that comes complete with rolling hills, wildflowers, old gnarled trees, and singing birds. Your dog will have the time of his life here, bounding up and down hills or trotting down the winding paved path to the bottom of the park—sans leash. You may be tempted to take some of the tiny dirt trails up the steep hills, but they tend to end abruptly, leaving you and your dog teetering precariously. The only thing the park lacks is water, usually a given at dog parks.

If you have a dog who likes to wander, watch out. There are a couple of potential escape routes near the two gates at the far ends of the park. The park is at Melendy and Portofino Drives. 650/802-4382.

31 Pulgas Ridge Open Space Preserve

🐾🐾🐾🐾 🦴 (See San Mateo County map on page 224)

A quick Spanish lesson: Pulgas means flea in Spanish, as my trusty researcher, Caroline Grannan, informed me. But don't let this park's moniker send you fleeing. There are no more fleas here than there are in other parks. In fact, Jake has never brought home extra vermin after a trip to Pulgas.

The name notwithstanding, dogs are thrilled to be here. Not only does this 293-acre Midpeninsula Regional Open Space District land permit leashed pooches, but on 17.5 acres in the middle of the preserve dogs are allowed to be leash-free.

The off-leash area is only for dogs under excellent voice control. That's always the case in off-leash, unenclosed areas, but it's particularly important here because of wildlife—and because of some vociferous folks who would love nothing better than to see leashes be mandatory here again. You know, *those* kind of people. The off-leash area is oak woodland and grassland, so dogs can explore a variety of landscapes. It's in the middle of the preserve and accessible via the Blue Oak Trail or the Cordilleras Trail.

Leashed dogs can explore the rest of this fairly flat, oak-chaparral area via three miles of trails that wind throughout. The best time to visit is in the spring, when the wildflowers come to life everywhere.

Exit I-280 at Edgewood Road and drive east almost a mile. Turn left at Crestview Drive and make an immediate left onto Edmonds Road. You'll see signs for the preserve. Roadside parking is limited here, but it's usually enough. 650/691-1200.

Menlo Park

PARKS, BEACHES, AND RECREATION AREAS

Menlo Park is now home to two parks that have off-leash hours. The areas are both small, but they make local dogs wag. We'll detail the one with longer hours below.

32 Willow Oaks Park

🐾🐾🐕 (See San Mateo County map on page 224)

The people here are super nice to newcomers. And if you visit during the park's Friday afternoon/evening hours, you may get to enjoy an informal "yappy" hour. The dog area within Willow Oaks Park is about a quarter acre. It's fenced, so I can't figure out why dogs can't be in it full time, but here are the hours: 7–9 A.M. and 4 P.M.–dusk. The dog area has poop bags, but no water. It gets two paws because of the friendliness. A big bow-wow to Rick Saletta, who

DIVERSION

Sniff Out a Good Book: Your dog doesn't have to be Mr. Peabody to appreciate fine books. In fact, even if your dog doesn't know his assonance from his alliteration, he could have fun accompanying you to **Kepler's Books.** Kepler's, one of the largest, very best, and most beloved independent bookstores around (it nearly went under not too long ago, but was rescued by community donations!), permits clean, leashed, well-behaved dogs to cruise the aisles with you. In fact, dogs who visit even get a tasty treat! Common sense and good manners apply. Please, no leg lifts on the merchandise; Kepler's frowns on yellow journalism. Dogs who lean toward the literary are welcome. Those who *jump* on the literature are not. After sniffing around the shelves, wander over to dog-friendly Café Borrone, right next door, for a tasty meal. 1010 El Camino Real, Menlo Park; 650/324-4321.

gave us the heads up about the park. The park is at Willow Road and Coleman Avenue. 650/330-2200.

33 Bayfront Park

😸 😸 😸 (See San Mateo County map on page 224)

This place used to be a dump—literally. It was the regional landfill site until it reached capacity in 1984. Then the city sealed the huge mounds of garbage under a two-foot clay barrier and covered it with four feet of soil, planted grass and trees, and voilà—instant 160-acre park!

Now it's a land of rolling hills with a distinctly Native American flavor. The packed dirt trails take you up to majestic views of the bay and surrounding marshes. There's no sign of garbage anywhere, unless you look down from the top of a hill and spot the methane extraction plant. Fortunately, very few vista points include that.

Our favorite part of the park is a trail studded with large, dark rocks arranged to form symbols, which in series make up a poem. The concept was inspired by Native American pictographs—a visual language system for recording daily events. At the trailhead, you'll find a sign quoting part of the poem and giving a map of the trail, showing the meaning of each rock arrangement as it corresponds to the poem.

Although leashes are required, dogs seem really fond of this park, sniffing everywhere, their tails wagging constantly. Perhaps they can sense the park's less picturesque days deep underground. Or they may be touched by the Native American magic that imbues these hills.

The park starts at the end of Marsh Road, just on the other side of the Bayfront Expressway. To get to the beginning of the rock poem trail, continue past the entrance on Marsh Road to the second parking lot on the right. 650/858-3470.

PLACES TO EAT

Bistro Vida: The French food here is quite good, and eating it at the patio tables with your dog is a treat. Dogs think everyone who visits should order the beef bourguignon. Humans love it, and dogs pray little bites will make it down to the floor. 641 Santa Cruz Avenue; 650/462-1686.

Café Borrone: The motto here is "Because Europe is too far to go for lunch." You and your dog may well feel like you've headed across the big pond when you come here. At least 20 tables, many topped by shade umbrellas, grace the large open patio in front of the café. Dogs are welcome. The delicious soups, salads, and sandwiches are made with quality ingredients. Café Borrone is conveniently located right next door to the dog-friendly Kepler's Books, at 1010 El Camino Real; 650/327-0830.

Flea Street Cafe: Dogs would normally flee from a restaurant with the word "flea" in it, but not from this dog-friendly eatery. (It's named for the word Pulgas in its street name, which, again, means "flea" in Spanish.) You can get upscale organic food here. Jake nearly wailed with grief when I passed on the organic grass-fed Marin beef and instead ordered a delectable warm baby spinach salad and vegetarian bagna cauda. The restaurant serves dinner only. Dine with doggy at the outdoor tables. 3607 Alameda de las Pulgas; 650/854-1226.

Iberia Restaurant: This restaurant is among the finest dog-friendly restaurants in the state. It's so elegant you can eat like a Spanish king. Dine with your dog in a stately garden under the canopy of an enormous 400-year-old oak tree. Flaming dishes are big here, so if your furry friend fears fire, try ordering something a little less dramatic. Owners, Jose Luis Relinque and his wife, Jessica, love dogs, and are always happy to see "our little friends" at the exquisite patio. 1026 Alma Street; 650/325-8981.

Atherton

PARKS, BEACHES, AND RECREATION AREAS

34 Holbrook-Palmer Park

🐾 🐾 (See San Mateo County map on page 224)

Roses. Gazebos. Bathrooms that look like saunas. Trellises. Jasmine plots. Tennis courts. Buildings that belong in a country club. People in white linen love it here; dogs are often just plain intimidated. Joe never did a leg lift at this park when we visited. Jake has, but only after checking around to make sure no one—not even a songbird—was watching. Leashes are a must. Please note that on weekends, this is a prime spot for weddings with lots of dressed-up people, so you might want to steer clear.

Holbrook-Palmer Park is on Watkins Avenue, between El Camino Real and Middlefield Road. Leave your car at one of several lots in the park. 650/752-0534.

Woodside

PARKS, BEACHES, AND RECREATION AREAS

35 Thornewood Open Space Preserve

🐾 🐾 🐾 (See San Mateo County map on page 224)

This 141-acre preserve is a former estate, and the views of the valley from parts of this land are magnificent. Dogs can peruse the preserve on leash. Thornewood is the smallest of the Midpeninsula Regional Open Space District's preserves, but dogs dig the one-mile trail that runs through the oak woodland, chaparral, and redwoods here.

Dogs have to stay away from Schilling Pond because swans call it home, and dogs and swans don't mix. In fact, although the pond is almost entirely surrounded by dense vegetation, rangers have spotted dogs swimming after these beautiful birds. If this happens very much, the entire preserve could be off-limits to all dogs, so let's be careful out there.

From I-280, exit at Highway 84/Woodside Road and drive west into the hills, about five miles. The road will make several sharp turns, but keep following Highway 84. Go left at the narrow, signed driveway. It winds through the woods for 0.3 mile before reaching the small parking lot on the west side of the driveway. 650/691-1200.

PLACES TO EAT

Alice's Restaurant: You can get almost anything you want at this restaurant, including a table for you and your dog on the large porch. Weekends here are packed with bikers, especially for Alice's colossal breakfasts. If your dog rides in your motorcycle sidecar, this is the place for you. It's at 17288 Skyline Boulevard, on the corner of Highways 35 and 84, just two miles north of Portola Valley's Windy Hill Open Space Preserve; 650/851-0303.

Portola Valley

PARKS, BEACHES, AND RECREATION AREAS

36 Windy Hill Open Space Preserve

🐾🐾🐾🐾 (See San Mateo County map on page 224)

You can look out from the top of the first big hill you come to and see for miles all around—and though you're on the edge of the suburbs, you'll see hardly a house. This 1,130-acre preserve of the Midpeninsula Regional Open Space District has as many different terrains as it has views, including grassland ridges and lush wooded ravines with serene creeks and drippy redwoods.

There are more than three miles of trails that allow you and your leashed canine companion to hike together. But watch out for foxtails; the park is so dry that foxtails seem to proliferate all year.

Start at the Anniversary Trail, to the left of the entrance. The hike is a vigorous 0.75 mile uphill, and that may be enough, especially when it's baking. But you can continue down the other side of the hill and loop right, onto the Spring Ridge Trail. Near the end of this 2.5-mile path, you'll come to a wooded area with a small, very refreshing creek. This is a good place to sit a spell before heading back. These two trails are the only ones that permit pooches, so don't try your paw at any others.

Park at the lot on Highway 35 (Skyline Boulevard), 2.3 miles south of Highway 84 and five miles north of Alpine Road. You'll see the big sign for the preserve and three picnic tables. 650/691-1200.

37 Coal Creek Open Space Preserve

🐾🐾🐾🐾 (See San Mateo County map on page 224)

Jake loves visiting this 493-acre preserve in the winter because of the little waterfalls that gurgle along a couple of creeks. In fact, year-round, this is one of the best of the Midpeninsula Regional Open Space District preserves for dogs, because it's generally cooler than most. The dense oak and madrone forests offer a real respite from the hot summer weather.

Banana slugs like this climate as much as dogs do, so don't be surprised to see a few lurking on the trails. When Joe Dog happened upon a banana slug here, at first he looked disgusted. Then he barked at it a couple of times and sat down and moaned at it when it didn't respond. I tugged hard on his leash to get him away, because I knew his next move would be to make a banana slug appetizer out of it.

If rolling meadows are more your dog's style, this preserve has those, too. The five miles of trails will take you through all kinds of landscapes. Let your dog choose his favorite, but make sure he's leashed.

The preserve has two entry points along Skyline Boulevard (Highway 35) in the southernmost part of the county (south of Portola Valley). One is about 1.2 miles north of Page Mill Road, at the Caltrans vista point, on the east side of the road. The other is at Skyline and Crazy Pete's Road, about two miles north of Page Mill Road, also on the east side of Skyline. This one has the closest access to the preserve, but there's only room for about three cars, and you'll need to walk down a fairly steep residential road to get to the trails. 650/691-1200.

Pescadero

PARKS, BEACHES, AND RECREATION AREAS

Beautiful Pescadero State Beach no longer allows pooches, even those with leashes and shamelessly pleading eyes. At least dogs still have Bean Hollow, and Arcangeli Grocery Company.

38 Bean Hollow State Beach

🐾🐾🐾 (See San Mateo County map on page 224)

This isn't a big sandy beach. In fact, it can be hard to find sand here at all. It's rocks, rocks everywhere, which is kind of fun. The rocky intertidal zone here is terrific for tidepooling, but only if you and your dog are surefooted. To get to the best tidepools, you must perform an amazing feat of team coordination—climbing down 70-million-year-old rock formations while attached to each other by leash. It's not that steep, just awkward. The pitted rocks can be slippery. This maneuver is not recommended for dogs like Jake, who goes deaf and senseless when the alluring ocean beckons him to swim. Besides, the surf can be treacherous in this area.

If you reach the tidepools, you're in for a real treat. But make sure your canine companion doesn't go fishing—we've seen a dog stick his entire head in a tidepool to capture a little crab. Fur and fangs aren't natural in the delicate balance of this wet habitat, so please keep dogs out of the tidepools. The mussels will thank you.

If you decide to play it safe and stay on flat land, you can still see the harbor seal rookery on the rocks below the coastal bluffs. Bring binoculars and you can really get a view of them up close and personal.

The beach is off Highway 1 at Bean Hollow Road. 650/879-2170.

PLACES TO EAT

Arcangeli Grocery Company: There's always fresh-baked bread here—still hot—waiting for you after a cold day at the beach. We like to buy a loaf of steaming herb-garlic bread and eat it at the picnic tables on the lawn in the back of the store. 287 Stage Road; 650/879-0147.

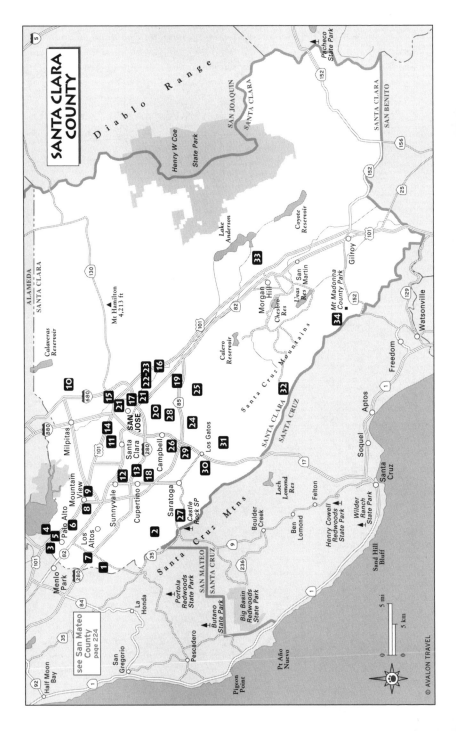

SANTA CLARA COUNTY

Diablo Range

Henry W Coe State Park

SAN JOAQUIN
SANTA CLARA

SANTA CLARA
SAN BENITO

Pacheco State Park

152

156

25

152

129

Watsonville

Freedom

Aptos

Soquel

Santa Cruz

Gilroy

Mt Madonna County Park

34

Uvas Res
San Martin

Coyote Reservoir

33

Lake Anderson

Morgan Hill

Chesbro Res

Calero Reservoir

Santa Cruz Mountains

32

SANTA CLARA
SANTA CRUZ

17

Felton

Loch Lomond Res

Ben Lomond

Henry Cowell Redwoods State Park

Wilder Ranch State Park

Boulder Creek

Sand Hill Bluff

9

236

Big Basin Redwoods State Park

Butano State Park

Portola Redwoods State Park

SAN MATEO
SANTA CRUZ

S a n t a   C r u z   M t n s

Pescadero

San Gregorio

La Honda

Pt Año Nuevo

Pigeon Point

1

© AVALON TRAVEL

5 mi
5 km

ALAMEDA
SANTA CLARA

Calaveras Reservoir

130

Mt Hamilton
4,213 ft

680

10

880

Milpitas

Palo Alto

Mountain View

4
3
5

82

6

Los Altos

7

280

Menlo Park

84

35

Half Moon Bay

92

1

2

Castle Rock SP

27

Saratoga

Cupertino

18
13
12

8 **9**

Sunnyvale

11
14

Santa Clara

SAN JOSE

15
21
17

22-23
16

19

20
28
25

24

Campbell

26
29

30

Los Gatos

31

85

280

101

82

101

152

San Martin

5

see San Mateo County
page 224

CHAPTER 9

Santa Clara County

While some parts of Santa Clara County are quite scenic, dogs have to face the facts: The place still revolves around Silicon Valley, and it's not a pretty sight. Cookie-cutter duplexes and townhouses abound. So do suburban-style office parks and strip shopping centers. Even dogs with questionable taste wince.

But if you get your dog out of the more populated areas and into the quieter county parks, you'll scarcely know you're in the middle of a megabyting, microchipping mecca. Some of the larger, wilder county parks may put your dog back in touch with the wolf inside herself. One dog we met on a trail at one park was sitting and howling every few hundred feet. Her person said she was just happy to be there. Joe Dog thought maybe the dog was just saying, "Get this leash off me!"

Fortunately, leash-free parks now dot the county. And for dogs who don't mind leashed hikes, trails in most of the Santa Clara County's 45,000 acres of parklands (www.parkhere.org) welcome dogs more than ever before. "We've opened so much more of our park system to dogs. There are very, very few

PICK OF THE LITTER—SANTA CLARA COUNTY

COOLEST HIKE
Mount Madonna County Park, Gilroy (page 277)

MOST DOG-FRIENDLY PLACES TO EAT
Bill's Cafe, San Jose (page 268)
Rock Bottom Restaurant and Brewery, Campbell (page 270)
La Fondue, Saratoga (page 272)
Classic Burgers of Los Gatos, Los Gatos (page 274)

RESTAURANT WHERE DOGS GET FREE FILET MIGNON
La Fondue, Los Gatos (page 272)

MOST DOG-FRIENDLY PLACES TO STAY
Cypress Hotel, Cupertino (page 264)
Doubletree Hotel, San Jose (page 269)
Hotel Los Gatos, Los Gatos (page 274)

BEST SHOPPING
Stanford Shopping Center, Palo Alto (page 256)
Santana Row, San Jose (page 256)

FRIENDLIEST PLACE TO BUY A PLANT
Yamagami's Nursery, Cupertino (page 263)

BEST SOCIAL GATHERING
Society Dog (page 271)

places where dogs are not allowed," says a park system representative. (Are you reading this, San Mateo County Department of Parks? Let this be a lesson to you!) We describe our favorite county parks in this chapter.

The Midpeninsula Regional Open Space District (www.openspace.org) is popular with pooches, with six dog-friendly Open Space preserves in the county. The district has unique rules about poop-scooping and six-foot leashes. (See the *San Mateo County* chapter for more on these rules, as well as the Diversion *Hike with a Like-Minded Hound* about the district's popular pooch hikes.) Its preserves are definitely worth sniffing out.

Palo Alto

For dogs, this town is the county's garden spot. Here, you'll find lots of other dog lovers and well-behaved dogs, enticing city parks—all of which allow dogs—and no fewer than three leash-free dog runs. At the Baylands, you and your leashed dog can watch birds and get a good workout at the same time. And many student-oriented restaurants with outdoor seating welcome your dog. If you're lucky enough to have a Palo Alto address, or a friend with one, you may bring your dog to the glorious Foothills Park on weekdays.

PARKS, BEACHES, AND RECREATION AREAS

Unless you have a working dog (and no, this does *not* mean a dog who is working on getting the dog treats out of your coat pocket—we're talking guide dogs and their ilk), you and your pooch can no longer walk together at the Stanford Dish. We know a good many dogs who have cried into their kibble because of this pooch ban. Fortunately, other pleasant Palo Alto areas still permit pooches to paw around.

1 Foothills Open Space Preserve

🐾🐾🐾 (See Santa Clara County map on page 252)

At 211 acres, this is the second smallest of the dog-friendly Midpeninsula Open Space District lands. It sports only a half-mile trail (one-mile roundtrip), but it's a fun place to take a dog who's happy with a moderate hike on leash. The trail leads up through chaparral-covered slopes to a ridge that leads to a grassy knoll with terrific views of the South Bay. It's not exactly an ocean or Golden Gate Bridge view, but it's rewarding. On temperate days we like to bring a little picnic along and plop down for some eats before heading back.

Trail access is at a two-car roadside pullout on the south side of Page Mill Road, 3.5 miles southwest of I-280. You'll see a brown pipe gate and wood rail fence there. Go over a step-over stile and follow the trail to the left. (The other trail quickly leads to a dead end.) 650/691-1200.

2 Long Ridge Open Space Preserve

🐾🐾🐾🐾 (See Santa Clara County map on page 252)

In order to hike here with a dog, you have to fill out a special permit, which is conveniently available at the Grizzly Flat parking area. You have to agree to keep your dog leashed and on restricted trails, namely the Peters Creek Trail, Ridge Trail, and a firebreak you'll see on the trail map there.

It's worth the tiny bit of extra effort to come to this 2,000-acre preserve. The trails make for many miles of superb hiking, and if you visit in spring, you'll be surrounded by a vast rainbow assortment of wildflowers, from purple lupines to cheery yellow buttercups. The dog-friendly trails take you through hilly grasslands as well as forests of oaks, bay, and Douglas firs that provide glorious shade. You may even encounter some wild turkeys along the way, so if you have a bird dog you'll be glad of your leash. (Nisha, the springer spaniel we had before she went to the happy hunting grounds in the sky, once brought Craig a live wild turkey in her mouth.)

The Grizzly Flat parking area is on Skyline Boulevard (Highway 35), 3.3 miles south of Page Mill Road and 3.6 miles north of Highway 9. (As a landmark, you'll see the Palo Alto city limits sign nearby if you're coming from the south.) 650/691-1200.

❸ Palo Alto Baylands
🐾🐾🐾 (See Santa Clara County map on page 252)

This is the best-developed wetlands park in the Bay Area for adults, children, and dogs. It's laced with paved bike trails and levee trails. Along the pretty levee paths, benches face the mudflats. Don't forget your binoculars on a walk here. A cacophony of mewling gulls, mumbling pigeons, and clucking black-

DIVERSIONS

Stop and Smell the Shopping Centers: Dogs are welcome to join you at **Stanford Shopping Center,** a 70-acre open-air mall that's disguised as a park. The grounds are home to 1,300 trees of 35 species, plus hundreds of hanging baskets and planters dripping with flowers. If a dog has to go shopping, this is one of the more pleasant places she could go. Many of the 120 stores allow dogs inside. Nordstrom and Neiman Marcus, two of the nation's most dog-friendly department stores, welcome dogs here. Rules at some of the others change frequently, so if you're interested in going inside with your dog, poke your head in and see if you can find someone to give your dog the thumbs-up. Chances are that not only will you end up sniffing out plenty of dog-friendly stores, but your dog will be offered some treats along the way. At El Camino Real and Sand Hill Road, in Palo Alto; 650/617-8200.

An intimate, slightly more trendy shopping center is the new **Santana Row** in San Jose. Charro, a San Jose pooch, wrote to tell us how much fun it is to be a dog there, and even though Jake isn't a shopping kind of dog, he enjoyed a trip there because he got so many pats from shopkeepers and fellow shoppers. (Plus there were plenty of palms and oaks to explore.) He was particularly interested in some leather shoes at Diesel (which only sometimes allows dogs), although he wasn't particular about which ones. Selecting shoes to chew is apparently a much quicker process than selecting shoes to wear. I quickly shooed him out of there. Santana Row is at Winchester Boulevard and Stevens Creek Boulevard, just off I-880 in San Jose. 408/551-4611.

birds fills the air. Small planes putt-putt into the nearby airport, and your dog will love the fishy smells coming from the marshes. This seems to be a popular spot for dog exercise. Keep your pooch leashed and on the trails.

Dogs shouldn't go near the well-marked waterfowl nesting area, but they're welcome to watch children feed the noisy ducks and Canada geese in the duck pond, as long as they don't think about snacks à l'orange.

From U.S. 101, exit at Embarcadero Road East and go all the way to the end. At the entrance, turn left for the trails, ranger station, and duck pond. A right turn takes you to a recycling center. 650/329-2423.

4 Greer Park
🐾🐾🐾 (See Santa Clara County map on page 252)

This is one of Palo Alto's parks with an off-leash dog run, but it isn't the largest (Mitchell Park holds that distinction). The park is green and pleasant, as are all the city's parks, but it's somewhat noisy because of nearby Bayshore Road. Dogs have to be leashed outside the dog run. There are athletic fields, picnic tables, and two playground areas. The dog run, near the Bayshore side, is small and treeless, but it's entirely fenced, if that's what your dog needs.

The park is at Amarillo Street and West Bayshore Road. The parking lot is off Bayshore, conveniently near the dog run. 650/496-6962.

5 Hoover Park
🐾🐾🐾 (See Santa Clara County map on page 252)

This park may be small, but dogs don't really care. It's home to a little-known dog park that's not as popular as the run at Mitchell Park, but that's part of the charm. There've been some improvements here recently, so if you haven't checked it out lately, it's worth a sniff.

The park is at Cowper Street between Colorado and Loma Verde Avenues. 650/496-6962.

6 Mitchell Park
🐾🐾🐾🐾 (See Santa Clara County map on page 252)

This generous, green park has some unusual amenities, including two human-sized chessboards and a roller-skating rink. The park is also a standout in the canine book: It has its own dog park that's completely fenced and has a row of pine trees on one side, water dishes on the other, and scrappy tennis balls everywhere.

The park has plenty of shade to delight a dog. Remember to leash outside the dog run. For kids, the playground area has sculptured bears for climbing and a water-play area (sorry, no dogs). The dog park is a short walk from the parking lot.

The park is on East Meadow Drive just south of Middlefield Road. 650/496-6962.

🔟 Pearson-Arastradero Nature Preserve

🐾🐾🐾 (See Santa Clara County map on page 252)

With 613 acres of rolling savanna grassland and broadleaf evergreen forest, Arastradero Preserve is one of the more peaceful and attractive parks in the area. Dogs dig it, but they have to be leashed. It's a good rule, because mountain lions, rattlesnakes, poison oak, and coyotes can be part of the scene here. And so can bikers.

Anglers are right at home in the preserve. A hike to Arastradero Lake takes only about 20 minutes from the main parking lot, and the fishing can be very good. (Sorry, no swimming, boats, or flotation devices.)

There are 6.25 miles of hiking trails. Jake Dog enjoys the hilly 2.8-mile Acorn Trail when he's in the mood to pant. Bring plenty of water; it can get toasty here.

From I-280, exit at Page Mill Road and go south. Turn right (west) on Arastradero Road (Refuge Road on some maps) and drive into the parking lot. 650/329-2423.

PLACES TO EAT

La Strada: Any place that shares a name with a Fellini movie is OK by Jake and me. Dogs are welcome to join you at the pleasant sidewalk seating—great for watching the University Avenue scene. The food here is good, the proportions generally large, and the breadth of selections wide. Thirsty dogs get water. Jake's good friend Zelda gives it two dewclaws up, and we have to agree with her assessment. 335 University Avenue; 650/324-8300.

Lulu's: This pleasant, affordable little Mexican eatery at the Town & Country Village offers several shaded outdoor tables for dogs and their people. If you come here at lunch on weekdays during the school year, you may be overrun by students from the local high school. Best to eat a bit later. 855 El Camino Real; 650/327-8226.

Palo Alto Sol: The friendly staff here will bring your thirsty pooch some water while he's drooling over your tasty Mexican food. The mole sauce is a must-order. 408 California Avenue; 650/328-8840.

Saint Michael's Alley: Dogs are welcome to join their people at the lovely shaded patio of this hidden gem. It's been around since 1959—ancient history in California! The California-classic cuisine here is delicious. I enjoy making a meal of starters here; they're too good to

pass up. Thirsty dogs get a bowl of water if they bat their eyes nicely at their server. 806 Emerson Street; 650/326-2530.

Tandoori Oven: Jake's beloved pen pal, Zelda, told him about the dog-friendly outdoor tables at this Indian restaurant. "You'll like it," she promised. What's not to like? The food isn't gourmet Indian, but it's quick, tasty, and reasonably priced, especially for this area. Try the chicken tikka masala wrap. 365 South California Avenue; 650/324-2111.

PLACES TO STAY

Garden Court Hotel: This newly renovated downtown Palo Alto hotel embodies a contemporary and luxurious Mediterranean esthetic that reflects the beautiful high-tech, historic college town in which it resides. It's a fusion of charming European and sophisticated Silicon Valley, and everything is top drawer here, from the bedding to the showerheads. Most rooms include French doors and private patios that look out onto the open-air tiled floor courtyard and fountains. Some rooms have fireplaces, others have spa tubs, and many feature breakfast nooks. Nice!

Dogs are just as happy to stay here as their people are: Upon check-in, pooches get a welcome mat, a fun gift, cleanup bags, and use of a couple of pet bowls. Rates are $199–389. Dogs pay a $50 fee per visit. 520 Cowper Street 94301; 650/322-9000 or 800/824-9028; www.gardencourt.com.

Sheraton Palo Alto: Dogs love staying here, not so much because of the rooms, which are comfy and more than adequate for a pleasant stay. What dogs (and their people) dig is the beautiful garden setting, complete with a large and tranquil koi pond. If the pond has you hankering for a swim, head to the pretty pool here. Dogs must be content to be landlubbers. Rates are $132–329. Dogs must be under 80 pounds. 625 El Camino Real 94301; 650/328-2800; www.sheraton.com.

Mountain View

PARKS, BEACHES, AND RECREATION AREAS

🕉 Rengstorff Park

🐾 🐾 🐕 (See Santa Clara County map on page 252)

This park is typically neat, green, and interesting for people, and it has another excellent feature: A sign reads, "Dogs must be on leash (except by permit)." This means that you can get a permit from the city that allows you to train a dog off leash, with the understanding that he'll be under control. Be fore-warned, though: If you don't bring the permit along with you when training, you will be ticketed.

Rengstorff Park is at Rengstorff Avenue between California Street and Central Expressway. Call for details on getting a permit. 650/903-6331.

9 Mountain View Dog Park

🐾🐾🐾🦴 (See Santa Clara County map on page 252)

Ahh, this fenced park has redwood trees. They're Jake's favorite arbors. Other amenities in this 0.75-acre park include benches and a separate area for smaller or more timid dogs. The ground cover is mostly grass, so it's easy on the paws. It's an off-leash oasis, and dogs seem mighty happy to be here.

The park is on North Shoreline Boulevard at North Road. 650/903-6331.

PLACES TO STAY

Best Western Tropicana Lodge: No Ricky Ricardo band here, but it's a decent place to stay with your pup-a-loo. Rates are $70–110. 1720 West El Camino Real 94040; 650/961-0220; www.tropicanalodge.com.

Residence Inn by Marriott: You and your dog will feel right at home at the suites at this attractive hotel. They have kitchens and lots of other extras you won't find in a regular hotel. But better than that is the very dog-friendly attitude here. "We take all pets, from snakes to rabbits. We see them as part of the family and try to accommodate the owner's needs," one manager told us. The place even has a little fenced area for exercising dogs, and the staff is happy to point you to nearby trails. Rates are $199–229. There's a $75 doggy fee per visit, so it's best to stay for a while to get the most bang for your buck. 1854 West El Camino Real 94040; 650/940-1300.

Milpitas

PARKS, BEACHES, AND RECREATION AREAS

10 Milpitas Dog Park

🐾🐾🐾🐾🦴 (See Santa Clara County map on page 252)

The big-dog side of this terrific two-acre park has smallish trees. And the small-dog section has big trees. Go figure! But some of that small-dog shade leaks over to the large-dog side, so it's a win-win situation.

This is a great place to bring a dog who longs to run like the wind. It's mostly grassy, and it's a very generous size. Dogs can really work up a sweat while chasing each other or running after lobbed tennis balls. The dog park is flanked by the scenic rolling hills of the surrounding 1,539-acre Ed Levin County Park. (Dogs are allowed only on one short segment of the Bay Area Ridge Trail there, and in the picnic areas, so don't be too tempted to sniff out Ed Levin.)

The dog park has all the usual pooch amenities, from water to picnic tables to poop bags. And it has an interesting extra one: A tiny concrete-floored fenced area with a bench. No one was using it when we visited, but it looks like a decent place for a child who wants to feel protected from the pounding paws.

There's an entrance fee to get into the county park, and therefore to get into the dog park. It's a steep $6 per car. But annual passes are available, should you want to make this a regular stomping ground. The dog park is at the very end of the county park. (If you're not confident you'll find it, just ask the park ranger at the fee gate.) The county park is at 3100 Calaveras Road, about 2.5 miles east of I-680. For dog park inquiries, phone the City of Milpitas at 408/586-3210. For questions about Ed Levin County Park, phone 408/262-6980 or 408/355-2200.

PLACES TO STAY

Best Western Brookside Inn: Rates are $89–129. Dogs are $15 extra. 400 Valley Way 95035; 408/263-5566; www.bestwestern.com.

Santa Clara

PARKS, BEACHES, AND RECREATION AREAS

The original Santa Clara Dog Park is no longer with us. It's been replaced by the lovely Reed Street Dog Park.

🔢 Reed Street Dog Park

🐾🐾🐾🐾🐕 (See Santa Clara County map on page 252)

This dog park is in a somewhat industrial part of town, but dogs don't mind a bit: Reed Street Dog Park has everything a dog could want in a pooch park: 1.5 fenced acres, grass (some months more than others), little mounds/mini hills

DIVERSION

Go on a Pilgrimage: Mission Santa Clara, on the Santa Clara University campus, allows leashed dogs on its grounds. You might make it part of your walk if you're exploring the campus. The building, dating from 1929, is a replica of one version of the old mission, first built in 1777 but destroyed five times by earthquake, flood, and fire. Preserved fragments of the original mission and the old adobe Faculty Club are the oldest college buildings standing in the western United States. The mission is on campus, off El Camino Real, Santa Clara. 408/554-4023.

for adding interest to the ball chase, separate areas for small and large dogs, lots of shade from shade structures, benches, water, poop bags, and most of all, friendly people and dogs, even when it's crowded. While it's not the fanciest park we've visited, it gets plenty of points for the nice people and pooches who frequent the place.

Keep in mind that it can get muddy in rainy season, and it's closed for maintenance on Thursdays. The park is at 888 Reed Street, at Lafayette Street. 408/615-2260.

PLACES TO STAY

Quality Inn: Rates are $70–135. Dogs are $20 extra. 2930 El Camino Real 95051; 408/241-3010.

The Vagabond Inn: Rates are $69–99. Dogs are $20 extra. 3580 El Camino Real 95051; 408/241-0771.

Sunnyvale

PARKS, BEACHES, AND RECREATION AREAS

12 Las Palmas Park

🐾🐾🐾🐾🦮 (See Santa Clara County map on page 252)

With its paved paths, green grass, and beautiful pond, this park is the best in town for a walk among rolling hills. But dogs consider it a real gem because of the two-acre dog park within. It has all the usual helpful dog-park amenities, including shade, water, poop bags, and even a fire hydrant. It's a kind of fenced-in nirvana. Dogs get deliriously happy when they visit. Some spend so much time rolling in the cool grass that they miss out on hanging with their fellow canines. But do they care? A look at their smiling snouts and flaring nostrils will answer that question.

A quick note about that fire hydrant. Enough dogs have run headlong into it that there was some thought about removing it. So far, it's still here. Doggies, keep your eyes open!

The park is at Danforth and Russet Drives. 408/730-7506.

PLACES TO STAY

Staybridge Suites: The suites are large and very livable, with kitchens and most of the amenities of home. Rates are $150–170. There's a $75 pooch fee per visit (this place caters to longish-term visitors). Dogs are supposed to be under 80 pounds, but they make exceptions. 900 Hamlin Court 94089, 408/745-1515 or 800/897-0084; www.wyndham.com.

The Vagabond Inn: Rates are $65–75. Dogs are $10 extra. 816 Ahwanee Avenue 94086; 408/734-4607; www.vagabondinn.com.

Cupertino

PARKS, BEACHES, AND RECREATION AREAS

13 Fremont Older Open Space Preserve

🐾 🐾 🐾 (See Santa Clara County map on page 252)

This 739-acre preserve smells sweet and clean, but that doesn't disappoint dogs. Pooches have enough trees and ground-level odors to keep them happily trotting along on their mandatory leashes.

Once you park in the small lot, you'll walk several hundred feet on a paved roadway, but be sure to turn right at the first sign for hikers. Otherwise you'll find yourself in the middle of a bicycle freeway. The narrow dirt trail to the right takes you on a three-mile loop through cool woodlands and rolling open hills up to Hunters Point via the Seven Springs Loop Trail. The view of Santa Clara Valley from the top of the 900-foot hill is incomparable. More trails may be open soon, so your dog's feet will be able to explore as never before.

Signs at the entrance warn of ticks, so be sure to give your dog (and yourself) a thorough inspection after your hike.

From U.S. 101 or I-280, take Highway 85 (Saratoga-Sunnyvale Road) south to Prospect Road. Turn right and follow the road to the park entrance. 650/691-1200.

DIVERSION

Nursery Tail Wag: Dogs love visiting **Yamagami's Nursery.** Not only do they get to help you pick out some great plants and flowers for your home, but dogs get treats when they visit Yamagami's. The treats are located at the information desk, should your dog ask. "We're extremely dog friendly," says a Yamagami plant doctor at this old and popular family business. 1361 South DeAnza Boulevard, Cupertino; 408/252-3347.

PLACES TO EAT

Bobbi's Coffee Shop: Charro the Dog told us about this eatery, where every dog gets a bowl of water upon arrival at the outdoor tables. It's a convenient place to stop for a bite before or after a visit to the dog-friendly Yamagami's Nursery (see the Diversion *Nursery Tail Wag*), right next door. It's only open weekends, so if you come on a Monday, you dog will cry and make you go to the nearest Starbucks. 1361 De Anza Boulevard; 408/257-4040.

PLACES TO STAY

Cypress Hotel: The word "Cypress" in a hotel name seems to confer ultra-dog-friendliness. Witness Doris Day's Cypress Inn in Carmel. The Cupertino Cypress, while larger and more hotelly than Doris Day's inn, makes dogs feel equally at home. They're not only welcome to join you at this fun boutique hotel, but they're encouraged to do so. There's even a package designed especially for pooches, called "See Spot at the Cypress." Included in your deluxe guest room or executive suite is a pet area with a dog bowl, biscuits, bottled water, chew toys, and a dog bed. Your dog will also get a dog tag stating, "I was pampered at the Cypress Hotel," and some other goodies, including free valet parking—something that comes in handy when you're traveling with luggage and a dog. The rate for the package is $129–299. If you want to simply stay here without the package but with your dog, your room will run you $89–229.

For a little more money, the concierge will arrange a pet massage, a grooming session, or even some time with a doggy psychic. (If a pet psychic were to read Jake's brain, she'd be hard-pressed to get beyond his ever-present thoughts of food, food, food.) 10050 South DeAnza Boulevard 95014; 408/253-8900; www.thecypresshotel.com.

San Jose

If you think San Jose offers little for dogs, think again. The city has added four new dog parks since the book's last edition (and it took away one, too). That's a grand total of eight city parks where dogs can run around naked as they day they were born! Except they couldn't run then, so this is better.

PARKS, BEACHES, AND RECREATION AREAS

San Jose's parks are slowly going to the dogs—in the best sense of the phrase. The goal here is that each of the city's 10 districts will have at least one dog park. We're at eight, and counting. (By the time you read this, the Raleigh Linear Dog Park, on the former campus of IBM/Hitachi, may be a reality. Keep your eyes peeled, because it's purported to be a big one!)

14 William Street Park

😸😸😸 (See Santa Clara County map on page 252)

This park is a boy dog's dream come true. It's only about 15 acres, but it has 200 trees and 400 shrubs. The acreage-to-trees/shrubs ratio makes it easy for boy dogs to sniff out just about every arbor. The trees make it a really pleasant, attractive place to visit, even in the armpits of summer. Head for the shade and let your happy, leashed pooch loll and roll in the green grass.

The park is at 16th Street and East William Street. 408/794-7275.

15 Emma Prusch Park

😸😸😸 (See Santa Clara County map on page 252)

This park, one of San Jose's most attractive working farms, is a museum. Like a symbol of the county, it lies in the shadow of the intersection of three freeways. Yet it's a charming place and, surprisingly, it allows your leashed dog to wander around the farm with you so long as he stays out of the farm-animal areas. A smooth paved path, good for strollers and wheelchairs, winds among a Victorian farmhouse (which serves as the visitors center), a multicultural arts center, farm machinery, a barn, an orchard, and gardens. Picnic tables are on an expanse of lawn with trees.

Ten more acres within the park are being developed, and there will soon be trails through demonstration gardens, row crops, pastures, and other agricultural areas. It's a great way to teach your dog about the origin of the ingredients for his dog treats.

The entrance is on South King Road, near the intersection of U.S. 101 and I-680/280. 408/794-7275.

16 Hellyer County Park

😸😸😸🐕 (See Santa Clara County map on page 252)

This county park, which surrounds the two-acre Shadowbluff Dog Run, is a generous, rustic area, popular with bicyclists. The best deal for dogs is the El Arroyo del Coyote Nature Trail, which by some miracle allows dogs. Walk to the left at the entrance kiosk and cross under Hellyer Avenue on the bike trail to find the entrance to the nature trail. Cross the creek on a pedestrian bridge to your right; once across, take the dirt path to your left. Bikes aren't allowed, making it all the better for dogs.

Willows and cottonwoods are luxuriant here, and in spring, poppies bloom. Eucalyptus groves provide occasional shade. Watch out for bees and poison oak. Otherwise, this is heavenly territory for your dog.

The park is closed Wednesdays for maintenance. Access is very easy from U.S. 101. Exit U.S. 101 at Hellyer Avenue and follow prominent signs to the park. The dog area is about 100 yards past the entry kiosk. A parking fee of $6 is charged, and that can add up fast, since there's really no good parking nearby. So if you're planning to be a regular, your best bet would be to buy a park pass for the year. It's a small investment to make for your dog's happiness. 408/355-2200.

17 Shadowbluff Dog Run

🐾🐾🐾🐾🐕 (See Santa Clara County map on page 252)

The two-acre enclosure within the large Hellyer County Park has just about anything a pooch could desire. You'll find shade from a few trees, water to slurp up, and lots of green grass. For humans, there are benches, poop bags, and garbage cans. (Seems the dogs get the better end of the deal.)

The park is closed Wednesdays for maintenance. From U.S. 101, exit at Hellyer Avenue and follow signs to the park. The dog area is about 100 yards past the entry kiosk. Parking fee is $6, so consider buying an annual pass ($80) if you're a regular. 408/355-2200.

18 Saratoga Creek Dog Park

🐾🐾🐕 (See Santa Clara County map on page 252)

There's room in this fenced 0.3-acre park for only about 20 dogs, the ground cover is artificial turf and decomposed granite, and there's water, a poop-bag dispenser, and a bench. It's small, neat, and a needed addition to the neighborhood. Thanks to good dogs Rusty and Kalman for having their human, Walter, give me the heads up about this park, the latest to join the San Jose fleet. It's at Graves and Saratoga Avenues. 408/794-7275.

19 Miyuki Dog Park

🐾🐾🐕 (See Santa Clara County map on page 252)

Dogs are happy to be at this tiny (0.37-acre) park without their leashes, even though the park isn't quite what it could be. The ground is covered with crushed granite, which can get a little dusty when everyone is running around. There's no water. The trees are small, but that will change. Meanwhile, many dogs enjoy sniffing and running around here. (Perhaps they haven't visited delightful Watson Dog Park yet.)

The park is at Miyuki Drive and Santa Theresa Boulevard. 408/794-7275.

20 Olinder Dog Park

🐾🐾🐕 (See Santa Clara County map on page 252)

Let's see how psychic your dog is. Ask her this: "What is the ground at Olinder Dog Park covered with?" If her reply is "Bark!" she may be clairvoyant. The vast bulk of the groundcover at this three-quarter-acre park is bark (wood chips, to be more precise, but most dogs can't pronounce that). Jake doesn't care for the feel, and tends to stick to the concrete path here. I've noticed the same for some other dogs. Otherwise, the park has all the usual good dog-park amenities, including water, a bit of shade from trees, separate large and small dog sections, picnic tables, and poop bags. A handy bonus: The park comes with 11 parking spaces designated for dog-park users. The dog park is within Selma Olinder Park, at 18th Street and East Williams Street. It can be a little challenging to find, but the dog park is at the south end. 408/794-7275.

🔳 Ryland Dog Park

🐾 🐕 (See Santa Clara County map on page 252)

This tiny park really utilizes unused space: The whole thing is directly under a major overpass. I've never seen such a setup. Jake kept looking up and flinching, apparently not all that comfortable being under the rumble and bumble of thousands of tons of heavy traffic.

On a positive note, at least there's no need for the city to worry about erecting a shade structure or growing shade trees. And if you forget your sunscreen, no worries! The thick asphalt and concrete over you is better than any sunscreen money can buy.

Only a cool mural and great dog-themed fence prevent this from getting our lowest rating—the dreaded hydrant. The park is under the Coleman Street overpass, at San Pedro and Ryland streets. It's across the street from Ryland Park, which is green and sees sun. 408/794-7275.

🔳 Delmas Dog Park

🐾 🐾 🐕 (See Santa Clara County map on page 252)

This a long, narrow, tree-filled park is great for dogs who like to retrieve. It's a clever use of a strip of land that's adjacent to the light rail. The park is only about one-third an acre, and the ground cover is nothing but dirt, but the city and the light rail (VTA) combined forces to include all the features a dog park could want, including a walking path, picnic tables, water, lighting, and mutt mitts. If it were a bit bigger, it would get more paws. The park is at Delmas Avenue and Park Avenue. 408/794-7275.

🔳 Butcher Dog Park

🐾 🐾 🐾 🐾 🐕 (See Santa Clara County map on page 252)

The name may not be inviting (the whole name, which no one uses, is Roy M. Butcher Dog Park), but the park is a gem. It's not huge, but there's usually adequate space for all the canine visitors. The people here are super friendly, and you and your dog will feel very welcome here, even as newbies. About 75 percent of the park is covered with what looks like lush, green grass, but on closer inspection is artificial turf. It's great for those rainy months, when all the other dog parks are swimming in mud. The park has everything a dog could desire, including shade from big evergreens, separate large and small dog sections, water, picnic tables, and poop bags. The park is located in Butcher Park, at Camden Avenue and Lancaster Drive. 408/794-7275.

24 Fontana Dog Park

🐾🐾🐕 (See Santa Clara County map on page 252)

This decent little fenced dog park is set in the larger Fontana park, named after San Jose police officer Jeffrey Fontana, who was shot to death in the line of duty not far from here.

It's quite a small dog park—about 0.3 acre, and that land is divided between large and small dog sections. But it has all the accoutrements that make for a pleasant dog park visit, including water, shade from trees, some little seating areas, and poop bags. The people are friendly, too, which definitely helps. The ground cover, formerly grass, was dirt when we visited, and dogs do tend to get a bit dusty if they're rambunctious here. The dog park section of Fontana is at Golden Oak Way and McAbee Road. 408/794-7275.

25 Almaden Quicksilver County Park

🐾🐾🐾 (See Santa Clara County map on page 252)

This rustic, 3,600-acre park allows dogs on all 30 miles of trails. Some of these trails are popular for horseback riding, so watch out; although leashes are the law here, they don't always stop dogs who like to chase hooves.

In the spring, the hills explode with wildlife and wildflowers. Any of the trails will take you through a wonderland of colorful flowers and butterflies who like to tease safely leashed dogs. Speaking of insects, there's a down side to this park: Ticks seem to hang out here. "We got 20 off our dog, then three more when big welts developed," an unfortunate San Jose resident writes. Keep your pooch in the center of trails, and the bloodsucking pests will have to go elsewhere for dinner.

You can enter the park at several points. We prefer the main park entrance, where New Almaden Road turns into Alamitos Road, near Almaden Way. 408/268-3883 or 408/355-2200.

PLACES TO EAT

Bill's Cafe: You and your favorite dog can munch on simple café cuisine at this bistro with umbrella-topped tables. Lucky dogs who visit get water and a biscuit! 1115 Willow Street; 408/294-1125.

Left Bank: Of course your dog is allowed at this lively brasserie. What self-respecting French restaurant wouldn't welcome dogs? The large, attractive patio seats 80, so you'll never feel alone. Your dog would like you to order the steak tartare for a starter and the *carre d'agneau* (roasted rack of lamb) for your main dish, but there are less meaty options. The Left Bank is at 377 Santana Row; 408/984-3500.

Pizza Antica: This upscale pizza, pasta, and salad restaurant at Santana Row is a very dog-friendly place. Our canine correspondent Dakota reports that he's not only welcome here, but also he gets a bowl of water. A manager confirms: "We enjoy dog guests," she says. 334 Santana Row; 408/557-8373.

Siena Mediterranean Bistro: A lovely patio graced by a beautiful mural is where you and your dog get to dine when you eat at this hidden gem. The food is really good, creative, homey European cuisine with a Mediterranean lilt. I could eat the risotto with goat cheese, pumpkin, butternut squash and fresh sage every day. Jake, however, would prefer I order the rosemary venison medallions. 1359 Lincoln Avenue; 408/271-0837.

PLACES TO STAY

Doubletree Hotel: This is a really comfy, contemporary place to stay with a dog. The hotel is set in two towers, with a total of 505 oversize guest rooms. It has all the usual amenities for humans that nice hotels do (decent fitness room, pretty pool, fluffy towels). It's not a Kimpton, but it's pretty close. What dogs like best is that they're welcomed with pet bed, bowl, and chew toy. (They chew toy is theirs to keep, which is a good thing when Jake is a guest. He is apparently known as a "destructive chewer" when it comes to dog toys. Even the indestructible ones destruct in his mouth.)

Rates are $99–329. Dogs are $50 per stay. Be forewarned: If your dog is noisy and disturbs another guest, if the guest complains, the hotel will offer him or her $100. And guess where it comes from? Your credit card deposit. Don't bring a big barker here (or to any lodging). 2050 Gateway Place 95110; 408/453-4000.

Homewood Suites: The suites here are comfy and much more like home than traditional hotels. Rates are $109–189. 10 West Trimble Road 95131; 408/428-9900.

Campbell

PARKS, BEACHES, AND RECREATION AREAS

Dogs aren't allowed in any Campbell parks except for one very suburban one that we won't spend time on here, and one fine dog park located within Los Gatos Creek County Park.

26 Los Gatos Creek County Dog Park

🐾🐾🐾🐾🐕 (See Santa Clara County map on page 252)

Jake seems to feel like a big man every time he enters this four-paw dog park. He trots right over to the sign that says Big Dogs, wags at it, and heads into the park with other large dogs. Some dogs that frequent this section are more like semi trucks, which probably makes Jake feel rather Toyota-ish, so he hangs with the medium-to-large dogs who make him look more sizeable.

The dog park (both the large and the small dog sections) is very well planned, with grass that is actually green, shade from trees and umbrellas, crushed granite pathways around the grassy areas, boulders and logs for adding interest for the human and canine set, water, benches, and poop-scoop areas. Jake particularly liked the logs and tried for minutes at a time to pry his jaws open wide enough so that he could carry around this prize stick of all sticks. Fortunately for everyone in the big dog section, his mouth wasn't big enough.

The park is located within Los Gatos Creek County Park, between the casting ponds (always a temptation for Jake) and the San Tomas Expressway. From Winchester Boulevard, travel east on Hacienda Avenue to the stop sign at Dell Avenue. The park is at the intersection of Hacienda and Dell. A $6 parking fee is charged in summer and on weekends and holidays, but if you want to avoid the fee, you can enter by paw on the beautiful Los Gatos Creek Trail. 408/355-2200.

PLACES TO EAT

Rock Bottom Restaurant and Brewery: The restaurant used to have a dog menu here, but most people were just ordering things such as bunless burgers for their dogs off the human menu (even before the low-carb craze), so it went back to human menus only. If you don't want to invest in your dog's carnivorous desires, you should know that the friendly servers here provide treats and water for pooches. For people, the signature microbrews are a big draw, as are tasty salads and interesting concoctions such as alder-smoked fish and chips. Dine at the full-service patio with your dog (it's even heated in the chilly months). It's at 1875 South Bascom Road, in the Pruneyard Shopping Center; 408/377-0707.

Yiassoo: Opa! The Greek food is tasty, inexpensive, and arrives quickly. Some call it Greek fast food. The servers here like dogs. "Absolutely, you come with your dog!" said a representative when I phoned about dog rules. I haven't made it down there yet, but friends reviewed it for me and gave it two paws up for friendliness. Dine at the patio with your pooch. 2180 South Bascom Avenue; 408/559-0312.

PLACES TO STAY

Residence Inn by Marriott: This is a convenient, comfortable place to stay when traveling with a dog. Residence Inns have only suites and apartments, and they all come with kitchens. Rates are $99–209. Extended stays get a discounted rate. Dogs have to pay a $100 cleaning fee. 2761 South Bascom Avenue 95008; 408/559-1551.

Saratoga

The Midpeninsula Regional Open Space District has added a chunk of land to its growing list of dog-friendly places. It's hard to find, so you may be better of setting your sites on the extremely dog-friendly and decadent restaurant, La Fondue.

DIVERSION

Drink Wine, Get Naked, Hop on a Bus: If you and your dog like to socialize, have we got a group for you: **Society Dog.** It bills itself as "a social club for dogs and their people," and boy, is it social. When we attended a doggy Easter egg hunt at a Saratoga winery, people were sipping wine and making new friends, and dogs were sniffing each other's heinies and making new friends too.

It's just one of many gatherings throughout the year for this South Bay group. It has monthly "naked" dog walks where dogs can be leash-free, and "bark in the dark" group walks on certain evenings. Some get-togethers culminate in hanging out at an alfresco restaurant together. Special events include winery tours, group sojourns via bus to fabulously dog-friendly destinations such as Carmel, and a field trip to the San Francisco Giants' Dog Days of Summer event (see *Dog-Ear Your Calendar* in the *San Francisco County* chapter), also via bus. Basic membership is free, but you pay for special events. See www.societydog.com for more info and a schedule of upcoming events.

PARKS, BEACHES, AND RECREATION AREAS

27 El Sereno Open Space Preserve

🐾 🐾 (See Santa Clara County map on page 252)

I'm pretty sure that once you find this place, and get a legal parking space, it's grand. But I wouldn't know for certain. I made the mistake of thinking the whole 1,415-acre preserve, with its 7.4 miles of trails, was dog friendly. I finally found the roadside turnout parking in the south part of the preserve, and Jake and I bounded out of the car. He needed to water the bay laurel, and I was pretty tired of driving around looking for the entrance to this hidden place. But before he could even get on the trail, a bearded fellow clambered up to us and said dogs weren't allowed here, just in the northern part. He was very pleasant, and rather grandfatherly, so I believed him—at least after he showed me his printout of the park's rules. So north we went, per his directions. And finally, finally, we found a tiny parking lot. Yes, a-hiking we will go—not! "Permit parking only" a sign read. What?! Were we on Canine Candid Camera? I didn't see Allen Funt jumping out of the bushes anywhere, so I parked for five minutes, took Jake on a wee hike (catch the double entendre), and left this disappointing excursion in the dust.

Back at home, I found out that what the hiker told me is true. Dogs can enter only on the northern portion of the preserve, and can use one trail only. It's a little more than a mile. Worth it? I don't know, but the trail is called Overlook, so I imagine the vistas are pretty sweeping. If you make it there, please go to my website, www.caldogtravel.com and send me an email letting me know of your adventure. To get that parking permit and directions (they're not even on the website), call 650/691-1200.

PLACES TO EAT

Big Basin Cafe: This very dog-friendly café serves the best mochas around. They're made with Ghirardelli chocolate and fresh, house-made whipped cream. The café also serves pastries and sandwiches, should you want a little nosh with your pooch. Speaking of dogs and noshing, dogs who visit get their very own treats! Dine together at the outdoor area's umbrella-topped tables. 14471 Big Basin Way; 408/741-1185.

La Fondue: This is one of the most decadent, gorgeous restaurants I've ever been to. Inside it's lush, plush, and exotic. But you and your dog will have to settle for the patio seating here. Don't cry into your kibble, dogs, because canines here have it very, very good. While humans get to dine on 50 varieties of fondue—including choices of kangaroo, python, alligator, and other "wild game,"—dogs get a bowl of cool water and (sit down for this) a bowl of filet mignon! It's true! OK, the filet mignon is apparently the trimmings from the filet mignon they serve humans, but what does a dog care? Why do they go to this kind of trouble? "Because my wife, Tracey, and I love dogs," explains restaurant co-owner Mitchell Scott Cutler.

Before rushing here, check your wallet. This is not a cheap place to grab a bite. If you want to sample a range of fondues, you'll be hard-pressed to get out of here for under $200. Hint for hounds on a budget: Stick with the traditional cheese or dessert fondues, and it's much more affordable. 14550 Big Basin Way; 408/867-3332.

Los Gatos

Dogs like the super dog-friendly community of Los Gatos, but they think it needs a name change. Jake suggests "Los Perros."

PARKS, BEACHES, AND RECREATION AREAS

28 Los Gatos Creek Trail
🐾🐾 (See Santa Clara County map on page 252)

This nine-mile-long paved trail (and growing as funding becomes available) stretches from San Jose through Campbell and Los Gatos, along the Los Gatos Creek (for the most part). We like to explore it on cold, rainy days, because it's not crowded then, and you can get a good feel for the nature that lurks not far away. But on most days, it's a rather crowded affair, with lots of bikes and pedestrians—not an ideal place for a relaxing walk with your furry friend. You can pick up the trail in any number of spots along the route. Handy entry points around here are at Vasona Lake County Park, and downtown Los Gatos, at the Main Street Bridge. Since the trail is a multi-governmental affair, there's no phone contact number.

29 Vasona Lake County Park

🐾🐾🐾 (See Santa Clara County map on page 252)

This is a perfectly manicured park, with grass like that of a golf course. Dogs find it tailor-made for rolling, although they tend to get tangled in their leashes—which the county demands they wear here.

Several pathways take you through this 151-acre park and down to the lake's edge. But no swimming is allowed. And dogs aren't allowed to visit the children's playground either. You can picnic in the shade of one of the large willows or lead your dog up to the groves of pines and firs for a relief session. You can access the Los Gatos Creek Trail here, too, should you care to take a flat, paved walk with many other people.

From Highway 17, take Highway 9 (Saratoga-Los Gatos Road) west to University Avenue. Go right and continue to Blossom Hill Road. The park will be on your left. Enter at Garden Hill Drive. The parking fee is $6. 408/355-2200.

30 St. Joseph's Hill Open Space Preserve

🐾🐾🐾 (See Santa Clara County map on page 252)

Want a quick escape from urban life? Visit this scenic, 173-acre preserve with your leashed pooch. Dogs are allowed on all four miles of trails here, but beware, it can get steep. The trails wind through oak woodlands and open grassland, and at the top of the 1,250-foot St. Joseph's Hill, you'll get magnificent views of the surrounding parklands. Joe used to love to sit here and let his nostrils flare.

From Highway 17, take the Alma Bridge Road exit and go across the dam. Public parking is available at Lexington Reservoir County Park. The trail to St. Joseph's Hill starts opposite the boat-launching area at the north end of the reservoir. 650/691-1200.

31 Sierra Azul Open Space Preserve (Kennedy-Limekiln Area)

🐾🐾🐾 (See Santa Clara County map on page 252)

The wildlife at this 5,000-acre preserve has it pretty good. There's so much steep, rugged terrain and dense chaparral that humans and their leashed doggy interlopers are pretty much forced to stay on the trails, out of critters' ways. Unfortunately for dogs and their people, mountain bikes seem to be everywhere on these trails, and they can go really fast. So on weekends especially, keep your eyes and ears peeled and be ready to dodge the traffic.

This is not a park for the fair of paw. A hike to the 2,000-foot ridge top can make even the fittest dog sweat. But the views from here or from the 1,700-foot

Priest Rock are worth a little panting, at least on your part. Take it easy on your dog, though, and don't let him pant too much. It can get very, very hot here in the summer, and there's virtually no decent shade. The folks at the Midpeninsula Regional Open Space District beg you not to take your pooch here on summer afternoons.

Parking here is a real problem. If you visit on a busy day, have a contingency plan in case you don't get one of the coveted spaces. Also note that the two other sections of the Sierra Azul Preserve (Cathedral Oaks and Mt. Umunhum; really, I did not make up that name) don't permit pooches.

From Highway 85, exit at Los Gatos Boulevard and drive west a little more than two miles. At Kennedy Road, turn left and follow the road about two more miles to the parking spot at the trailhead. There's room for only two cars here. This is utterly inadequate, and the district is working to do something about this. In the meantime, there's room for about seven cars across Kennedy, on Top of the Hill Road. Please be considerate of the residents here, and keep noise to a minimum and don't litter. 650/691-1200.

PLACES TO EAT

Classic Burgers of Los Gatos: This dog-friendly eatery has fine burgers. Dogs drool over them at the four tables on the patio. In fact, they've drooled so much that the café's proprietors now offer dogs their very own ice cream for $0.50. Pooches can get water if thirsty, too. 15737 Los Gatos Boulevard; 408/356-6910.

Dolce Spazio Gelato: On warm days, this is the place to come. The homemade gelato is creamy and delicious. When there's a chill in the air, try something from the café's espresso bar. The good-sized patio has heat lamps, which helps dogs and their people cozy up to a winter visit. Thirsty dogs get water on request. 221 North Santa Cruz Avenue; 408/395-1335.

Johnny's Northside Grill: Barbecue is the specialty here, and dogs appreciate this deeply. Dine with your drooling friend at the outdoor tables. 532 North Santa Cruz Avenue; 408/395-6908.

Viva: Not to be confused with the Elvis hit of a similar name, Viva Los Gatos is a fun, upbeat place with friendly servers and a patio that welcomes dogs. The cuisine is generally of the World Food variety and is really tasty. 15970 Los Gatos Boulevard; 408/356-4902.

PLACES TO STAY

Hotel Los Gatos: Your dog will feel like she's in the lap of Mediterranean luxury when you bring her as your guest to this villa-like boutique hotel just a couple of blocks from beautiful downtown Los Gatos. From the richly hued interior décor to the lush courtyard with heated pool, it's like you've traveled to Tuscany without that pesky plane ride. French (Tuscan?) doors and fireplaces come with some rooms, and decadent bedding, robes, and towels are standard, as is free internet (Wi-Fi is in lobby only).

As with most dog-friendly Joie de Vivre hotels, dogs get special treatment for no extra cost. Waiting in your room will be a dog bed (if you want one), pet bowls, and gift bag of treats and other goodies. Wow! I think your dog is handing you the phone to make a rezzy... Rates are $189–309. 210 East Main Street 95030; 408/335-1700; www.jdvhotels.com.

Los Gatos Lodge: The rooms here are clean and comfortable, but dated, and with thin walls. If you want high end, look at the hotel above this one. But this lodge has something many others don't–something that your dog will appreciate much more than fancy digs: 10 acres of lovely grounds to sniff around. Leashed dogs are welcome to explore the gardens, grass, and trees. Back at the ranch, you'll have use of a decent swimming pool and free Wi-Fi in your room. Some rooms come with kitchenettes, and you can get a mini fridge in any room for the asking. A continental breakfast comes with your stay. Rates are $89–199. Dogs are $30 per stay. 50 Los Gatos/Saratoga Road 95032; 408/354-3300 or 800/231-8676; www.losgatoslodge.com.

Morgan Hill

PARKS, BEACHES, AND RECREATION AREAS

32 Uvas Canyon County Park

🐾 🐾 🐾 (See Santa Clara County map on page 252)

This is a pretty, clean park of oak, madrone, and Douglas fir trees in cool canyons. The Uvas Creek Trail is a favorite trail. Dogs always appreciate a creek on a warm summer day, and this one doesn't dry up in hot weather. You might also try the wide, dirt Alec Canyon Trail, 1.5 miles long, within sight of Alec Creek, or the Nature Trail Loop, about one mile long, beside Swanson Creek. You may see some waterfalls in late winter and early spring. A ranger tells us that leashed dogs may now peruse all trails, even the Knibbs Knob Trail, which has a No Dogs sign (apparently left over from less-enlightened times). There's a $6 day-use fee.

Dogs are allowed in the campgrounds and picnic areas of Uvas Canyon. The park has 25 campsites, available on a first-come, first-served basis, for $24 a night. The campground is open daily April 15–October 31, and Friday and Saturday November–March. It's crowded on weekends during late spring and summer, so arrive early or camp during the week. Phone 408/355-2201 for reservations.

From U.S. 101, exit at Cochrane Road; go south on Business 101 to Watsonville Road, then right (west) on Watsonville to McKean-Uvas Road. Turn right on Uvas (past Uvas Reservoir) to Croy Road. Go left on Croy to the park. The last four miles on Croy are fairly tortuous. 408/779-9232 or 408/355-2200.

🔢 Morgan Hill Dog Park

🐾🐾🐾🐾 🐕 (See Santa Clara County map on page 252)

This is how dog parks should be made. Morgan Hill Dog Park is a big three acres of rolling terrain. There's really room here for dogs to cut loose and for people to go for a stroll.

The park is grassy, fenced, and has separate sections for large and small dogs. There's water, and people like to bring their own dog bowls to prevent transmissible illnesses like kennel cough. If you just want to sit and rest while your dog sniffs about, you have your choice of plenty of benches. The park is the south section of the attractive Morgan Hill Community Park, where you can walk on leash. It's on Edmundson Avenue, just west of Monterey Road/Highway, and next to the Centennial Recreation Center. You'll see the big sign with the dog illustration that's reminiscent of a cave painting. Jake and I thank Marlys Warner-Hussey for giving us the heads up about this park. 408/782-0008.

PLACES TO STAY

Doubletree Hotel: This is a great place to come if you want a good night's sleep in spacious, clean, comfy accommodations. The rooms are quiet, and they're quite large, so your dog will have plenty of space to stretch out. And between the pool, the fitness room, and the free Wi-Fi, you'll be a happy camper. Dogs don't care much about the latter three amenities, since they can't take advantage of them, but they do give a wag about the hotel's special treatment of pooch guests: Dogs who stay here get use of a lovely pet bed and pet bowls. They also get some yummy treats, and sometimes a chew toy. They feel perfectly at home among all the business travelers here. Rates are $99–299. Dogs are $50 per stay. 2050 Gateway Place 95110; 408/453-4000; www.doubletree.com.

Quality Inn: Rates are $70–100. Dogs are $15 extra. 16525 Condit Road, 95037; 408/779-0447.

Residence Inn by Marriott: This is an all-suites hotel, and the suites are spacious, with full kitchens and comfy beds. Your dog will have a choice of rooms for snoozing. A hot breakfast and afternoon social hour are included in the price. There's a decent little indoor pool and OK exercise room. Rates are $149–209. Dogs are $100 extra for the length of their stay. 18620 Madrone Parkway 95037; 408/782-8311.

Gilroy
PARKS, BEACHES, AND RECREATION AREAS

34 Mount Madonna County Park
😺😺😺😺 (See Santa Clara County map on page 252)

This magnificent 3,700-acre park is midway between Gilroy and Watsonville (in Santa Cruz County). No matter where you're coming from, it's worth the drive. The mountain, covered with mixed conifers, oak, madrone, and bay and sword ferns, is wonderfully quiet and cool—especially appreciated by San Jose dwellers, whose parks are almost never far from the roar of freeways. You may hear the screech of jays and little else.

Try driving on Valley View Road (to the right from the ranger station) to the Giant Twins Trail, where you can park in the shady campsite of the same name—at least when no one is camping there. (When we were there on a perfect Indian summer day in late September, the park was deserted.) Two huge old redwoods, green with lichen, give the trail its name. After half a mile, the trail becomes Sprig Lake Trail and continues for another two miles. Sprig Lake, really a pond, is empty in summer, but in spring it's stocked for children's fishing.

This walk isn't much of a strain. If you'd like more exercise, there are plenty of longer and steeper trails—18 miles in all, and as of this writing, your dog may enjoy every one of them. From the Redwood Trail or the Blackhawk Canyon Trail, you'll be rewarded with views of the Santa Clara Valley, the Salinas Valley, and Monterey Bay. For a walk almost completely around the park, try the Merry-Go-Round Trail.

The park's deer are only one of many reasons you should keep your dog securely leashed, tempting as it might be to let her off. "Dogs have instincts," a friendly ranger said.

Your dog might enjoy a camping vacation here. There are 113 large, private campsites. Sites are $24–30 per night. Phone 408/355-2201 for reservations. A $6 day-use fee is always charged on weekends and daily Memorial Day–Labor Day.

From U.S. 101, exit at Highway 152 west to Gilroy. Continue on 152 (Hecker Pass Highway) through part of the park. The entrance is a right (north) turn at Pole Line Road. 408/842-2341 or 408/355-2200.

PLACES TO STAY

Quality Inn & Suites: Rates are $80–220. Dogs are $10 extra. 8430 Murray Avenue 95020; 408/847-5500.

Index

S

TUV

Keeping Current

Note to All Dog Lovers:
While our information is as current as possible, changes to fees, regulations, parks, roads, and trails sometimes are made after we go to press. Businesses can close, change their ownership, or change their rules. Earthquakes, fires, rainstorms, and other natural phenomena can radically change the condition of parks, hiking trails, and wilderness areas. Before you and your dog begin your travels, please be certain to call the phone numbers for each listing for updated information.

Attention Dogs of the San Francisco Bay Area:
Our readers mean everything to us. We explore the Bay Area so that you and your people can spend true quality time together. Your input to this book is very important. In the last few years, we've heard from many wonderful dogs and their humans about new dog-friendly places, or old dog-friendly places we didn't know about. If we've missed your favorite park, beach, outdoor restaurant, hotel, or dog-friendly activity, please let us know. We'll check out the tip and if it turns out to be a good one, we will include it in the next edition, giving a thank-you to the dog and/or person who sent in the suggestion. Please write us—we always welcome comments and suggestions.

The Dog Lover's Companion to the San Francisco Bay Area
Avalon Travel
1700 Fourth Street
Berkeley, CA 94710, USA
email: atpfeedback@avalonpub.com
or go to www.caldogtravel.com and write the author directly.